Games Ancient and Oriental and How to Play Them, Being the Games of the Ancient Egyptians, the Hiera Gramme of the Greeks, the Ludus Latrunculorum of the Romans and the Oriental Games of Chess, Draughts, Backgammon and Magic Squares

GAMES ANCIENT AND ORIENTAL

AND

HOW TO PLAY THEM.

BEING

THE GAMES OF THE ANCIENT EGYPTIANS
THE HIERA GRAMME OF THE GREEKS,
THE LUDUS LATRUNCULORUM OF THE ROMANS
AND THE
ORIENTAL GAMES OF

CHESS, DRAUGHTS, BACKGAMMON
AND
MAGIC SQUARES.

BY

EDWARD FALKENER.

LONDON:
LONGMANS, GREEN AND Co.
AND NEW YORK: 15, EAST 16th STREET.
1892.

CONTENTS.

BACKGAMMON.

MAGIC SQUARES

INTRODUCTION.

The present age is distinguished for discovery of the records and monuments of antiquity, and for the wonderful discoveries of the secrets of nature; for searching after things long past, and for making progress with rapid strides into the future. These two studies frequently go hand in hand together. We study the buildings and the sculptures of the ancients, and the paintings of the old masters, and we apply the principles thus learnt to the requirements of the present day; we study ancient authors, not merely to improve our taste and intellect, but also to enable us to exert our faculties to the best advantage in the affairs of life. The past, the present, and the future are woven together in all the studies and occupations of man. As a healthy recreation from pursuits of more severe study, necessity and usefulness, the following pages are offered in the hope that some of the amusements of past ages may take their place among the relaxations of modern times.

The author directed his attention many years ago to the games of chess, draughts, and backgammon, and to the formation of magic squares. After the elaborate works which have been written on the history of these games, he feels, now that he proposes to publish his researches, it would be presumptuous were he to attempt to add to what has been already done so well; he has confined himself therefore exclusively to the practical rules and principles of each game, so that anyone, without further application, may be able to play any of these games, as if they were modern games invented for the present times; and he thinks it will be found that these games which were established in years gone by, whether of greater or less antiquity, contain merits which are not always to be found in the new and fanciful conceits which are brought out each day, and set aside by others to be introduced on the morrow, which will again in their turn soon be forgotten.

In the examples of games given for each description of chess, the reader, and more especially the chess-player, will understand that the examples are merely given to show the moves; being frequently played by friends who were not chess-players, but who kindly learnt the moves so as to enable the author to score the game.

Chess, draughts, and backgammon, or games resembling these, have been played in all civilized countries, and at all times. In some instances there is little or no variation of the same game in different countries: in others the difference is such as to constitute a new game, and very frequently a game of great interest. It is the object of this book to show some of these varieties, and what is more, by giving examples of these games to enable anyone to learn the games and play them. We have not as yet found them in Nineveh or Babylon, though we are convinced they were played there; but we see them depicted on the walls of Egypt; and the most ancient of all the games of chess, the details of which are known to us, comes from India. Kings and princes, bishops and laymen, are depicted on ancient monuments and in mediæval MSS., playing at these games. Learned men in all ages have sought relaxation in such pursuits, after hours of severe study; and to all of us as we advance in years a game at whist or backgammon relieves the eyes and keeps us awake, when the faculties of the mind and body have become enfeebled. The invalid also, and the afflicted, forget their troubles when absorbed in the intricacies and difficulties and the excitement of the game. The remembrance of our friends is often associated with the games we have played together; sometimes even when we have played only a single game, and have never met again.

The formation of a magic square is an occupation which we can enjoy when alone, as it presents countless varieties of ingenious solution. Men in the present age of necessity and practical industry are apt to look upon such occupations as trivial, and as a waste of time; but they forget that the mind requires relaxation as well as the body; and that as some of the first wranglers have been the first athletes; and as the most illustrious Greeks thought it their highest glory to be a victor in the Olympic games; so Euler and other eminent mathematicians have not despised the solution of such problems.

"Deficiet sensim qui semper tenditur arcus."

The utilitarian therefore is wrong in declaiming against such recreations as a waste of time; as much so as when he affirms that classics and mathematics are useless in this age of science. Every man who has risen to the highest grade of science will tell us that he could not have been where he is were it not for the education he received at college; and in like manner a man who has never looked into the works of a Greek or Latin author, or worked a problem in Euclid, or solved an equation in algebra, since he left school, will acknowledge that though he has never had occasion to apply these studies in after life, he has found them of immense advantage to him in improving and strengthening his mental faculties in the position which he occupies. But whether these games are useful or not, they form the means of rational amusement and social amusement far superior to many of the amusements which are resorted to in the present day: and no apology therefore is needed either for the study or for the practice of any of these games. But of all these games chess is the most useful; for as mathematics is a handmaid to logic, and teaches the lawyer to build up and establish his proofs before he goes on; so chess teaches the soldier not merely the science of attack, but instils caution in the mind of a prudent general to avoid surprises, to fortify his base of operations, and to despise no foe. Talleyrand regarded the pieces on a chess-board as applicable to mankind:—things to be made use of, whether of higher or lower degree; and it is thus that priests regard the laity:—"Les hommes sont, à ses yeux, des échecs à faire mouvoir: ils occupent son esprit, mais ils ne disent rien à son cœur."[1]

Of late years indeed it has become the parent of the Kriegs-spiel. And are not such habits essential and necessary to us all, whatever our position of

[1] Mémoires

life may be, enabling us to concentrate all our efforts to the accomplishment of the task before us, and to stand on our guard constantly against all the temptations and dangers with which we are surrounded?

Were we writing a history of chess and other games, we should have to narrate how kings and emperors, shahs and sultans, princes and bishops, conquerors and captives have played at chess; and how provinces have been staked, lives lost, and others saved only by the delay in finishing a game; how one who was summoned to execution in the middle of a game begged to finish it, and at the end of the game was proclaimed king; and we should be able to give many other anecdotes connected with the game; but these have been narrated many times and by better hands, and of late by Professor Forbes, from whose interesting history of Chess one anecdote we will give, which Mr. Bland had however previously narrated,[1] and others before him.

"Two Persian princes had engaged in such deep play, that one of them having lost his whole fortune, was rendered desperate, and staked his favourite wife Dilārām to retrieve it. He played, but with the same ill success, and at last saw that he must inevitably be checkmated by his adversary at the next move. Dilārām, who had observed the game from behind the *parda*, or gauze screen that separates the female from the male portion of the company, cried out to her husband in a voice of despair: —

"Ai Shah! do Ru*kh* bidih, wa Dilārām rā madih;
Pil wa Piyāda, pesh kun, wa zi Asp Shāh-māt."
"O Prince, sacrifice your two rooks, and save Dilārām;
Forward with your bishop and pawn, and with the knight give checkmate."

[1] *Persian Chess*, p. 23.

BLACK.

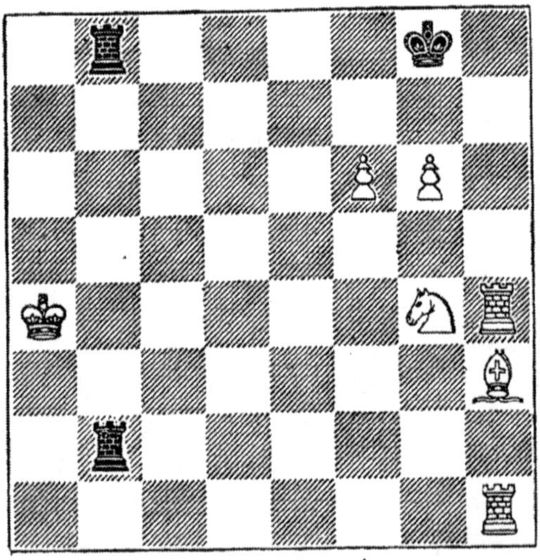

WHITE.

Solution.

DILARAM.	BLACK.
1. R. to R. 8th (check).	1. K. takes R.
2. B. to K. B. 5th (discovering check).[1]	2. K. to his Kt's. square.[2]
3. R. to R. 8th (check).	3. K. takes R.
4. Kt's. P. gives check.	4. K. to his Kt's. square.
5, Kt. to R. 6th (mate).	

There is one anecdote, however, connected with our own history, which ought to be recorded. When the noble-minded, but weak and unfortunate King, Charles I. received a letter to inform him that the Scots had agreed to hand him over to the Parliamentary forces, he was playing at chess. "Painful as the tidings must have been to him, his countenance betrayed no change;

[1] The Bishop moves two squares always, with power of hopping over an intermediate square, whether occupied or not.

[2] Black might have interposed Rook from his Q. Kt's. 7th to his K. R's. 7th, but this would merely have delayed the game one move.

and he continued the game with the same placidity of manner and apparent interest, as if the letter had remained unopened.[1]

But it is our purpose, not to give a history of chess and other games, but to give the games themselves, with examples of games, so that anyone may play them; such examples being given, as we have said, not for the superior play exhibited in such games, but simply to show the moves, and the nature and genius of the game.

"O thou whose cynic sneers express
The censure of our favourite chess,
Know that its skill is science self,
Its play distraction from distress.
It soothes the anxious lover's care;
It weans the drunkard from excess:
It counsels warriors in their art,
When dangers threat, and perils press;
And yeilds us, when we need them most,
Companions in our loneliness."

From the Persian, of Ibn ul Mutazz.[2]

[1] John Heneage Jesse, *Memoirs of the Court of England during the reign of the Stuarts*, 1. 405.

[2] *Persian Chess*, by N Bland Esq., M.R.A.S., 1850.

II.

THE GAMES OF THE ANCIENT EGYPTIANS.

The illustration on front book-cover is from a photograph of the bust of Queen Hatasu in the Berlin Museum. She lived about 1600 B.C.; and we shall presently describe her draught-board and other games. But these games were played as early as the time of Râshepses and we can trace them even to the fourth dynasty; which we will leave to Egyptian chronologists to determine whether it was three or four thousand years B.C., or twice the age of Queen Hatasu before the Christian Era. The illustration on back book-cover is of the time of Trajan, A.D. 100, and thus we see through what a long period these Egyptian games continued to be played, begining in the earliest ages, and going down to the time of the Romans.

We have said that many of our modern games have descended to us from ancient times, and that some are depicted on the walls of Egyptian temples and tombs. As Indians believed that the enjoyments of life with the Great Spirit in the future state would consist in hunting; as the Romans placed theirs in the symposial enjoyments prefigured by the lectisternium, as evidenced by the recumbent figures so frequently found on their sarcophagi; and as the Mahometans look forward to the solace of houris, so the Egyptians are represented as passing their time in the future state in anointing (and therefore we may conclude in previous bathing,) in music, and dancing, and song, and in playing at various games. What these ancient games were will be seen by the following paper which was given to me in 1864, by the eminent Egyptologist, and founder of the Biblical Archæological Society, the late Dr. Birch, of the British Museum, and which will be read with great interest. We have added the illustrations to make it more intelligible.

"B. M.
1 April, 1864.

"My dear Sir,

"Herewith I send you the representations of the games of draughts on the monuments, which I have long promised you:—

"On the Games of Ancient Egypt.

"The earliest appearance of games is in a tomb of Râshepses, a scribe and functionary of the King of Tat-Ka-ra of the 5th Egyptian dynasty. Amidst the diversions of music and singing are seen two games:—

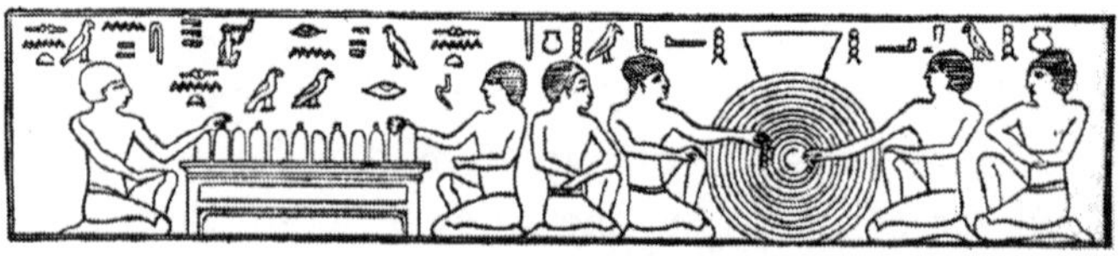

Lepsius, Denkmäler, 11.61, *Tomb* 16.

1. "A low stand or table,[1] at each side of which is a player seated on the ground, each placing a hand on

[1] About 16 inches high. E.F.

one of the pieces. These pieces, twelve in number, are of two different kinds, those of the player on the left being conical, while those of the player on the right having a small cap or stud at the top of the cone. The pieces are placed alternately, plain and capped. Each player is represented as about to take up a piece. Hieroglyphical inscriptions are written over. Above the board is *maa sen't,* "see the sen't," *i.e.* the game. The word *sen't* has many meanings in hieroglyphs, and being here written without any determinative, is very ambiguous.[1] It might be connected with *sen*, a "robber," and if so, would be the *latrunculus.* Over the player on the right is "ar en" (*That makes*) "shamt" (*three*) "m" (*from*) "sen't" (*the board*): evidently alluding to the pieces taken. Over the player on the left is inscribed "Fa" (*Lifts*) "shamt" (*three*) "sen" (*pieces*) or *two* "m" (*from*) "sen't" (*the board.*)

2. "The other game represents a circular board" (placed upright in order to show it). The description which follows is not very accurate, and the reader is referred to the description of the game further on. Prof. Lepsius's drawing, as noted by Dr. Birch, makes the two innermost rings pen-annular, but this arises

[1] "This word is not (*sten*) as sometimes inaccurately written, but (*sendt*) or rather . It is also written (*sendt*). Now the apparently kindred word (*sen*) has unquestionably the sense of 'passing, (moving from one place to another)' and in the Tablet of Canopus is rendered in the Greek *μετατίθημι*, 'to alter, transpose, place differently. The word *sen* has however another meaning (which may possibly have given the name to the game) viz. to *remove, take away, cut off*: hence perhaps 'game of take.' This however does not appear to me as probable as the former, because the verb in this sense has usually the termination of *cutting*." P. le P. Renouf.

probably from an imperfection in the painting, or from an intentional desire of the artist to give space for drawing the hands of the players.[1]) "Above the board is a jar. The game is called  Hab em han," *the game of the jar*. The arrangement of the board has great similarity to that of the circular Cretan labyrinth, as seen in the coins of Gnossus.

3. "Some other representations of the first game occur in the tombs of Beni-Hassan. They are of the time of the twelfth dynasty.

On a low table of painted wood (coloured yellow, with grey markings, E.F.), the men, twelve in number as before, are placed. They are conical, and tipped cones, as before; the conical ones coloured yellow, the tipped ones green. They are placed, as in the already described representation of the fifth dynasty, alternately yellow and green, conical and tipped, along the board. Each player is touching with delicate hand the piece nearest to him.

4. "A second representation has a similar board with players: but the green and tipped men are on one side of the board, and five in number: while the yellow cones on the other side are six in number. Over them is written the word  *aaseb*, which is erroneously translated *leisure* by Rosellini. It probably means some particular form of the game: or possibly *Lost.*"[2]

5. "There is also an historical representation of this game. The monarch, Rameses III, or Maimoun, is represented at Medinet-Haboo seated on a chair.

[1] E.F.

[2] It is hopeless to attempt interpreting the word, until we find it with some kind of context Mr. P. le P. RENOUF.

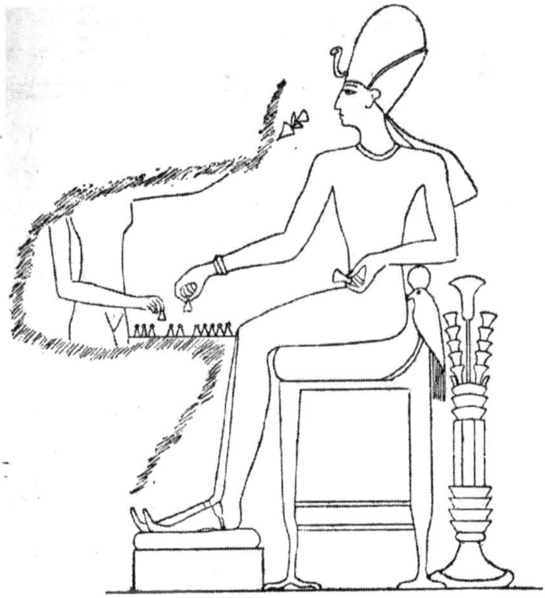

"Before him is a female standing, supposed to be his queen.[1] Between them[2] is the table and board. The pieces are all alike, with tipped heads, (but probably of different colours, yellow and green[3]) each player lifts a piece. The men, (as in the last representation,) are placed at each end of the board, with a space between them. There are six close together on the king's side of the board, and five on the female's, who has taken

[1] In his article published in the Trans. of R. Soc. of Lit. he quotes Herodotus II, 122, who says that Ramsinitus (Rameses III. the head of the 20th dynasty, and founder of the palace at Medinet Haboo at Thebes) played (at draughts) with Isis (Ceres) the wife of Osiris, and that sometimes he won, and sometimes he lost. Rameses is often represented with his queen sitting behind him, and looking at his play. It must therefore be either Isis, or his Queen, but not a slave.

[2] Dr. Birch writes here—"Between them is a chess or draught table." Chess is quite out of the question.

[3] E.F.

up the fourth piece. This makes the number of men eleven, which is probably an error in the drawing." (The queen has five men with a gap between them, and she has one piece in her hand; while Rameses also has five on the board, and one in each hand. He therefore is the winner: and he seems to show it in his countenance.[1])

6. "At a late period, viz. in the age of Trajan and the Antonines, the game was still played, as appears by the caricature papyrus in the British Museum.

"A lion is seated on a stool playing at the game with a goat. On the board are eight pieces, four on each side, with tipped heads on the goat's side, and flat heads on the lion's side. Each player is lifting up a piece with his right forefoot.[2]

"Thus it will be seen that though the number of pieces varied in the representations, the proper number was six to each player; that the number of squares on

[1] E.F.

[2] As Queen Hatasu's pieces are lion-headed, and as the name of the pieces *abu* has some relation to a goat, it is probable that the caricature merely represents a battle between the two sides, in which the lion-headed pieces have got the mastery. E.F.

each side of the board was six; and that the pieces were arranged parallel to the player, as in modern draughts. When the game advanced, the pieces were played side by side, and probably took laterally. The first move too was, it appears, one of the end pieces; or at least that was the favourite move.

7. "Different from this game are those shown on a board in the collection of (Dr.) Abbott.

"On one side is a board formed of three lines of squares in width, the central one of which has twelve squares in length, and the two side ones four squares in length. A drawer underneath held the pieces, some

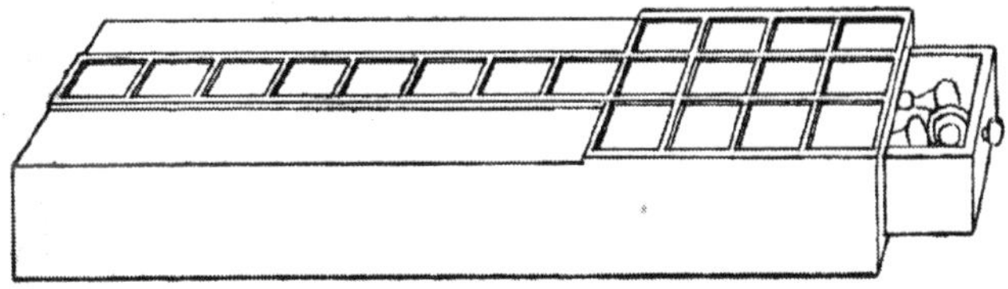

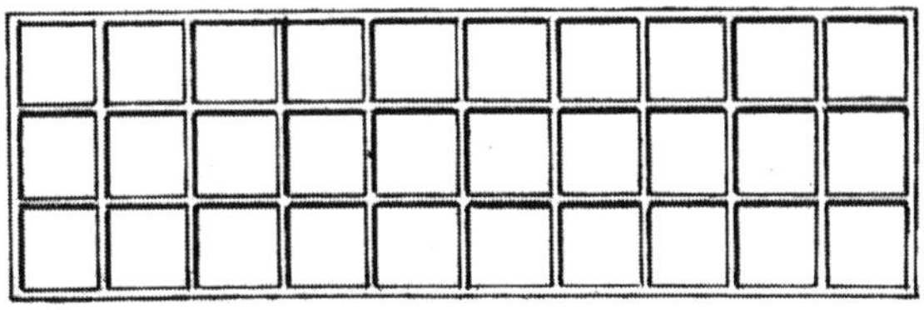

of which are tipped, and others reel-shaped. M. Prisse thinks the game was probably played like the πεττεία of the Greeks, said to have been invented by Thoth, (Plato, *Phædr*, p. 227^{D}) and that the central line was the line called ἱερὰ γραμμὴ or sacred line. He also considers that it may have been the origin of the Greek game διαγραμμισμός.

8. "On the other side is a board of thirty compartments, having three squares at each end, and ten on each side.[1]

9. "Another kind of game is said to have resembled the game of draughts. This game was also supposed to afford diversion to the deceased in the future state. The pieces are found with different heads, as those of a man, a jackal, and a cat; and are generally of porcelain or wood."

In the following year Dr. Birch sent a contribution on the same subject to the *Revue Archéologique*, Vol. ix. 1865.

And in 1866 he published a paper entitled "Adversaria Ægyptiaca" in the *Zeitschrift fur Egyptischer Sprache*, in which he states:—

"In my paper in the *Revue Archéologique* I gave the explanation of the word  as signifying the Egyptian game of chess, and also that of  *han*, the game of the vase. To this I will add the  *tau* or game of "Robbers," the prototype of the Latrunculi of the Romans which is found in an inscription at Thebes published by Mr. Brugsch in his Monuments Egyptiens, Pl. LXVIII f. h., and in Champollion, Notices Descriptives, p. 566. From a comparison of these inscriptions it is evident that the hieroglyph  often in full texts represented chequered is really a chess-board with the pieces arranged ready for the game.

[1] It will be noticed that the cells are sunk in each of these games, to keep the pieces in their places. In Queen Hatasu's board they are not sunk. E.F.

"The text in Champollion differs from that of Brugsch. It reads:

sχχm *m* *hab* *m* *han* *m* *stn-t*
delectatus in ludendo, in ludo vasis, in abaco,

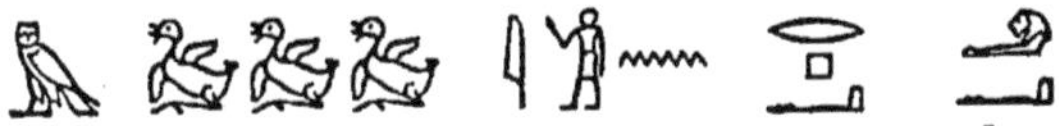

m *t'au* *ȧn* *rpa* *ha*
in latrunculis, fuit dux princeps.

"Here it is necessary to correct the form of the Notice descriptive to , the form in which it occurs in the inscription published by Brugsch, while the form in other passages is *sn-t* as already elsewhere shown, which is the correct form, the being the homophone of and the phonetic complement as I have elsewhere shown of the or . In Brugsch the text is larger.

"The text in Brugsch, Pl. LXVIII. f. reads:

'ma *bu* *nefr* *n* *sχm* *suta* *m*
visus est locus bonus delectationis valetudinis. In

at *nefr-t* *ma* *hes* *χbt* *urhs*
horâ bonâ videntur cantus, saltatio, unctus,

ana *m* *χt* *nbt* *hâb* *m* *han*
thura, cum rebus omnibus, ludus in vase,

m *stnt* *m* *tau* *an*
in abaco, in latrunculis, a (duce) etc. [1]

[1] We are indebted to Messrs. Harrison & Sons for the use of this Egyptian type.

"That the game *snt* means chess in general, there can not be a doubt from the evidence which I have already given. That of the *tau* or "Robbers" connects it with the Roman game of Latrunculi which both by name and probably as arranged had been derived from Egypt. This last game indeed is described as different from that of the vase and the chess-board. Perhaps future researches may throw some light upon its nature. It is mentioned however as *latrones* and not *latro* in the Egyptian texts."

In 1867 I received a copy of this article in the *Zeitschrift*, with the accompanying letter:

"British Museum,
4th December, 1867.

"Dear Falkener,

"You can keep the dissertations in the journal, as other copies of the Zeitschrift are in my possession. Some years ago, about three as I remember, I wrote a short paper in French in the *Revue Archéologique* entitled "Rhampsenite et le jeux d'echecs." In it I showed that the unknown Egyptian word 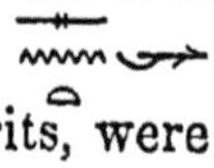 meant chess; and that the dead, or their spirits, were supposed to play at it in the future state. Something of this, as far as memory serves, takes place in the Greek or Roman Elysium, where the dead play at *tali*, or knuckle-bones, an Elysian pleasure which I formerly realized when a boy at school. Since then Lepsius has published a coffin, with the very chapter of the Ritual which I illustrated; in which are depicted the chessmen. This time it is my intention to amalgamate the two papers for the Royal Society of Literature in English, and add some additions and observations.

"The 'Vase' game was played over a circular board, and the pieces moved on concentric circles. It is represented on early tombs. My article in the *Revue Archéologique* is in Vol. xii, 8° Paris 1865, p. 65 and foll. No copies of my paper were sent me, or I should have distributed them amongst my friends.

Yours very truly,
S. BIRCH."

These two articles were incorporated together with some additions in a paper read before the Royal Society of Literature, Feby. 28, 1868, and published in its Transactions, Vol. ix, new series, in 1870.

Here, in game No. 4 preceding, he gives the signification of *aaseb* as "consumed" or "extinguished." Relative to game No. 5, he mentions that, as already stated, Rameses III. played at draughts with Isis. Game No. 6 he thinks may represent Rhamsinitus "the old lion" playing with Isis, on whose head was placed a solar disk entwined with goats' horns. In the 17th chapter of the *Ritual for the Dead* we read—"Making transformations at their will; and playing at (draughts) being in a pavilion, a living soul."

Lastly, in 1878, we have some further observations by Dr. Birch in his notes in the second edition of Sir Gardner Wilkinson's *Ancient Egyptians*:—

"The board of the game was called 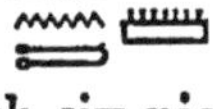 or 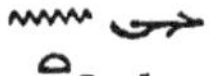 *sent.* They generally played with six pieces, and the set of each player was alike, but distinct from that of his opponent. The most ordinary form was the cone or conoid, either plain, or else surmounted by a pointed or spherical head: but there were several varieties of shape. A very old type of porcelain in the

British Museum, No. 6143^a is a human head, and no doubt expresses  the *tau*, or robber, the latro of the Roman draught-board, said to be made of glass, and supposed by some to be a single piece. Another type was cat–or possibly dog-headed, B.M. 6414, and another decidedly dog or jackal-headed, 6414^b, of black porcelain probably represented the *kuon*, or dog, as the Greeks called their pieces. One remarkable one has traced upon it, in darker colour, the name of the monarch Nechao, or Necho II of the 26th dynasty, 600 B.C. It is numbered 6414^a." (It was originally white: another 5575^a is black. They are represented below, the former of full size, the latter of half size.)

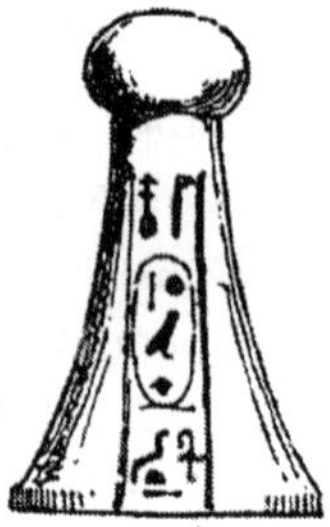

"The game was one of the delights of the Egyptian Elysium, and played in the future state, according to the 17th chapter of the *Ritual of the Dead*; and boards and men—five of one kind, and four of the other—are sometimes represented in the sarcophagi of the eleventh dynasty. The boards had nine squares one way, and seventeen the other: in all 153 squares. They were alternately coloured red and black. The draught-men were called *ab* or *abu*." In another place he says—"The Egyptian chess-board had thirty squares, black and white," p. 259.

It will be seen that these remarks of Dr. Birch extend from 1864 to 1878. Making no further progress, I then laid aside my labours as hopeless, and turned my attention to the Ludus Latrunculorum of the Romans. But there also—notwithstanding all that had been written on the subject by learned students and antiquaries—as no board had been discovered, we had no clue to the game; and the wildest theories were advanced for its solution; and we got no further than the poets left us. For the reader will have observed from the foregoing that although numerous representations of the Egyptian draught-board exist in Egyptian wall-painting, no plan of the board has been so represented; neither have any remains of a draught-board been discovered till very recently, although numerous draught-men have been found from time to time. As it was considered probable, as stated by Dr. Birch in the foregoing extracts, that one of the Egyptian games was the prototype of the famous Ludus Latrunculorum of the Romans, a game which is now lost to us, and of which likewise we have no remains of a board, or even a description which we knew to apply to this game, of the number of squares or the number of men; the reader will imagine how when after so many years of study, we had only got to the bare commencement of our work, we were struck with startling amazement and joy when we read the following announcement in the *Times* of June 22, 1887 :—

III.

"Ancient Royal Egyptian Relics at the Manchester Exhibition.

"In the place of honour at Manchester—that is to say, on the dais, immediately under the dome in the centre of the exhibition building—stands an Egyptian-looking glass case containing a group of relics described in the catalogue as "The throne, signet, draught-board and draught-men of Queen Hatasu, B.C. 1600."

"*Draught-board and draught-men.*" "1600 years B.C,"—I said "we shall now know the number of squares, and the number of men: and it will be no difficult matter then to find the game." But we must go on with the description by the *Times*' Correspondent, for the particulars are most interesting:—

"The date is sufficiently startling, but, due allowance being made for chronological difficulties, it is no doubt fairly correct. As for the contents of the case, whether as regards their extreme antiquity or their historical associations, it is not too much to say that they are the most remarkable objects in the exhibition. The throne is unique. Specimens of ancient Egyptian stools and chairs, some beautifully inlaid with marqueterie of ivory and various woods, may be seen in several European museums; but in none do we find a Pharaonic throne plated with gold and silver, and adorned with the emblems of Egyptian sovereignty. It is not, of course, absolutely intact. The seat and back (which may have been made of plaited palm-fibre or bands of leather) have perished; but a leopard skin hides the necessary restoration of these parts, and all that remains of the original piece of furniture is magnificent. The

QUEEN HATASU.

wood is very hard and heavy, and of a rich dark colour resembling rosewood. The four legs are carved in the shape of the legs of some hoofed animal, probably a bull, the front of each leg being decorated with two royal basilisks in gold. These basilisks are erect, face to face, their tails forming a continuous coil down to the rise of the hoof. Round each fetlock runs a silver band, and under each hoof there was originally a plate of silver, of which only a few fragments remain. The cross rail in front of the seat is also plated with silver. The arms (or what would be the arms if placed in position) are very curious, consisting of two flat pieces of wood joined at right angles, so as to form an upright affixed to the framework of the back and a horizontal support for the arm of the sitter. These are of the same dark wood as the legs and rails, having a border line at each side; while down the middle, with head erect at the top of the upright limb, and tail undulating downwards to the finish of the arm-rest, is a basilisk carved in some lighter coloured wood, and encrusted with hundreds of minute silver annulets, to represent the markings of the reptile. The nails connecting the various parts are round-headed and plated with gold, thus closely resembling the ornamental brass-headed nails in use at the present day. The gold and silver are both of the purest quality. Of the royal ovals which formerly adorned this beautiful chair of state, only one longitudinal fragment remains. This fragment measures some 9in. or 10in. in length, is carved on both sides, and contains about one-fourth part of what may be called the field of the cartouche. Enough, however, remains to identify on one side the throne-name, and on the other side the family name, of Queen

Hatasu, or, more correctly, Hatshepsu. The carving is admirable, every detail—even to the form of the nails and the creases of the finger-joints in part of a hand—being rendered with the most perfect truth and delicacy. The throne-name, "Ra-ma-ka," is surrounded by a palm-frond bordering, and the family name, "Amen-Knum Hatshepsu," by a border of concentric spirals. The wood of this cartouche is the same as that of the basilisks upon the arms, being very hard and close-grained, and of a tawny yellow hue, like boxwood. Some gorgeously coloured throne-chairs depicted on the walls of a side chamber in the tomb of Rameses III. at Thebes show exactly into what parts of the frame-work these royal insignia were inserted, and might serve as models for the complete restoration of this most valuable and interesting relic.

"Among other objects in Queen Hatshepsu's case is a fine female face—part of an effigy from a sarcophagus lid—carved in the same rich dark wood as the throne. In profile, this face not only bears a close resemblance to the face of the seated statue of Hatshepsu in the Berlin collection, but it is almost identical with the profile of Hatshepsu's grandmother, Queen Aah-hotep, as carved in effigy upon her sarcophagus lid in the Boulak Museum. It is a beautiful, low-browed, full-lipped Oriental face, of Egyptian type *pur sang*, without the least touch of Semitism. Is it a portrait of Hatshepsu? This question (which it is perhaps impossible to answer) is one of no ordinary interest; for Hatshepsu was not only a principal actor in the long and splendid drama of Egyptian history, but she was also one of the most extraordinary women in the history of the ancient world. A daughter of Thothmes I., she appears to have inherited certain sovereign rights by virtue of her descent in the female line from the old legitimate XIIth Dynasty stock. Intermarrying with her brother, Thothmes II., she ratified that Pharaoh's succession, and after his death she reigned alone, literally as Pharaoh, for many years. As Pharaoh, she is represented in the garb of a king, crowned with the war helmet, and wearing a false beard. She was one of the most magnificent builder-Sovereigns of Egypt; her great temple at Dayr-el-Baharee, in Western Thebes, being architecturally unlike every other temple in Egypt, and her obelisks at Karnak being the most admirably engraved and proportioned, as well as the loftiest, known. One yet stands erect beside the fallen fragments of its fellow. The most striking incident of her reign was, however, the expedition which she despatched to the "Land of Punt," now identified with the Somali country, on the east coast of Africa. For this purpose she built and fitted out a fleet of five ships, which successfully accomplished the voyage and returned to Thebes laden with foreign shrubs, gums, spices, rare woods, apes, elephant-tusks, and other treasures. The departure and return of this fleet, the incidents of the voyage, the lading of the ships, and the triumphal procession of the troops on re-entering Thebes, are represented on the terrace walls of Hatshepsu's temple in a series of sculptured and painted tableaux of unparalleled interest. This is the earliest instance of the fitting out of a fleet, or of a voyage of discovery, known in history. Meanwhile, it may be asked what route they followed. That the ships started from and returned to Thebes is placed beyond doubt by the tableaux and inscriptions. It is incredible that they should have descended the Nile, sailed westward through the Pillars of Hercules, doubled the Cape of Good Hope, and arrived at the Somali coast by way of the Mozambique Channel and the shores of Zanzibar. This would imply that they twice made the almost complete circuit of the African continent. If we reject this hypothesis, as we must, there remains no alternative route except by means of a canal, or chain of canals, connecting the Nile with the Red Sea. The old Wady Tûmilat Canal is generally ascribed to Seti I., second Pharaoh of the XIXth Dynasty and father of Rameses the Great; but this supposition rests upon no other evidence than the fact that a canal leading from the Nile to the ocean is represented upon a monument of his reign. There is really no reason why this canal may not have been made under the preceding dynasty, and it is far from improbable that the great woman-Pharaoh who first conceived the notion of venturing her ships upon an unknown sea may have also cut the channel of communication by which they went forth. The throne which is now to be seen at the Manchester Exhibition, the broken cartouche, the exquisitely-sculptured face, the elaborate draught-men, may all, perchance, be carved in some of that very wood which the Queen's fleet brought back from the far shores of Punt. This, perhaps, is to consider the question too curiously; but the woods, at all events, are not of Egyptian growth.

"These rare and precious objects are the property of Mr. Jesse Haworth, and are, by his permission, now for the first time exhibited."

In the catalogue of the Manchester Exhibition is the following description of the objects, written previously to the above, by Mr. A. Dodgson of Ashton-under-Lyne.

"THE THRONE, CARTOUCHE, SIGNET, DRAUGHT-BOARD AND DRAUGHT-MEN OF QUEEN HATASU. DATE B.C. 1600.—These remarkable relics, the workmanship of royal artists 3,500 years ago, *i.e.*, before the birth of Moses, are now being exhibited for the first time, by the kind permission of their owner, Jesse Haworth, Esq. Queen Hatasu was the favourite daughter of Thothmes I., and sister of Thothmes II. and III., Egyptian kings of the XVIII. dynasty. She reigned conjointly with her eldest brother; then alone for 15 years, and for a short time with her younger brother, Thothmes III. She was the Elizabeth of Egyptian history; had a masculine genius, and unbounded ambition. A woman, she assumed male attire; was addressed as a king even in the inscriptions upon her monuments. Her edifices are said to be "the most tasteful, most complete, and brilliant creations which ever left the hands of an Egyptian architect." The largest and most beautifully executed Obelisk, still standing at Karnak, bears her name. On the walls of her unique and beautiful Temple at Dayr-el-Baharee, we see a naval expedition sent to explore the unknown land of Punt, the Somali country on the east coast of Africa, near Cape Guardafui, 600 years before the fleets of Solomon, and returning laden with foreign woods, rare trees, gums, perfumes, and strange beasts. Here we have (1) Queen Hatasu's Throne, made of wood foreign to Egypt, the legs most elegantly carved in imitation of the legs of an animal, covered with gold down to the hoof, finishing with a silver band. Each leg has carved in relief two Uræi, the sacred cobra serpent of Egypt, symbolical of a goddess. These are plated with gold. Each arm is ornamented with a serpent curving gracefully along from head to tail, the scales admirably imitated by hundreds of inlaid silver rings. The only remaining rail is plated with silver. The gold and silver are each of the purest quality. (2) A fragment of the Cartouche or oval bearing the royal name, and once attached to the Throne; the hieroglyphics are very elegantly carved in relief, with a scroll-pattern round the edge and around one margin, and a palm frond pattern around the other. About one-fourth of the oval remains, by means of which our distinguished Egyptologist. Miss Amelia B. Edwards, L.L.D., has been able to complete the name, and identify the Throne. On one side is the great Queen's name, "Ra-ma-ka." On the other the family name, "Amen-Khnum-Hat-Shepsu," commonly read Hatasu. With all its imperfections, it is unique, being the only throne which has ever been disinterred in Egypt. (3) A female face boldly but exquisitely carved in dark wood, from the lid of a coffin, the effigy strongly resembling the face of the sitting statue of Hatasu in the Berlin Museum; the eyes and double crown are lost. (4) The Signet: this is a Scarabæus, in turquoise, bearing the Cartouche of Queen Hatasu, once worn as a ring. (5) The Draught Box and Draught-men: the box is of dark wood, divided on its upper[1] side by strips of ivory into thirty squares, on its under[2] side into twenty squares, twelve being at one end and eight down the centre;[3] some of these contained hieroglyphics inlaid, three of which still remain, also a drawer for holding the draughts. These draughts consist of about twenty pieces, carved with most exquisite art and finish in the form of lions' heads—the hieroglyphic sign for "Hat" in Hatasu.

[1] *lower.* [2] upper. [3] ambiguous: see p. 33.

Also two little standing figures of Egyptian men like pages or attendants, perfect and admirable specimens of the most delicate Egyptian art. These may have been markers, or, perhaps, the principal pieces. Two sides of another draught box,[1] of blue porcelain and ivory, with which are two conical draughts of blue porcelain and ivory and three other ivory pieces. (6) Also parts of two porcelain rings and porcelain rods, probably for some unknown game. (7) With the above were found a kind of salve or perfume spoon in green slate, and a second in alabaster."[2]

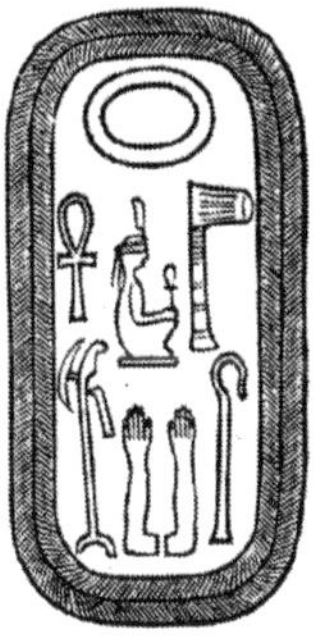

RA-MA-KA.
(The throne name.)

AMEN-KNUM-HATASU.
(The family name.)

NUTAR HIMET HATASU.
The divine spouse,
(wife of the King.)

[1] *board.*

[2] [The coffin of Thothmes I., and the bodies of Thothmes II. and III. were found at Dayr-el-Baharee in 1881—that of their sister, Queen Hatasu, had disappeared, but her Cabinet was there, and is now in the Boulack Museum, and "I have no doubt whatever," says Miss Edwards, "that this Throne and these other relics are from that Tomb."]

The "dark wood bust," though not found with the other objects, was supposed to be that of Queen Hatasu, and to "strongly resemble the face of the sitting statue of Queen Hatasu in the Berlin Museum," a copy of which, in plaster, we have in our Museum; but I must acknowledge that I see no resemblance whatever between them. Its identification being very uncertain, Mr. Haworth did not present it to the British Museum. Queen Hatasu erected the magnificent obelisk at Karnak. Her father gave her the name of Mat Ka ra, Queen of the south and the north, that is to say, of the whole world.

I naturally went to Manchester immediately after reading this account in the *Times*, but was disappointed to find that the "draught-board" is only the fragment of a draught-board, and so my conjecture of the Egyptian draught-board being a board of twelve squares on each side could not be verified. It is broken off at the end of the sixth square in length, and has only a square and a half in width remaining, so that it is a mere fragment. But the sixth square has the hieroglyph 𓄤 *nefer*, good, upon it, and I take this as half the length.[1] The squares are about $1\frac{5}{16}$ inch, and the ivory divisions nearly $\frac{1}{4}$ inch. The squares are filled with porcelain, and the black hieroglyph is burnt into the porcelain. The board stands three inches high, with an inch and a half porcelain pannel on each side, bordered with $\frac{3}{4}$ inch ivory. The dark wood squares under the porcelain are veneered on rough wood.

There are twenty pieces remaining of this game: ten

[1] The same sign, *nefer*, is seen in three examples extant of the game of the *Sacred Way*, which we shall describe presently, and which there seems to denote a division in the board.

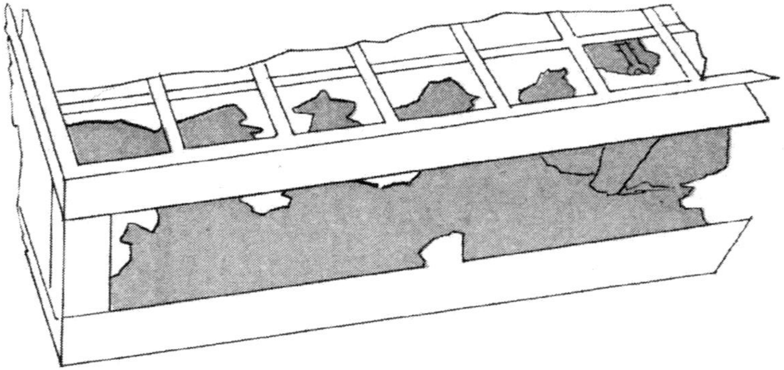

FRAGMENT OF QUEEN HATASU'S DRAUGHT-BOARD
OF IVORY AND PORCELAIN.

of light colour wood, and nine of dark wood, and one of ivory; all these pieces have a lion's head. These lions' heads are not all of exactly the same size; one is rather larger than the rest, and one is smaller. But there is not sufficient difference of size to lead to the supposition that they were of different powers, though they may have belonged to different sets. Together with these pieces are two reel-shaped pieces, one astragal, and two upright draught-men of the form represented in Egyptian paintings; one white, the other of blue enamel, and a dark wooden one a little larger. These are evidently the sole remnants of another set or sets.

A double game was also found in Queen Hatasu's tomb, similar to that formerly belonging to Dr. Abbot of Cairo which is now in the Louvre. It is inlaid or veneered with dark wood like the draught-board; and the squares are divided in like manner by ivory slips. It is $12\frac{1}{2}$ inches long by $4\frac{1}{8}$ wide, and $2\frac{1}{2}$ deep with a drawer in the middle to contain the men. On one side the board has ten squares in length, and three in breadth, the cells being a little more than an inch square. On the other side the middle row has twelve squares and the sides only four. Some of these "squares" are of oblong form, in consequence of there being ten in length instead of twelve as on the other side. This game appears to be the game of the Sacred Way. The other game differs from that of Dr. Abbot's in having hieroglyphics in two of the squares. In a similar board discovered by Mr. Petrie, and exhibited by him in London in 1889, two squares are marked by I and II, thus appearing to denote position: consequently, the two figures in one of these squares, and the three figures in the next, in this example, denote II and III. The next square in Mr. Petrie's board has two diagonals across it, thus dividing it into four parts, and the fifth square has the *nefer* (good), as in this example. All these objects have been given to the Nation by Mr. Jesse Haworth, and are now in the British Museum.

The reader will have perceived from the preceding article how much we are indebted to the learning and research of Dr. Birch, in collecting all the evidence relative to the games of ancient Egypt; the more so as it would appear from his belief that these games, or one of them, represented chess, that he was occupied far more in Egyptian and Assyrian and Chinese literature and antiquities, than in these so-called "idle" amusements. No one can for a moment suppose that chess was invented in those ancient times. Draughts of some kind were certainly played then, but as there are various kinds of draughts in the present day—English, Polish, Turkish, and many others—so "draughts" as played by the ancients were very different to the games we know. That the Roman game of Latrunculi was known to the Egyptians, was taken for granted by Dr. Birch, and the probability of its being so is shown by his researches. In his paper of 1864 he thought *sen* signified a robber, and so he identified it with *latro* and *latrunculus*.[1] But in his paper of 1868 he identified the game of *Tau* (robbers) with the latrunculi. Consequently *senat* must mean something else; and accordingly he there gave a different interpretation of the word, stating that *seni* means "to traverse, or to open the gates." Possibly it had some other meaning, more appropriate to our purpose, and indeed, he tells us that *sen* has many meanings in hieroglyphics.

In the inscriptions given us by Brugsch and Champollion, we have a distinction between the games of *Senat* ("abacus" or "draughts"), and *Tau* (robbers). The word *Senat* is inscribed over Dr. Birch's No. 1 (p. 10). That therefore cannot be the game of *Tau*. It will be observed that the game of *Senat* is there coupled with the game of *Han* or *the Vase*; just as Dr. Birch's No. 3 and No. 4 are coupled together, and as in a representation of the Egyptian game called *Mora* by the Italians, which we shall presently consider, two different games are represented; one where only one player throws out his fingers, while the other guesses; the other where both do so, and each guesses. Nos. 3 and 4 therefore of Dr. Birch's description are different games, though the board appears to be the same, with the exception of the pieces being differently placed; and so we may conclude that one is the game of *Senat* ("draughts"), and the other the game of *Tau* or *Robbers*. The word *Aaseb* written over the latter is acknowledged by Dr. Birch to be of doubtful meaning. From what is just stated that these grouped games represent different games, we cannot accept Dr. Birch's supposition that this word signifies "lost," as being the

[1] But this was a mistake, for the word here is differently spelt.

conclusion of the other game; but rather that it represents the other game of *Tau*, or *robbers*. If so, we see that the board, like that of the game of *Senat*, or "draughts," contained twelve cells each way, or 144 in all. As these two games of "draughts" and *robbers*, were played apparently on the same board, and are represented in the paintings with the same men, it would be impossible to tell in these paintings which game is represented, where the name *Senat* or *Tau* is not given, were it not from other circumstances, which we shall mention presently. In some examples we find the men, instead of being placed in a continuous row, are divided between the two players. In Dr. Birch's No. 5 (p. 12) that of Rameses III. and Isis, or his queen, there are ten men on the board. In No. 6 each side has four men remaining, while each player holds a piece *en prise*, and the lion has a bag in which he holds his captive pieces. In No. 4 one player has six pieces, and the other five, but relative to this also we will speak presently. We have seen that in 1878 Dr. Birch thought that "the board had nine squares one way and seventeen the other, in all 153 squares." This idea was evidently taken from the painting on Mentuhotop's sarcophagus, published in Lepsius's *Ælteste Texte.*

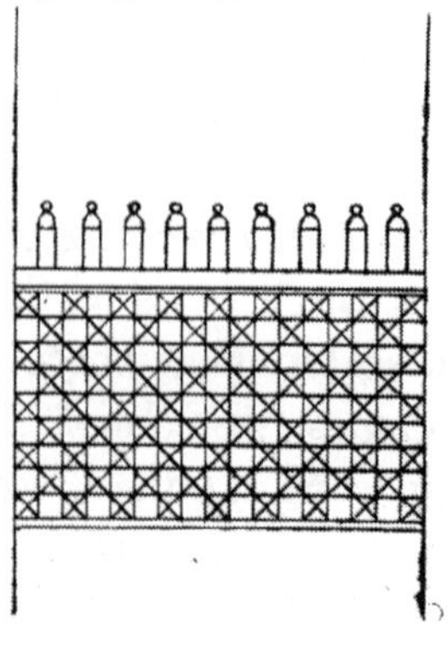

On examining Prof. Lepsius's work however it will be seen that this painting is in the middle of a long upright pannel, and that the so-called board is merely a piece of diaper ornament figuratively representing a board, but not the board itself. The diaper is a mere indication of the game, and goes for nothing in the argument. In this same article Dr. Birch said: "The Egyptian chess-board had thirty squares, black and white," and "they generally played with six pieces." Dr. Birch therefore cannot be trusted for the details of the game. Thirty also is the number given by Souterius, p. 60.

IV.

THE GAME OF TAU

OR GAME OF ROBBERS.

AFTERWARDS THE

LUDUS LATRUNCULORUM,

OR LUDUS CALCULORUM, OR PRŒLIA LATRONUM, OR BELLUM LATRONUM

OF THE ROMANS.

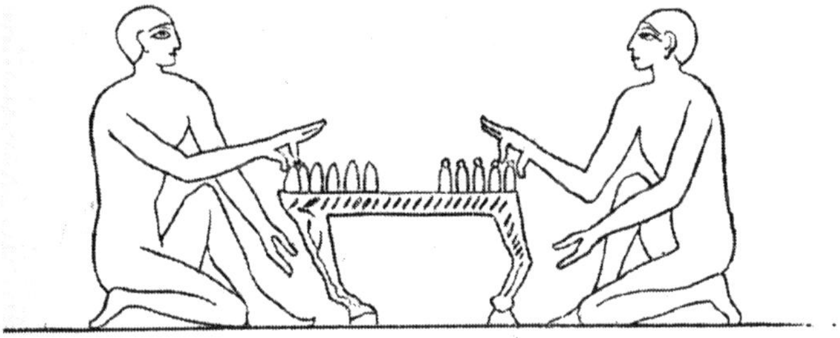

Salmasius, Historiæ Aug. Scriptores Sex - -	1620
Souterius, Palamides - - - -	1625
Bulengerus, De ludis Veterum - - -	1627
Semptlebius, De alea Veterum - - -	1667
Severinus, Dell' antica Pettia - - -	1690
Hyde, Historia Nerdiludii, h.e.d. Trunculorum -	1694
James Christie, Inquiry into the ancient Greek game	1801
Becker, Gallus - - - - -	1838
Van Oppen, in "Schachzeitung," for - -	1847
Herbert Coleridge, on Greek and Roman Chess -	1855
" " in Forbes' History of Chess -	1860
L. Becq de Fouquières, Les Jeux des anciens -	1869

IT is wonderful that this game should ever have fallen into dissuetude, that it should ever have become so completely forgotten, that the most zealous and learned antiquaries should have failed in restoring it to light. The goodly array of names at the head of this article is evidence sufficient to show that all has been done which learning and diligence could do. All passages from ancient poets and historians have been collected; the bones of the entire skeleton have been put together, but there they remained; the game was not played, and it could only be regarded as an interesting fragment of antiquity—curious, but incomplete, and useless.

Few visitors to the British Museum, previous to the present time, could have failed to notice on the wall of the further staircase,[1] the Egyptian caricature drawn on papyrus, referred to in the first section, which represents a lion and goat—and looking very much like our famous lion and unicorn—playing at a game which, from the appearance of the pieces, might be easily mistaken for chess. In the galleries upstairs may be seen some wooden and bone pieces of similar appearance, viz., lofty pieces like chess-men, and not flat, like draught-men. Several references have been given in the last section of Egyptian pictures of kings and other persons playing at a game which seems in every case to be identical. The pieces are always upright pieces, and there is a difference of colour, or else a slight difference of form observable between the two sides. In all these representations, there is but one form discernible in each colour or side, and this form is indicated with great precision. Thus it is evident that

[1] It is now removed, in order to protect it from the light.

the game so represented cannot be the game of chess; but a game like draughts. Some of the pieces in our Museum, and of those in some foreign collections, have the heads of animals; and this seems to connect the game with the game played by the Greeks and Romans, the pieces of which were called dogs, κύνες, by the Greeks.[1] Such heads of animals are observable in Queen Hatasu's pieces, but in general the pieces represented in the Egyptian monuments were of cylindrical form rounded at the top, or tapering pieces surmounted by a bead or knob. The latrunculi or latrones of the Roman game were originally soldiers, but by degrees the name became significant of licentiousness and audacity, as the soldier became a robber. Just so in our own language the terms knave, brigand, villain, have lost their original significance. But whether we regard the pieces in the Roman game of draughts as soldiers or thieves, they are equally deserving of their name: we have equally to guard against the strategies of war, and the stratagems of thieves. Sometimes we find our pieces taken by superior force or by skilful marshalling: sometimes we find them stolen from us when we least expect it. When most intent on taking an adversary our enemy comes with subtlety and robs us of our own piece. It is a lively inspiriting game, and likely to be a favourite in modern, as it was in ancient times.

In the preceding sections we have shown the probability of the Ludus Latrunculorum having its origin in Egypt. We have the myth of Thoth (Hermes) having invented the game of draughts; we have inscriptions and wall paintings from tombs of the 4th dynasty; we have the actual draught-board and draught-men used

[1] Bulengerus says they were called so on account of their impudence.

by Queen Hatasu shortly after the time of Joseph; we see on the wall-paintings Rameses III. playing the game in the time of the Exodus; we find in every tomb and sarcophagus, from the earliest to the latest times, evidence that the Egyptians believed that in the future state those who were weighed in the balance and found worthy would play at these games; and from the papyrus painting in our Museum we know that the Egyptian game was still played in the time of Trajan and the Antonines, say A.D. 100. We thus have evidence that it continued to Roman times. Instead then of its being an idle assumption, a mere hypothesis, to connect the Ludus Latrunculorum of the Romans with the Egyptian game of *Tau*, it seems to be a most strange, and unaccountable, and incredible thing to imagine that a game with a history of say 3000 years, and which, as we have seen, was played in the time of the Romans and early Christians, should not have been continued in practice by them, though under another name. But it is not another name: for *Tau* and *Latrones* or *Latrunculi* are synonymous; as are the dogs (κύνες) as the Greeks called their Ψῆφοι, with the dogs, kilab, as the Arabs still call their draught-men. The upright form also of the Egyptian piece (1) was merely

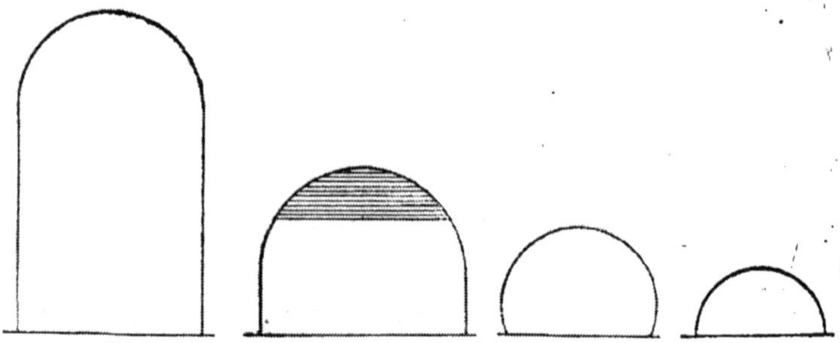

(1) (2) 1859. (3) 1853. (4) 1888.

diminished in height by the Romans, as we may judge from the Græco-Roman latrunculus found by Mr. Newton[1] at Halicarnassus, (2) and now in the British Museum; $^{12\text{-}20}_{215}$; the numerous pieces found in the tombs of Cuma,[2] and other Etruscan cities; (3); and from the still smaller and shorter latrunculus found at Rome in 1888, (4), in my possession.

The difference in size of these latrunculi is interesting as showing the habits of the various peoples. The Egyptians in the earliest times played the game sitting on the ground, as we see by their pictures, whereas the Greeks and Romans sat on chairs.

It is therefore only through neglect of this evidence that we have hitherto not been able to determine the details, and to recover the game of the Ludus Latrunculorum.

It will be observed that as the pieces diminished in height they became more difficult to handle. Other forms were therefore devised, gradually advancing to the reel-shape, so as to give greater stability, and greater facility of handling, though even in the old shape we see this attempted in the latrunculi of Cuma already given.

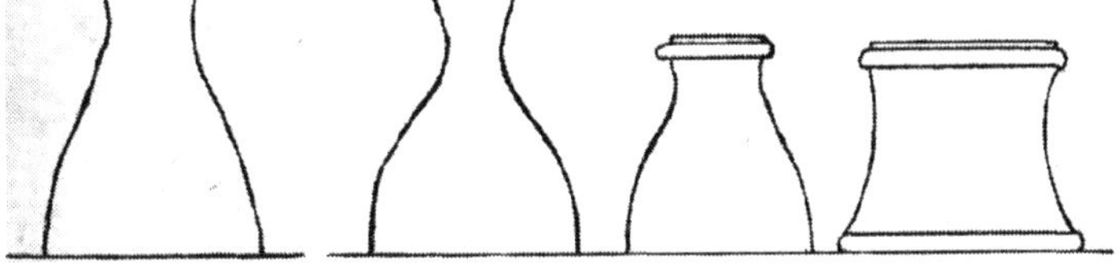

[1] Sir Charles Newton, K.C.B. [2] Bullet. Archeolog. Nap. N.S. 1883.

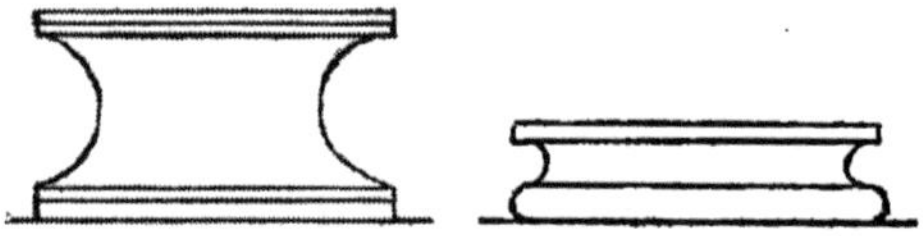

Those of Cuma were found in a tomb, the plan of which is seen below. It contained three graves, and on the podium round the walls were placed the latrunculi, ready for the dead to play with when they arose from their lethal state. No doubt there was the full

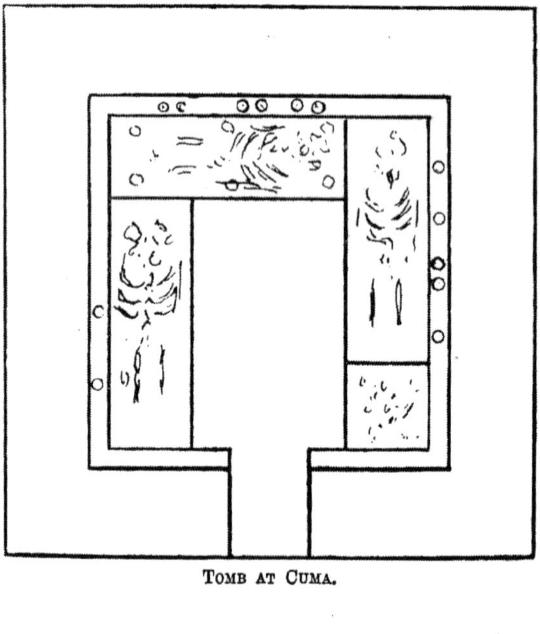

TOMB AT CUMA.

number of them originally, sixty, but most of them must have been taken away by the workmen or others, and sold to travellers or dealers before Sigr. Minervini visited the tomb.[1]

It was probably with latrunculi similar to that of No. 4 that Quadratilla played.[2]

. We will now proceed to connect together what we know of each. While we have only disconnected references to the game by the Latin poets, but no representation of the board; in the Egyptian paintings and hieroglyphics we have only a profile of the board, and the name of the game, but no description. We will therefore endeavour to discover the game by applying the Roman description to the Egyptian board. We will begin with the board.

There were two Egyptian games, the boards of which, and the pieces of which appear to be the same. The *Senat*, as we have seen, was supposed to be the game of "Draughts;" and the *Tau* the game of Robbers. Although in our Museum we see pieces of various forms, it is important to bear in mind that in the paintings the boards are always in profile, and of the same size, and the boards and pieces are alike.

The games are represented also in hieroglyphics, In

[1] Sigr. Minervini thus describes these objects :—"In a Cuman tomb of Roman construction were found the objects we publish, of the size of the original . . There were several hemispherical pieces of three different colours, white, yellow, and black . . . . With these were found two dice, with fragments of a carved ivory box, in which probably they were kept; and similar fragments are seen in the work of the chev. Fiorelli's *Monumenti Cumani*, tav. ii, No 6." The Brit. Mus. has no copy of this book. Speaking of these hemispherical pieces, he continues—"è che in gran numero fuori da altri sepolchri, a me pare siano da riputarsi reservienti al giuoco de *Calculi o Latrunculi*." He then refers to the passages in Pollux, Ovid, Martial, and Sidonius Apollinaris, and lastly to the poem by Saleus Bassus, and then concludes—"Non saprei giudicare quai movimenti si additassero dal latino poeta." *Bullettino Archeologico Napolitano*. Nuova Serie, del P. R. Garucci e di Giulio Minervini, anno primo, 1853.

[2] Pliny's *Letters*, vii, 24.

general the board appears as a block with men on it: this will be seen in the hieroglyphic description in p. 17. The hieroglyph did not pretend to indicate the exact number of men, but merely a board with men upon it. But in larger hieroglyphic paintings the board is represented with a greater number of men. The men are sometimes all of one height, and sometimes of high and low pieces placed alternately: and in the double group of the Benihassan tomb, p. 12, we find these two distributions of the men. These therefore are the two games. The left group will be seen to be the same as the left group in Rashepses' tomb p. 10, over which is the name "*Senat.*" The right hand group therefore must be the *Tau.* It is this which we are now considering. It will be observed that, unlike the other game, the men are placed in close ranks on either side prior to commencing the game.

The larger hieroglyphics represent the board with six, eight, ten or twelve men. Where the men are of unequal height there was a reason for this, as we shall presently see: but where they are of equal height, we may hold it as certain that the painter or engraver would never take the trouble to show more men than were necessary. We may conclude then that the greatest number shown in such hieroglyphs, twelve, was the full number. This number, twelve, is the exact number shown in all the paintings. The Egyptian board therefore was a square of twelve, having 144 cells: for the men do not represent the number of men played with, but the number of cells on each side of the board. Thus in the papyrus Burton in the British Museum we see a fictitious board represented,

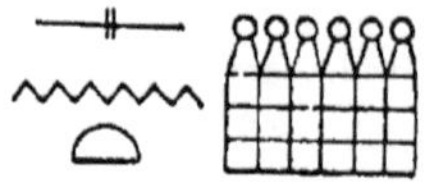

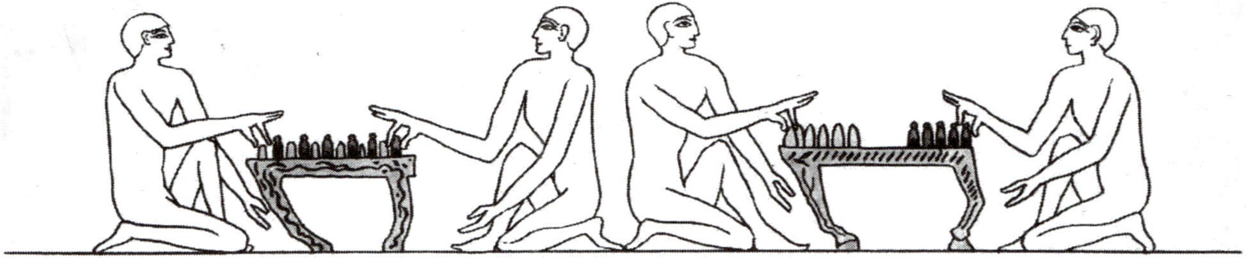

FROM TOMBS AT BENIHASSAN.

of six by three squares, and having six men on the top over the six squares.

Eustathius and Hesychius, as we learn from Pollux, tell us that the Greek game, *grammismos*, or *diagrammismos*—and from this we may draw the inference that the Roman game we are treating of, though it had its origin in Egypt, was known to the Greeks as well as the Romans—was played with many pieces (πολλῶν Ψήφων), Hesychius says sixty, (ἑξήκοντα), and that the *plinthion* or board had certain parts of it called a *city* (πολις), applying probably to groups or masses of pieces in different parts of the board, so firmly intrenched that their opponents could not touch them. Thus if the board was twelve-square, and there were thirty men on each side, and the men were placed, as with us, on alternate squares, they would occupy five rows: and this number, five, is what is shown in right hand group of Benihassan painting,[1] and in that of the Lion and Goat.[2] There would then remain only two vacant rows, so that the pieces would soon come *in medias res.*

Here we find the fragment of Queen Hatasu's board of use: for if the sign *nefer* 𓄤, on the sixth square, marks the half of the board, it is probable that the other half was marked in the same way: and thus we have the two vacant rows of the Ludus Latrunculorum indicated.

One of the meanings of the word 𓄤 *nefer*, given us by Mr. le Page Renouf in his letter which we will give presently, is *door*; which probably may mean here *open.* If so, its appearance on these two lines would be very

[1] The left hand figure appears to have six men; but on examining it we see that the artist had drawn five only· but finding he had left too wide a space between two of them, he endeavoured to rectify it by squeezing in another to fill it up.

[2] Four on the board, and one in each hand.

appropriate, to designate the open space between the two armies at the commencement of the battle; and this again would constitute a further argument both for the size of the board and the number of the men. In the game of the Sacred Way, which we shall consider further on, we find the same sign *nefer* again used to mark a division in the board.

We see now that Rameses III, and the lion and the goat, are playing at the game of *Tau*; not the game of *Senat*, or "draughts."

As Dr. Birch collected all the authorities for the Egyptian games, without discovering the games themselves; so Dr. Hyde brought together all the passages from the Latin poets without discovering the Ludus Latrunculorum. But we are equally indebted to both these writers for their diligent and learned researches. The following are the chief materials collected by Dr. Hyde, though his work will be found to contain many more of philological and antiquarian interest.

Sive latrocinii sub imagine calculus ibit,
Fac pereat vitreo miles ab hoste tuus.
Ovid. *Ars Amandi*, ii, 207.

Cautaque, non stulte, latronum prœlia ludat;
Unus cum gemino calculus hoste perit.
Bellatorque sua prensus sine compare bellat,
Æmulus et cœptum sæpe recurrit iter.
Id. iii, 357.

Discolor ut recto grassetur limite miles,
Quum medius gemino calculus hoste perit:
Ut mago velle sequi sciat, et revocare priorem;
Nec, tuto fugiens, incomitatus eat.
Id *Trist.* ii, 477

OUEEN HATASU'S DRAUGHT-BOARD RESTORED.

Sic vincas Noviumque Publiumque,
  Mandris et vitreo latrone clausos.

Mart. *Epig.* vii, 72.

Hic mihi bis seno numeratur tessera puncto:
  Calculus hic gemino discolor hoste perit.

Id, xiv, 17.

Insidiosorum si ludis bella latronum,
  Gemmeus iste tibi miles, et hostis erit.

Id. xiv, 20.

Vultisne diem sequentem, quem plerique omnes abaco et latrunculis conterunt . . . . a primo lucis in cœnæ tempus.

Macrob. *Sat.* i, 5.

Calculi partim ordine moventur, partim vage. Ideo alios Ordinarios, alios Vagos appellant. At vero qui omnino moveri non possunt Incitos dicunt.

Isidor. *Orig.* xviii, 67.

But the principal authority adduced by Dr. Hyde is the following panegyric to Calpurnius Piso, for his efficiency in this game; written by Saleius Bassus—

Te si forte juvat studiorum pondere fessum,
Non languere tamen, lususque movere per artem:
Callidiore modo tabulâ variatur apertâ
Calculus, et vitreo peraguntur milite bella:
Ut niveus nigros, nunc ut niger alliget albos.
Sed tibi quis non terga dedit? Quis te Duce cessit
Calculus? Aut quis non periturus perdidit hostem?
Mille modis acies tua dimicat, ille petentem
Dum fugit, ipse rapit: longo venit ille recessu
Qui stetit in speculis: hic se committere rixæ
Audet, et in prædam venientem decipit hostem.
Ancipites subit ille moras, similisque ligato,
Obligat ipse duos: hic ad majora movetur,
Ut citus et fractâ prorumpat in agmina mandrâ,
Clausaque dejecto populetur mœnia vallo.
Interea sectis quamvis acerrima surgunt.

Prœlia militibus, plenâ tamen ipse phalange,
Aut etiam pauco spoliatâ milite vincis,
Et tibi captivâ resonat manus utraque turba.

Which may be thus freely rendered :—

When wearied in the studious hours,
And yet you would not idle be,
The *Tabula* invites your skill
The sly *latrunculi* to move.
The vitreous *soldiers* see engage:
The whites by times a black ensnare;
The blacks again a white destroy.
But who is there can play with thee?
And under you what knave can yield?
See how in death their foes they slay,
For in a thousand ways they fight.
That *calculus* pretends to fly:
But lo, his follower he slays.
There comes a man from his retreat,
Who ever has been on the watch.
See there a man who boldly comes
His laden foe to intercept.
And there one braves a double foe,
That dying, he two more may slay.
See how that man from conquests fresh,
To other conquests now proceeds.
Swift how he breaks the ramparts dense,
And now the (*city*[1]) walls lays waste.
But though in such fierce contests held,
Thy phalanx still remains intact,
And scarce a soldier hast thou lost.
(The victory now, O *King*,[2] is thine!)
And each hand rattles with the captive crowd.

Now from these passages all that writers were agreed upon was that the pieces on each side were of different colours, and that a piece was captured or held in check

[1] Pollux, *Onom*, ix, 7. Segm 98.

[2] The conqueror in the game was called Dux, or Imperator. Vopiscus, *Procul.* 13. He is called Dux in the sixth line of this poem: and the same word *dux* is given by Champollion in his *Notices Descriptives*, p. 556. See p. 17.

when an enemy attacked him and held him in on each side. This is supposed by some to be understood by the word *alligatio*; and the piece so *bound* is supposed by some to be able to escape capture if there is an empty cell adjoining into which it can move: while others supposed that the piece so *bound* is *incitus*, unable to move, like the check-mate in Double Chess, only so long as it is thus bound. But neither of these suppositions can be correct: for the board is too large, the men too numerous; and so the game could never come to an end, if there were so many means to escape capture. The "alligatio" then occurs when two opposite pieces are in contiguous squares on the same line: then each is *joined to*, and attacks, or is attacked by the other. But when a piece is "alligatus" by an enemy on *each* side, it is "incitus," unable to move, and consequently is slain, or dead:—

> Fac pereat vitreo miles ab hoste tuus. Ovid. *A.A.*
> Unus cum gemino calculus hoste perit. Id.
> Quum medius gemino calculus hoste perit. Id. *Trist.*
> Calculus hic gemino discolor hoste perit. Mart.

and the piece so slain is taken off:—

> Dum fugit, ipse rapit . . . .
> Et tibi captivâ resonat manus utraque turbâ. Bassus.
> Ludi hujus ars est, comprehensione duarum tesserarum concolorum, alteram discolorem tollere. (ἀναιρεῖν) Pollux. *Onom.* ix, 7. § 98.

and this is shown in the Egyptian painting of Rameses and Isis; and in the caricature of the lion and goat, where the lion is seen to hold a bag full of captive pieces in one paw, and to take up a piece in the other.

Much confusion has also arisen relative to the moves as described by St. Isidor. He appears to say that some of the pieces move in a right, or "straight forward" line, as in Ovid:—

Discolor ut recto grassetur limite miles.

and some in a *wandering*, supposed to be a diagonal line: and he appears to accentuate this by calling the pieces by different names according to their moves—"ordinarios" and "vagos." Accordingly more than one recent writer on the games of the ancients, suppose that the men on either side consisted of inferior and superior pieces—but, as we have seen, there is no authority for this. One writer indeed supposes that, as in chess, so in this game, there was first a line of eight pawns, which he calls infantry, and behind them a line of eight queens, or cavalry, on an ordinary eight-square board. But if the word *vage* means diagonally, then they would be like bishops, not like our queens. But even with this lower power, imagine eight bishops on either side fighting against eight pawns. What chance would the poor pawns have? and what a fierce battle it would be between the bishops! It would be like the bishops of Antioch and Alexandria, of Constantinople and Ephesus fighting against each other, and ravaging their flocks! But I doubt whether Isidor meant anything of the kind: for after mentioning the "ordinarios" and the "vagos," he describes the "incitos," or dead pieces. Now if the pieces had different moves and different powers, we should not, if we had taken two of each, say we had taken four captives, or four "shut up" pieces; but two bishops and two pawns, or names denoting the respective powers of such pieces. I apprehend therefore that the passage merely means that all the pieces move both in an ordinal or straight line, forwards, sideways, and backwards, and in a diagonal line; and that those that "cannot move" are called by such a name, and are then taken off. That the pieces can move backwards is shown by Ovid :—

> . . . et cœptum sæpe recurrit iter.
> Ut mage velle sequi sciat, et revocare priorem.

With these data we began the game: but we soon found, although we made several trials, that as we moved up the pieces we arrived at a dead-lock. For if two solid lines of twelve pieces are advanced on either side, not a man could advance: we thus came to a stand-still, and so felt convinced that something was missing. Some pieces with increased power, like the bishop, as above suggested, would have got over this difficulty; but queen Hatasu's draught-men being all alike, as those are also which have been found in Etruscan tombs, we see that there was no such difference of power between the pieces, and that the pieces were all alike.

I was thus on the point of giving up the game in despair. But fortunately I remembered that Dr. Birch stated that the name of the Egyptian draughtman was *ab* , and I perceived that this sign is exactly like the representation of draught-men in Egyptian paintings, and like the draughtmen themselves so frequently seen in the British Museum, and Museums abroad, and three of which, two white and one black, were found in Queen Hatasu's tomb with the twenty lion-headed pieces, forming pieces of another set: and on making enquiry, I found that this word *ab* means *to leap*. But I must here give Mr. le Page Renouf's letter :—

"18 August, 1887.

"DEAR SIR,

"The hieroglyphic sign  representing what we may call a draught-man has the phonetic value *ab*, and the meaning of the Egyptian *ab* is 'leap,' 'jump,' 'hop,' hence 'play.' The heart in Egyptian is called *ab* on account of its motion, just as our own word 'heart,' the German herz, the Latin cor (cord-is), the Greek καρδία, and other Indo European words have their origin in a root *skard*, which signifies 'spring,' 'hop,' 'play.' The Sanskrit *kurd* has these meanings. The Greeks, as we know from the *Etymologicum Magnum*, were aware of the sense of κραδία, ἀπὸ τοῦ κινεῖσθαι. They called the extremity of the branch of a tree the *dancing part* κράδη, and an especially lively dance was called κόρδαξ, a word which in Egyptian would be rendered by 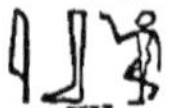 *ab.*

The Egyptian name of the piece in draughts, thus drawn from a verb of motion, is analogous to our own pawn, or the French 'pion,' or the German 'laüfer,' (for the bishop in chess). It is, I believe, quite true that the original word for pawn was *paon* (peacock), but this does not alter the fact that the idea of *motion* in connection with the game was so strong in people's minds as to obliterate the original signification derived from the *shape* of the piece.

The Egyptian word 𓄤 *nefer* originally signifies 'fair,' 'beautiful,' and hence 'good.' It is used as a substantive in the sense of a youth, a damsel, a pony, young cow, and even of wind (*fair* wind). Festal robes were called *neferu.*

There are other meanings: *nefer* is once found signifying 'door,' and once in the sense of 'fire.' A string is also called *nefert. Neferu* also signfiies corn, but this is probably only a form of the more common *nepru.*

The object 𓄤 is undoubtedly a stringed instrument, and its name *neferit* looks as if it were connected with the Semitic נבל or the Greek *νάβλα*. But it means probably the 'stringed.' One of the Egyptian constellations was called the Lute-Bearer, *t'ai-nefert*.

Believe me,
Very faithfully yours,
P. le P. Renouf."

This solved the difficulty, and completed the game. Each piece was an *ab*, and therefore all the pieces, though moving only one square at a time in any direction, could *leap* over an adversary occupying a contiguous square, provided the next square were open, as in draughts, but without taking it. I then tried a game, and the following is the result:—

19*b*	29*b*	39*b*	49*b*	59*b*	69*b*	79*b*	89*b*	99*b*	109*b*	119*b*	129*b*
19*a*	29*a*	39*a*	49*a*	59*a*	69*a*	79*a*	89*a*	99*a*	109*a*	119*a*	129*a*
19	29	39	49	59	69	79	89	99	109	119	129
18	28	38	48	58	68	78	88	98	108	118	128
17	27	37	47	57	67	77	87	97	107	117	127
16	26	36	46	56	66	76	86	96	106	116	126
15	25	35	45	55	65	75	85	95	105	115	125
14	24	34	44	54	64	74	84	94	104	114	124
13	23	33	43	53	63	73	83	93	103	113	123
12	22	32	42	52	62	72	82	92	102	112	122
11	21	31	41	51	61	71	81	91	101	111	121
10	**20**	**30**	**40**	**50**	**60**	**70**	**80**	**90**	**100**	**110**	**120**

Game I.

White.	*Black.*	*White.*	*Black.*
14—15	127—126	43—44	78—77
15—16	126—125	85—86	116—106
34—25	107—116	44—35	98—97
54—55	118—127	66—88+87	99*a*—99+88
23—14	47—36	14—15	107—96
94—85	98—107	86—85	57—56
74—65	109—118	63—74	38—47
83—94	58—47	25—26	47—46
55—66	47—57	65—55	67—57
94—95	89—98	26—37+36, 46	57—47+37

Here 26 by moving to 37, takes 36 and 46, but is lost itself; thus illustrating Bassus :—

> Ancipites subit ille moras, similisque ligato,
> Obligat ipse duos.

16—17	47—36	15—25	29—38
17—16	36—34	17—18	98—87
32—33+34	56—46	25—16	118—117
33—44	69—68	23—24	97—106
44—34	79*a*—79	21—22	66—56
34—25	99—98	54—55	56—54
16—17	27—36	55—44	54—45
55—37+36	18—28+37	24—35	45—36
35—36	28—37	44—45	36—47
52—53	46—35+36	16—26	46—44
53—44	35—46	45—55	44—66
44—45	46—44	22—33	87—97
45—54	44—55	33—44	117—108
54—65	37—46	55—77+86	79—88+77
25—36	46—35	35—46	88—77
12—23	77—66	74—75	47—57
65—54	35—46	72—63	57—56
[1] 36—56+55, 56	96—86	75—65	56—57
103—94	106—84+85, 84	63—74	77—86

[1] The piece 56 should not have been lost : as the rule is probably similar to that of Senat or Seega, in which a piece can place itself between two opponents without loss. This rule should occur again three moves afterwards, with 84, and in other places ; and is rectified in the next game. See page 64

White.	*Black.*	*White.*	*Black.*
61—62	49—58	26—36	38—47
62—53	108—107	95—77+66, 77	47—25
44—55	119*a*—109	36—35	

Here *Black's* 25 is lost: but 58 comes up to the rescue, and *White* neglecting to cover 46—45, it jumps from 47—45, and takes 35, thus releasing his partner 25.

. . . . Hic se committere rixæ
Audet, et in prædam venientem decipit hostem.

	58—47		
18—17	47—45+35, 45	78—76	97—87
46—37	25—36	54—55	69—78
55—56	57—48	92—93	109—98
17—26	48—38+37	41—42	39—48
56—46+36	68—57	42—43	48—26
94—95	38—47	37—27	26—17
46—68	57—79	27—26	19*a*—19
68—77+86	47—57	43—34	29*b*—39*a*
77—67	79—78	57—48	39*a*—39
67—47	39*a*—39	48—47	17—27
65—66	57—67	47—36	27—38
47—57	67—58	26—17	49*b*—59*a*
26—37	59*a*—59	17—18	39—29
53—54	78—68	36—37	58—48
66—67	68—77	55—56	48—26
67—78	59—69	37—46	19—17

Here by moving 17 to 18 four moves ago, *White* gradually detached a piece from its support, and must have inevitably lost it, had it not by good fortune eventually found shelter in 19*b*.

Bellatorque suo prensus sine compare bellat.
Nec, tuto fugiens, incomitatus eat.

18—19	29—19*a*	46—47	78—68
19—19*b*	59*a*—49*a*	31—32	77—67
34—25	38—37	47—58+67	37—48+58
25—15	49*a*—39	56—57	48—47
30—31	26—16	57—46	19*a*—19

White.	*Black.*	*White.*	*Black.*
74—75	68—58	35—44	87—86
76—66	47—45	57—46	78—67
46—55	58—67	75—65	67—56+46
55—65	45—55	44—45	14—34+45
66—44	55—66	32—43	34—14
65—56	66—46	43—33	36—25
56—66	46—36	24—13	39—48
66—68	67—78	33—34	14—12
68—57	36—37	[1] 13—23	86—76
44—45	16—14	95—85	76—66
15—24	69*b*—69*a*	65—55	56—54
45—35	37—36		

White's piece 55 is here hemmed in. It cannot move into 44, 46, or 64, without losing 34; which would also be lost eventually if it moved into 56. In 45 or 65 it would be taken immediately. Its only escape is by leaping into 53. It is to such a position as this that Seneca alludes in *Epist.* 117:—

> Nemo qui ad incendium domus suæ currit, tabulam latrunculariam perspicit, quomodo alligatus exeat calculus.

White.	*Black.*	*White.*	*Black.*
55—53	54—43+34	84—75	66—76
23—33+43	12—22	114—105	98—87
[1] 50—41	25—34	54—65	76—74
33—11	22—23	75—84	74—56
11—12	23—14	45—46	56—36
53—43	106—96	41—42	36—35
93—84	96—74	46—45	58—57
85—63	74—75	42—33	107—106
63—64	66—65	33—34	35—25
64—66+75	48—58	84—85	127—117
66—75	65—55	112—103	87—96
75—66	55—44	105—107+96	117—108+107
66—55	44—35	103—104	125—115
55—45	34—52	123—124	108—97
70—61+52	35—55	124—125	115—116
43—54	55—66	104—105	106—104

[1] Should have been 10—11: but the 10 had accidentally slipped off the board.

White.	*Black.*	*White.*	*Black.*
105—114	104—124	47—37	25—26
114—123 + 124	129—118	34—35	26—48
123—114	118—107	37—47	19—28
114—105	97—106	19*b*—29*a*	28—37
101—102	17—16	35—46	48—57 + 47
61—62	69*a*—69	29*a*—29	37—47
81—82	69—78	29—38	47—45
85—86	78—77	46—47	45—36
86—76	57—67	47—58	57—68
45—56	67—78	65—56	68—67
56—67	107—97	56—66	67—78
125—107 + 106	116—117 + 107	105—96	98—97
105—96	117—106	124—125	97—95
96—116	89*b*—89*a*	96—105	107—116
82—83	77—57	105—96	78—87
67—47	78—77	96—107 + 116	95—96
76—67 + 57, 67	106—126	107—85	36—46
116—105	126—115	125—126	46—56
105—125	97—106	66—46	16—26
83—94	115—126	46—47	56—46
94—95	106—116	85—75	87—76
95—105	126—124	75—65	76—54
125—126	116—127	62—53	54—45
126—116	77—87	53—44	14—24
121—122	124—125	12—23	26—35
122—123	87—97	65—54	96—86
116—115	97—107	54—55	24—22
123—124	89*a*—99	38—37 + 46	35—24 + 23
115—126 + 125, 126	99—98	44—35 + 45	Black resigns.

Et tibi captivâ resonat manus utraque turbâ.
And each hand rattles with the captive crowd.

Reminding us of the jeering laugh with which the old lion shakes the bag of victims in the face of the poor goat.

The preceeding game was played before we had discovered the game of Senat, and consequently before we knew that a piece voluntarily going between two opponents is not forfeited. We therefore give another example of the game, subject to this condition: as it may be regarded as certain that the same law would be common to each game.

GAME II.

White.	*Black.*	*White.*	*Black.*
14—15	27—26	35—45	36—46
15—16	47—46	24—35	58—57
23—24	46—36	74—65	57—56
34—35	38—37	65—75	87—86
16—17+26	37—26	63—64	107—96
17—16	67—66	43—44	127—116
16—17+26	36—26	54—55	118—107
17—16	26—36	55—57+46, 66	49—58+57

White's 55 moving to 57 takes 46 and 66, but is taken itself.

Ancipites subit ille moras, similisque ligato,
Obligat ipse duos.

White.	*Black.*	*White.*	*Black.*
64—65	58—47	45—36	86—64
35—36	56—66	[1] 75—76	64—75+76
36—46	86—64+65	124—125	98—97
52—53+64	78—77	94—95	89—88
123—124	96—95	125—126	18—27
83—84	129—128	44—45	27—37
103—104	107—106	46—55	47—56
114—115	69—68	126—117+106,116	97—106+117
104—105	95—86		

Here again the same quotation applies. It would appear that this was a favourite move in the game.

White.	*Black.*	*White.*	*Black.*
115—116	106—107	116—115	118—107
95—85	37—26	75—85	88—87
36—25	66—65	53—64	29—38
16—27+26	56—66	64—65	38—48
55—56	66—67	56—66	67—56+66
84—74+65	75—76	45—67+76	56—66+67
85—96	128—118	65—56	66—67
74—75	107—125	72—73	109—98

Here it is evident that if *White's* 72 could get up to 76, and then jump over to 78, it would take *Black's* 67 and 87 : though it would be taken afterwards. He therefore tries it,

> ——— Longo venit ille recessu
> Qui stetit in speculis.

but is not so successful as in the game described by Bassus: for on reaching 74 *Black* moves from 68 to 78, and thus stops him.

[1] 75—65. [2] 76—85 and taking 96.

White.	*Black.*	*White.*	*Black.*
73—74	68—78	44—55	58—67
115—124	19*a*—29	66—75	98—97
74—75	29—38	55—65	129*a*—129
105—116	38—16	95—85	97—87
27—17	16—27	117—107	129—118
56—47	27—38	107—96	86—97
47—46	38—47	75—86	76—66
116—126+125	47—45	92—83	119—108
46—56	48—47	47—57	69—68
25—34+45	67—45	65—75+66	68—58
56—46	47—57	57—66	87—88
34—44+45	57—67	85—95	118—107
46—57	59*a*—59	32—43	39*a*—49
75—76	59—58	86—87	77—86+87
57—47	119*a*—119	66—76+86	108—117
124—115	79*a*—69	96—106	117—116
126—117	107—116	106—126	116—106
117—127	77—86	126—117+106	109*b*—109*a*
127—117+116	67—66+76	112—113	109*a*—99
85—76+86	66—65+76	95—96	107—98
96—86	87—85	113—114	98—87
86—75	65—76	117—107	87—86
75—66	129*b*—129*a*	107—98+97	88—97+98
115—106	85—86	[1] 76—87	[2] 97—106+96
106—95	78—77	75—85+86	67—76

Black's men are now reduced to one half of *White's*, and so he gives up the game.

The above being the first attempts to play the game, exhibit no brilliancy of movement. On the contrary they are full of oversights and mistakes, only two or three of which are noted; but they will serve to show the genius of the game. The chief peculiarities of the game are the leaping power of the pieces, and the great facilities of attack and escape. The double capture

[1] 96—85. [2] 86—77 and taking 97.

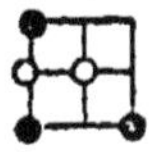

as shown in the beginning of the game, and the pinning in of two pieces as indicated in the last part, are

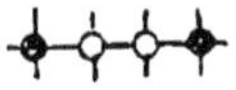

pretty moves. In the latter case if one of the pieces moves, the other is taken captive. But even from this first effort at a game, and with unpractised players, it is evident that the game is not only unlike any other game, but that it possesses great variety of movement, and owing to the leaping power of the pieces, these moves come upon us quite unexpectedly, like those of a thief, as indeed the name of the game indicates, so that it requires the greatest attention and circumspection to prevent an attack.

Cautaque, not stulte, Latronum Prœlia ludat.

And thus, as we have seen from Seneca, and as we learn from the Scholiast in Juv. *Sat.* v. 109, people were accustomed to stand round the tables to watch the players, especially when men like Novius or Publius or Cneius Calpurnius Piso played. Like all other games of Oriental origin it is somewhat long: but this agrees with what we are told by Macrobius—"Vultisne diem sequentem, quam plerique omnes abaco et latrunculis conterunt . . . . a primo lucis in cœnæ tempus."

The above game occupied about two hours: but no doubt with the celerity with which Orientals play, it might be accomplished in half that time, and indeed, it would be wrong to play a game like this, as if one were playing at chess, fearful of making a wrong move; for the game would then become very tedious: but the players should be expected to play rapidly, as if at Atep, or Mora; and to laugh at the mistakes that are made, instead of lamenting them, especially when the ardour of conquest has so carried us along, that we forget our own danger, and find ourselves taken captive. But this does not invalidate the maxim we have just quoted from Ovid : the game must not be played carelessly or ignorantly, but with quickness of eye, and intelligently.

It is to be hoped that Egyptian students will now be able to find some interpretation of the word  *aaseb*, having connection with this game. It cannot be, as Dr. Birch supposed *lost*, for the game as depicted is not yet begun. Rosellini's interpretation, *leisure*, if correct, has some meaning, denoting it as a game of *leisure* or recreation.

The game can be played, as an experiment, upon a paper board, or paste-board, with thirty bone counters on each side of different colours, or with gun-barrel wads, some left white, and others blackened over; as we ourselves have played the game.

V.

THE GAME OF SENAT

THE ANCIENT EGYPTIAN GAME.

SEEGA—THE MODERN EGYPTIAN GAME.[1]

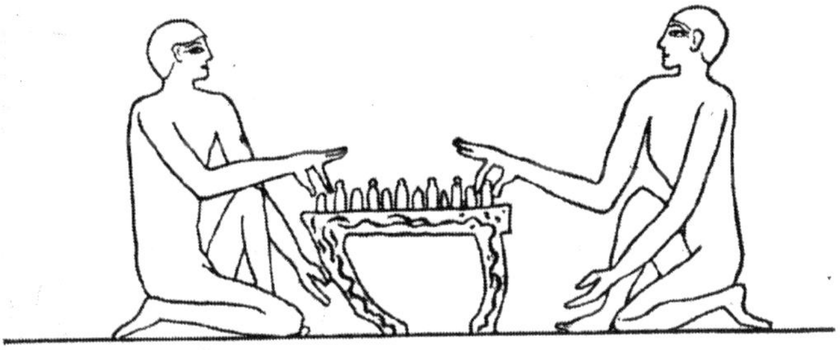

Dr. Hyde—De ludo dicto Ufuba Wa Hulana, -	1694.
E. W. Lane—Manners and Customs of the Modern Egyptians, - - -	1846.
H. Carrington Bolton, Ph.D., *Seega*, in "Field," June 1,	1889.

The modern Egyptian game of Seega has been lately again brought to our notice by Dr. Carrington Bolton, of New York. It is described by Lane more than forty years previously, and is mentioned under another name by Dr. Hyde, two hundred years ago. The Wa-Hulana,

[1] Dr. Riou, of the British Museum, says the word Seega is not noticed by native Lexicographers; and that it seems to be a local name.

or *people* of Hulana, appear to be natives of the lake district in Equatorial Africa, like the *Wa*-Humas, *Wa*-Tusi, *Wa*-Ima, *Wa*-Chevezi, *Wa*-Witu, *Wa*-Nyassa, and other tribes mentioned by Stanley, who describes them as being the finest race in Africa, and all speaking the same language.

There can be no doubt that this was a very ancient game. As the ancient Egyptian games of Draughts and Robbers were very large games, and played with a great many pieces, it is evident that such games would be inconvenient and unsuitable to the common people, who generally play at short and simple games: and it is probable that this game, and that of Dabs, were played by the lower orders among the ancient Egyptians. Lane tells us that many of the fellaheen of Egypt frequently amuse themselves with the game of Seega. They dispense with a board by scooping holes in the ground or sand: and stones, or beads, or beans, or pieces of wood of different colours serve as pieces, which they call *Kelbs*, or dogs, as the Greeks called the men in their use of the game of Robbers or Latrunculi. The mode of capturing a man also in Seega is precisely similar to that of the ancient game of the latrunculi, namely by confining him, or manacling him on each side, and thus taking him prisoner. But here the similarity ceases. There are no diagonal, or "wandering" moves; and the men are not arranged, at starting the game, in two hostile bands.

The following is Lane's description of the game:—

"Seega consists of a number of holes generally made in the ground, most commonly of five rows of five holes in each, or seven rows of seven in each, or nine rows of nine in each: the first kind is called the Khams-áwee

Seega, the second the Seb-áwee, the third the Tis-áwee." We will take the first.[1]

4			1	3	
3					4
2	2				2
1	4				
		3	1		
	10	20	30	40	50

"The holes are called ''oyoon,' or eyes, in singular ''eyn.' In this seega they are twenty-five in number. The players have each twelve 'kelbs,' similar to those used in the game of '*Tab*.' One of them places two of his kelbs in the 'eyns marked 1, 1; the other puts two of his in those marked 2, 2. (1).[2] They then alternately play two kelbs in any of the 'eyns that they may choose, except the central 'eyn of the seega. All the 'eyns but the central one being thus occupied,—most of the kelbs being placed at random, (2)—the game is commenced. The party who begins moves one of his kelbs from a contiguous 'eyn into the central. The other party, if the 'eyn now made vacant be not next to any one of those occupied by his kelbs, desires his adversary to give him, or open to him, a way: and the latter must do so by removing, and thus losing (3) one of his own kelbs. This is also done on subsequent occasions, when required by similar circumstances. The aim of each party, after the first disposal of the

[1] The notation of the board is that which we have given previously: the cells of each column starting from the base.

[2] See following page.

kelbs, is to place any one of his kelbs in such a situation that there shall be, between it and another of his, one of his adversary's kelbs. This, by so doing, he takes; and as long as he can immediately make another capture by such means, he does so, without allowing his adversary to move. (4) These are the only rules of the game. (5) It will be remarked that though most of the kelbs are placed at random, (2) foresight is requisite in the disposal of the remainder. Several Seegas have been cut upon the stones on the summit of the Great Pyramid by Arabs who have served as guides to travellers."

Remarks on this description.

1. Dr. Carrington Bolton says the Bedouins usually begin with 3, 3, and 4, 4, followed by 2, 2, and 1, 1.

2. They appear to be placed at random, and moved at random; but by experience and practice they know which are the best positions, and which to avoid.

3. In the games which we have played we have not met with this necessity: and we would suggest reading—and the latter must do so by *moving* one of his own pieces.

4. By studying Dr Carrington Bolton's example, we are able to define this more clearly. On taking a piece, the player may make another move with the same piece, provided if, by so doing, he can take another piece.

5. An additional rule suggests itself in the necessity of not allowing a player to make the same move more than twice, when it occasions a "see-saw."

The Rules therefore are:—

The first move to be determined by lot.

Each player places two kelbs alternately. It is desirable to place these two kelbs on opposite sides of the board.

The central square is to be left open, and all the other squares are to be filled in.

The kelbs move perpendicularly and horizontally, not diagonally.

A kelb is taken by placing one on each side of it, as if manacling it: but a kelb so placed in filling in the squares before beginning the game, is not lost: and a kelb can, in the game, go between two hostile pieces without being taken.

On taking a piece, the player may make another move with the same piece, provided if, by so doing, he can take another piece.

If a player cannot move any of his pieces his opponent plays again.

When a see-saw takes place, another move must be made by the attacking party.

A player surrounded by the enemy, and refusing to come out, surrenders the game.

If both parties are blocked up, it is a drawn game.

It will be seen in playing this game that it is advisable to get command of as many outside squares as possible: and Game III will show the advantage of enclosing the enemy if possible. This is often done even when each party has the same number of pieces.

Dr. Carrington Bolton devised the following game in order to show the moves, and to accomplish certain ends: whereby "*White's* first move being most unfortunate, gave *Red* the power of forcing nearly all *White's* moves."

GAME I.

Placing.

White.	*Red*
34, 33	42, 52
12, 22	31, 30
23, 21	43, 41
53, 51	24, 40
44, 20	13, 11
10, 54	14, 50

Playing.

White.	*Red.*
33—32	43—33+23, 32
22—32+33	13—23
12—13	23—22+32 and 12+13
34—33	24—34
33—23	14—24
23—33	42—32+33
53—43	32—42
54—53+52	42—52+51
43—33	31—32+33, and 31+21
44—54	34—44
20—21	30—20
21—22	31—32+22
53—43	41—42+43
54—53	44—54+53
———	20—30
10—20	11—10+20. *Game.*

In this game *White* made several bad moves, in addition to a bad starting: but the game was prepared merely to show the moves. We will now accept the placing—which we may presume is in favour of *Red*—and play *White's* men differently.

GAME II.

White.	*Red.*	
22—32	———	
12—22	11—12	
21—11	31—21	
32—31+21, 41	42—32+22, 31 :	and 22+23 :
34—33+43	24—34	and 23+33
53—43	23—22	
54—53+52	22—32+33	
51—52	50—51	
43—42	32—33	
53—43	30—31	
42—32	31—41	
32—42	40—30	
11—21	12—11	
21—22	33—23	
22—12+11	14—24	
10—11	41—31 oversight	
42—41	31—32	
41—40+30	32—33	
40—50+51	23—22	
20—21	24—23	
52—42	33—32	
43—33	32—31	
42—32+22	31—41	
50—51	41—40	
11—10	40—30	
21—31	30—40	
51—50	23—22	
31—30+40	22—21	
12—11	21—31	
50—51	34—24	
33—23	24—14	
51—41	31—21	
41—31+21	14—24	
44—34	24—14	
34—24	13—12	
23—13+12	———	
13—12	14— 8	
24—14—13 *Game.*		

But we will now not only accept the placing of the first game, but also *White's* "most unfortunate first move," as it is described in the "Field;" and *White* still wins the game:—

GAME III.

White.	*Red.*
33—32	43—33+23, 32
22—32+33	13—23
32—22	23—13+12
22—12+11	13—23
12—13	23—33
44—43	33—32
54—44	32—33
13—23+33	14—13
53—54	42—32
43—42	32—22+23
54—53+52	13—12
10—11	22—23
44—43	23—13
43—33	13—23
42—32	23—13
32—22	31—32+22
21—31+32, 41	12—22
31—32	22—12
53—52	13—23
52—42	23—13
42—41	13—23
41—31	23—13
31—21	13—23
21—22	23—13
33—23	24—14
34—24	40—41
32—31+41	30—40
31—41	40—30
41—40+30	———
40—30	50—40
51—50+40	———
11—10	12—11
22—12+11	———

White.	*Red.*
12—11	13—12
23—13+12	———
13—12	14—13
24—14+13 *Game.*	

From the examples we have given it is evident that the game is one of great variety and interest, and one that requires a quick eye and close attention.

We will now show the connection between this and

THE GAME OF SENAT.

We have seen in the description of the amusements of the blessed in the future state, that among the games they were then supposed to play were the *Senat* and the *Tau*. The "Tau" means *Robbers*. We have identified the Tau with the Ludus Latrunculorum of the Romans. The other game, represented on the left hand of the tomb-painting at Benihassan, p. 44, and on the Tomb of Rashepses, p. 10, has the name of *Senat* attached to it.

The game "Senat," (Birch, 1, 3) was at first translated *chess*, and afterwards *draughts*. Certainly it could not be chess : and there is no reason whatever—except that it is not chess— for calling it draughts. We will therefore merely call it *Senat*. In this game we observe that the pieces are not separated, as in the game of Tau, half on one side, and half on the other; but they are all mixed together. The pieces are represented as of different sizes alternately, and of different colours. We cannot for one moment suppose that one player played with tall pieces, and the other with short ones : neither can we suppose that this difference of size was merely to distinguish the different sides : for the difference of colour would be quite sufficient to so distinguish them. This difference of size therefore must have some other interpretation. We have stated that the picture of the game of *Tau*, p. 44, represents the position of the pieces before the game begins. It follows that the picture of the game of *Senat* must also represent the position of the men before beginning the game. Instead then of placing the men in two opposite camps as in the game of *Tau*, the pieces are placed on the board, one by one, or two by two, alternately, as in the game of Seega ; thus having a confused and promiscuous appearance, as if seen in perspective ; and the game is represented in the picture as it would appear when all the pieces are thus placed, and the game is about to begin.

Lane tells us that Seega is played by the fellaheen on "boards of five, seven, or nine rows of so many squares." Now it is curious that in the sarcophagus of Mentuhotop[1] we have boards depicted of nine, eleven,

[1] Lepsius, *Die Aelteste Texte des Todtenbuchs*, Berlin, 1867.

and thirteen pieces, representing the number of squares in each board: under each of which is the word "Senat." It will be objected—as we ourselves have already stated—that in the smaller hieroglyphics the artist's intention was merely to show a "draught"-board, without indicating the exact number of squares. No doubt this was generally the case; and so on different monuments we should expect to find that the artist represented the board with a greater or fewer number of squares, as he chose at the moment: but here we find the same artist has represented boards of different numbers of squares on the same sarcophagus; and we are justified therefore in attaching a motive for his thus treating them.

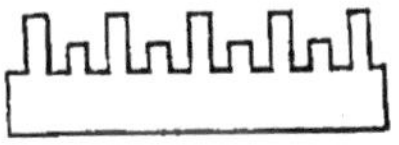

(1)

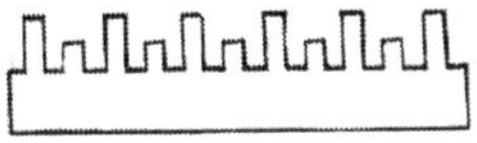

(2)

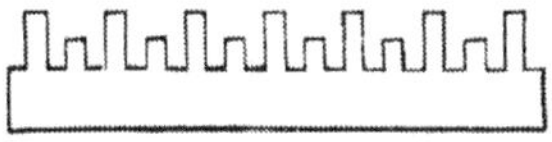

(3)

1. On left hand, inside the sarcophagus.
Two others with checkered diaper under.
2 On inside, right and left.
3. On inside of lid of sarcophagus,
and on right hand inside.

These different representations of the game then would seem to indicate that the ancient Egyptians had, like the present fellaheen, boards of different sizes, intended for more or fewer pieces, and consequently for longer or shorter games, according to the time they had to spare. Thus it is evident that while the full game was played on a board having eleven or thirteen squares on each side, the principle of the game consisted only of having an odd number of squares, so as to have a vacant square in the middle: and thus the same game could be played with fewer pieces, and less trouble, and less time, by reducing it to squares of nine, seven or five cells. This proves the identity of the two games.

We find a similarity between the two games of *Tau* and *Senat* in the mode of taking; namely, by confining a man on each side, as soldiers march off a deserter: but in *Senat* we do away with the necessity of leaping, in the game of Robbers, by placing the men promiscuously on the board in starting.

There remains only the difficulty of the board appearing to be the same in each game, (Birch, 3 and 4,) though one game requires a board of an even number of squares, and the other of an odd number. But though we have supposed the boards to be represented by the men, the artist of the pictures considered he could not give a greater number of pieces to one player, than to the other; so he was obliged to make them equal in number, though the board itself had an odd number of squares; while the scribe who wrote the hieroglyphics considered that he could not make the figure of his board lop-sided by having a tall piece on one side, and a short one on the other; and thus in the larger hieroglyphics we have given it will be seen that the game is represented with an odd number.

Though the two games appear to be so much alike in some particulars we have mentioned, in others they are very dissimilar. In one the pieces jump, in the other they do not; in one the pieces are arranged in two serried phalanxes, in the other they appear in a confused melée; in one the game is played with 60 pieces, in the other with 24, 48, 80, 120, or 168.

But it will be asked—what sort of game would it be

if played with so many men? So I thought I would try: and I give the result. As I anticipated, the greater number of pieces on the board gives an opportunity of taking a great many pieces at one move. On examining the game it will be seen that the captures were not only very frequent, but that two, three, and even four pieces were sometimes captured at one move. The game occupied an hour and three-quarters, including scoring; say an hour and a half without scoring. There were about a hundred and thirty moves on each side: whereas in the game of Latrunculi there were about two hundred and twenty on each side, occupying about two hours. The full game of thirteen squares is

1	2	3	4	5	6	7	8	9	10	11	12	13
14	15	16	17	18	19	20	21	22	23	24	25	26
27	28	29	30	31	32	33	34	35	36	37	38	39
40	41	42	43	44	45	46	47	48	49	50	51	52
53	54	55	56	57	58	59	60	61	62	63	64	65
66	67	68	69	70	71	72	73	74	75	76	77	78
79	80	81	82	83	84	85	86	87	88	89	90	91
92	93	94	95	96	97	98	99	100	101	102	103	104
105	106	107	108	109	110	111	112	113	114	115	116	117
118	119	120	121	122	123	124	125	126	127	128	129	130
131	132	133	134	135	136	137	138	139	140	141	142	143
144	145	146	147	148	149	150	151	152	153	154	155	156
157	158	159	160	161	162	163	164	165	166	167	168	169

a very different game to the smaller one of five squares, because the game of thirteen squares is played rapidly, from there being so many pieces: whereas the game of five squares is played very cautiously, step by step, and with careful calculation. The smaller game therefore will be the favourite in the present day when time is more valuable than it was before the properties and powers of steam and electricity were discovered.

PLACING THE MEN.

Red.	*White.*	*Red.*	*White.*
44, 128	157, 13	31, 146	81, 82
55, 125	79, 78	48, 161	102, 103
20, 136	1, 169	77, 92	139, 152
29, 114	105, 52	40, 117	56, 57
17, 110	27, 143	66, 130	120, 121
134, 9	4, 166	131, 24	142, 156
18, 126	7, 164	90, 91	135, 147
38, 148	11, 159	163, 168	42, 54
34, 122	104, 53	133, 150	45, 58
15, 154	132, 64	59, 60	123, 124
2, 127	43, 113	80, 97	21, 22
5, 115	118, 39	94, 10	6, 8
67, 141	41, 129	138, 140	3, 23
30, 155	107, 37	119, 106	145, 93
16, 153	83, 74	68, 69	100, 101
14, 167	108, 62	49, 165	61, 63
19, 137	149, 151	76, 51	35, 36
12, 158	46, 47	70, 50	71, 72
26, 144	111, 112	162, 116	73, 95
28, 65	88, 89	75, 109	96, 84
160, 25	32, 33	99, 87	86, 98

THE GAME.

Red.	*White.*
———	86— 85
87— 86	100— 87+86
	——100+99
———	100— 99
———	74— 87
75— 74+61	62— 61+48, 74
	—— 62+49
60— 61	47— 60+59, 61
	—— 47+34
50— 49	62— 61
49— 50+63	
—— 63+64	[1] 51— 50+37
65— 64	78— 65
91— 78	104— 91+78, 90
77— 90+103	36— 37+24, 38
25— 24+37	102—103+116
115—116+103	101—102
116—103	91—104+103
90— 91+104	102—115+114
117—116	115—114
116—115	129—116+115
130—129	116—103
128—115	103—116+129, 115
127—128	142—129
128—115	129—128
115—102+89	114—101
102—115+128	101—114+115
76— 89	116—103
89—102	114—101+102
140—127	139—140+153
	——139+126
	——126+125
	——125+138
91—104	166—153
167—166	61— 48

[1] Through some confusion *Red* plays here instead of *White*, thus having three moves.

Red	*White.*
141—140+153	
——139+152	151—152
127—128	152—151+150
	——150+137
	——137+136
163—150+149	164—163+150
165—164+163	123—136
128—115	136—123+122
	——122+109
	[1] ——109+108, 110
	——110+97
115—102+103	135—136
24— 37	35— 36
12— 25	39— 38+37
	—— 39+26
25— 12+11	52— 51
50— 37	39— 38+37
148—135	147—148
135—122	136—123+122
146—147	159—146+147, 133
	——159+158
134—133+132	
—— 146+145	120—133+146
	——120+119
	——119+106
144—145	159—158
145—144	107—108
94—107	105—106+107
	——105+92
160—147	81— 94
162—149+148	82— 81+80
	—— 82+69
	—— 69+70
139—138	137—136
149—150	79— 80+67
	—— 79+66
	[1] —— 66+53
	—— 53+40

[1] 108 and 53 appear to have been *Red* instead of *White*, by mistake.

Red.	*White.*
1501—37	{ 54— 67+68
	{ —— 54+55
147—134	136—149
12— 25	{ 149—150+137
	{ ——151+138
25— 26	38— 39+26
63— 50	48— 49+50
10— 11	23— 10+9
11— 24	27— 40
24— 25	13— 26
25— 38+51	36— 37+38
166—153	40— 27+14
153—140	143--142
140—139	151—138
104—117	142—141
139—126	138—139+126
164—151	141—140
161--148	140—153
151—152+153	27— 14
102—115	101—114
115—128	65— 78
154—153	49— 62
153—140	62— 63
64— 51	37— 50
128—127	113—126
117—116	123—136
116—103	114—115
127—128	115—102
152—151	125—138
128—127	39— 52+51
127—114	88—101
148—135	112—113
114—115	78— 91
151—150	124—137
135--122	110—123+122
150—151	137—150
151—164	139—152
164—151	152—153

Red.	*White.*
151—164	{ 126—127+140
	{ ——128+115
155—142	91—104+103
28— 27	153—154
142—129	154—167+168
164—165	167—166
165—152	138—139
152—165	150—163
129—142	163—164+165
27— 40	14— 27+40
15— 28	27— 14
2— 15	1— 2
134—133	121—134
133—132	158—145+132
142—129	134—133
129—130	104—117
28— 27	53— 40+27
15— 28	2— 15+28
29— 28	42 — 29+16
28— 27	29— 42
17— 16	4— 17+16, 30
31— 30	3— 4+5
27— 28	4— 5
30— 31	43— 30+31
18— 31	30— 43+44
28— 27	43— 30+31
19— 18	32— 19+18, 20
27— 28	14— 27
28— 29	27— 28+29
131—132	118—131+132, 144
130—129	117—130+129
	Game.

We have thus, we believe, not only discovered the Ludus Latrunculorum of the Romans, which has hitherto been the puzzle of antiquaries, but we have identified this game and that of the supposed modern game of Seega with the two Egyptian games depicted on monuments of the earliest antiquity. And it is interesting to see how an idle Egyptian caricature of a lion and a goat, of the time of the Antonines, should enable us at the same time to discover the origin of a forgotten Roman game, and assist us to discover the meaning of an obscure Egyptian hieroglyphic of the remotest antiquity, representing a game that the patriarch Joseph may have played as an ancient game in his time: and again how watching the fellaheen of the desert making holes in the sand for a game with twenty-four stones, and hearing the name which they called the stones, should enable us to discover the meaning of another obscure hieroglyphic representing a game played with 120 or 168 pieces, according to whether the board was a square of eleven, or a square of thirteen.

In the accompanying gem, formerly in the possession of the Duc de Luynes, and published in the *Bullet. Archeol. di Napoli,*[1] we see two figures playing at a game, the board of which has five squares in width, and, owing to the difficulty of perspective, only four in length. It is evidently intended to represent a game of five squares each way, and therefore the Senat. It appears to be of the Græco-Roman period, and thus is interesting as representing a medium between the fourth Egyptian dynasty, three thousand years B.C., from which all these games appear to date, and the present time when the fellaheen of Egypt play the game; and consequently showing how the game has been handed down. It represents the ordinary and favourite way of playing the game, on a board of five squares. The interest attached to the game is indicated by the two figures in the back ground intently looking

[1] *Tav.* viii. 5.

at the board. It will be seen that the squares are marked by double lines, showing that the squares were sunk in, to keep the pieces in their proper places, similar to Dr. Abbot's board; and that a bag is suspended under the board, probably not merely for keeping the men, but for holding the stakes in playing: and here again this gem affords another proof that the pieces were placed on the squares, and not on the lines, as has been supposed.

VI.

HAB EM HAN.

THE GAME OF THE BOWL.[1]

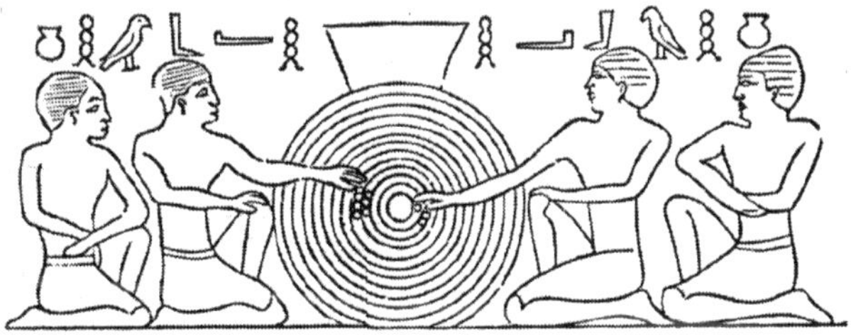

We have no extraneous aids for determining the nature of this game, as we have for those of *Senat* and *Tau*. We have indeed nothing but this picture, and the name of the game. But however puzzling it may look, we think the difficulty may be solved by comparing it with the other Egyptian games.

Evidently it was a game of great interest: for spectators are seen looking on, which we do not see in the other Egyptian games, as represented in the tomb paintings; though we find them represented in the Roman intaglio at the end of the game of *Senat*, and we find them referred to by the poets in their description of the Ludus Latrunculorum, the Egyptian game of

[1] This is generally described as the game of the Vase: but in the picture it is represented as a bowl, for the greater facility of putting in pieces, and taking out the stakes.

Tau. It always formed one of the supposed recreations of those in the future state who had been "weighed in the balances, and (not) been found wanting."

The artist has represented it upright, like a target, with a bowl standing on the top of it, because he could not represent it in profile as he represented other games. It was played on a circular board, having a

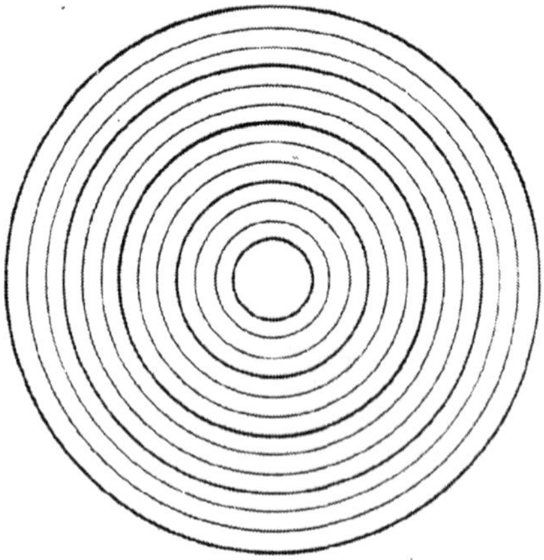

bowl in the middle, containing the stakes for which the game was played, as also the pieces which succeeded in getting home; and this would account for the interest and excitement shown by the spectators who are watching the game. As it was a game for money, it was evidently played with dice. This is proved by the hieroglyphic sign for this game, ʊ, the bowl for holding stakes, appearing between the two games of *Atep*, given us by Sir Gardner Wilkinson, as we shall see in a following game.

The pieces were entered by throws of dice, and had to begin at the outer rim, and to proceed gradually to the centre as their home.

The pieces were taken, as in the games of *Senat* and *Tau*—and we are justified in believing in this analogy—by attacking them on each side. Being in a circle, *a piece would operate all round the circle, whether to the right or left.*

We will suppose a player has entered one of his pieces. On his adversary having the same throw, he would enter a piece in the same ring on his side. Each of these pieces would then attack the opposite one. Whichever side next entered a piece in the same ring would take the opponent's piece; for he would have two pieces to his opponent's one, and *one of these would attack it on the right side, and the other on the left.* But should his opponent have two pieces already entered when he enters his first piece in the same ring, he will not lose such piece, as he put it voluntarily in that position: and his opponent must enter a fresh piece in the same ring before he can take it. This accords with the rule in the game of *Senat*, which we are bound to consider.

We will now discuss the dice. The ordinary dice and the tarsal bone, called a *cube* and an *astragal* by the Greeks, and a *tessera* and a *talus* by the Romans, were used for games of chance, for purposes of gambling, and for divination and other purposes, from the earliest antiquity. The astragal from its form may be regarded as a double or elongated cube; and among the Romans it was occasionally numbered 1, 3, 4, 6;[1] leaving the ends unmarked. The dice which the Indians use in their game of Pachisi are elongated cubes with the

[1] Or it signified these numbers according to whatever side was uppermost, the concave or bottom 3; the convex or upper, 4; the right side 1, and the left 6. See Hyde, *Hist. Nerdiludii*, p. 143.

numbers 1, 2, 5, 6, on their four sides. But the astragal of the Egyptians is not numbered, the flat or concave side probably counting for *one*; and the convex side as *two*, or vice versa. They were frequently imitated in ivory, and one such is observable in the group of "draught-men" of Queen Hatasu. We may conclude therefore that astragals were used in this game.

The pieces would enter, or move, two at a time, as at *Senat*, into the ring indicated by the throw of the astragals. This would cause a constant state of excitement, for if each of the two players had a piece in the same ring, and each piece was getting near the centre, they would each be in the greatest apprehension, lest, having so many adversaries behind his piece, the other should throw the exact number and take it up.

Thus the aim of each player would be two-fold. He would endeavour to protect his pieces by getting always two or three in the same ring, and then gradually moving them up towards the goal; and he would be constantly on the watch to take his opponent's pieces.

It will be seen that several pieces would be taken on either side. We cannot suppose that these pieces would enter again, as in Pachisi and Backgammon; but that they would be slain as in *Senat* and *Tau*, and Chess, otherwise there would be no end to the game, or at least it would be too long. If this, however, were the case, the game would then consist—as all the pieces on each side would be in action, or expected action—in getting out first, as in the games we have mentioned: but we must assume rather that the game would resemble the kindred games of *Tau* and *Senat* in which the pieces are killed outright.

In the picture before us we observe that the left hand player has seven pieces, the right hand player only three. These are the pieces which have successfully reached the innermost rings, notwithstanding all the dangers which beset them. There were therefore, probably, twice as many at starting: so we may conclude that the number of pieces on each side originally was a dozen. It would appear that the artist's intention was to represent the moment in the game immediately before taking off by entering the home. If so, the player on the left has the advantage, although his pieces are two rings further backward; for the game is determined, not by which side enters all his men first into the home—for this might be the weaker side, having the fewer number of pieces to take off, but by which side has entered the greatest number of pieces, and taken most men by the time one side is out; or in other words, by which side has the greatest number of warriors come out safely from the battle, and which has taken or slain the greatest number of the enemy.

As, therefore, the taking a prisoner counts the same as the getting a man home, it is desirable to use every endeavour to take pieces; and this is done by keeping behind the opponent's pieces, and so being able to take advantage of any "blot" he is obliged to make. Having thus marked the enemy's pieces, he can now push on his advanced forces to enter into the citadel or home, before he can get there.

We have divided the board into sub-divisions of three rings each, for facility of counting. No doubt the Egyptians thus marked the rings, either by thick lines, or by colours, as yellow, green, and red, alternately; most probably the latter.

THE GAME.

White. Throws.	Enters	Moves.	Takes	*Black.* Throws.	Enters.	Moves	Takes.
1	1			1	1		
2	2			1	1	———	1
1	1			1	———	1—2	
1	1			2	2	———	2
1	1	———	2	1	1		
2	2			1	1		
1	———	1—2		1	1		
2	2			2	———	1—3	
2	———	1—3		1	———	1—2	
2	———	1—3	— 3	1	———	1—2	
1	1			1	1		
1	1			2	———	2—4	
1	———	3—4		1	———	2—3	
2	———	2—4	— 4	2	———	1—3	— 3
2	———	1—3		1	1		
2	———	1—3		2	———	1—3	
1	1			1	1		
1	1			1	1		
1	———	1—2		1	———	3—4	
2	———	1—3		2	———	2—4	
1	———	3—4		1	———	3—4	
2	2	———	2	2	———	1—3	
1	———	2—3		1	1		
2	———	2—4		1	———	1—2	
1	———	4—5		1	———	2—3	
1	———	4—5		2	———	1—3	
1	———	5—6		1	———	3—4	
1	———	5—6		1	———	3—4	
1	———	6—7		1	1		
1	———	6—7		2	———	1—3	
			4				3

White. Throws.	Moves.	Takes,	Out.	*Black.* Throws	Moves.	Takes.	Out.
		4				3	
1	7— 8			1	4— 5		
1	7— 8			1	4— 5		
1	2— 3			1	5— 6		
1	2— 3			2	5— 7		
1	3— 4			2	3— 5		
1	3— 4			2	3— 5		
1	4— 5			1	6— 7		
2	3— 5			1	4— 5		
1	3— 4			1	7— 8		
2	3— 5			2	5— 7		
2	4— 6			1	7— 8		
2	6— 8	8		1	7— 8		
2	4— 6			2	8—10		
2	6— 8			2	8—10		
1	8— 9			1	4— 5		
1	8— 9			2	3— 5		
2	4— 6			2	5— 7		
2	4— 6			2	5— 7		
1	5— 6			1	4— 5		
2	6— 8			2	5— 7		
1	5— 6			1	10—11		
1	5— 6			1	10—11		
2	8—10			1	5— 6		
2	6— 8			2	5— 7		
1	8— 9			1	11—12		
2	6— 8			2	11	———	Out
1	10—11			1	12	———	Out
2	9—11			2	7— 9		
2	11	———	Out	2	7— 9		
2	11	———	Out	2	7— 9		
		5 + 2				3 + 2	

White.				*Black.*			
Throws.	Moves	Takes.	Out	Throws	Moves.	Takes.	Out
	———	5 + 2			———	3 + 2	
1	8— 9			2	7— 9		
2	9—11			2	6— 8		
1	6— 7			1	9—10		
1	6— 7			1	9—10		
1	7— 8			1	8— 9		
2	11 ———		Out	1	9—10		
1	9—10			1	10—11		
2	8—10			2	11 ———		Out
1	8— 9			1	9—10		
2	8—10			1	9—10		
1	10—11			1	10—11		
2	11 ———		Out	2	11 ———		Out
1	10—11			2	10—12		
2	11 ———		Out	2	10—12		
1	9—10	10		1	12 ———		Out
2	9—11			2	———		
1	10—11			2	———		
2	11 ———		Out	2	———		
1	10—11			1	12 ———		All Out
2	11 ———		Out	2			
		6 + 7 = 13				3 + 6 = 9	
	On the board	2					
		15 *Game.*					

This forms a very capital and original game, subjected to uncertain but calculated dangers, and requiring great caution.

Cowries can be used instead of astragals.

VII.

THE GAME OF THE SACRED WAY.

THE HIERA GRAMME
OF THE GREEKS,

LUDUS DUODECIM SCRIPTORUM
OF THE ROMANS.

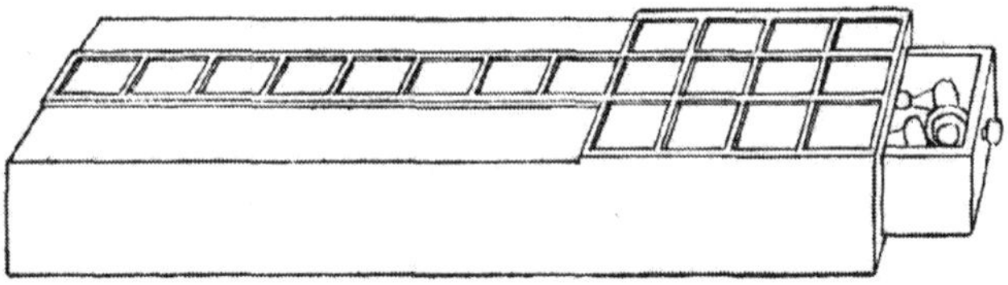

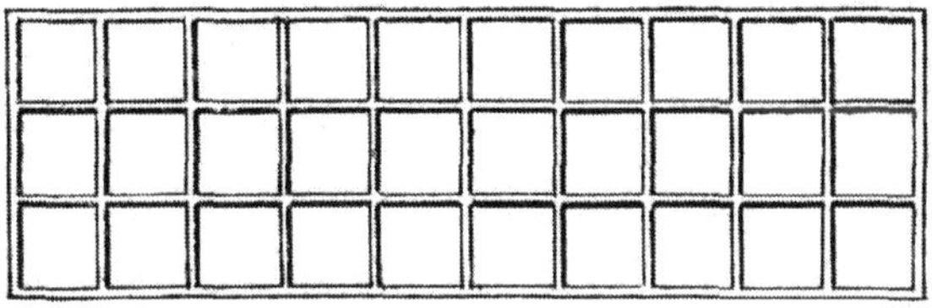

As the Egyptian game of *Tau*, or Robbers, and the Roman game of the Latrones or Latrunculi, or Thieves, were incapable of solution when considered separately, and resisted all attempts of the learned to explain them; though each has explained the other when the references to the Roman game were applied to the board of the Egyptian game: so the Greek and Roman games we are now about to consider have remained up to the present time mere abstract ideas, known only by name; while the Egyptian game, when seen in our Museums, was known only by form. But no sooner do we compare the two together, than we find them one and the same thing; and are thus enabled to make each intelligible; and thus, as in the games of *Tau* and the *Latrunculi*, in finding out one game, we discover two.

The Egyptian name of this game is not known, but we have many examples of the board. One is in the Louvre which was obtained from the collection of Dr. Abbot of Cairo: it measures 28 ins. by 7 ins. and was found in Thebes; and has been published in the *Revue Archéologique* in 1846 by M. Prisse d'Auvennes. Another, which belonged to Queen Hatasu, was presented by Mr. Jesse Haworth of Manchester to the British Museum. Another, which also belonged to Queen Hatasu, and which, like it, has the squares inlaid with green porcelain, in now in the Salle Historique of the Egyptian gallery of the Louvre,[1] and is described by M. Paul Pierret, in his *Musée du Louvre*, 1873. Another, which belonged to Amon-mes, an officer in the Egyptian Court, who lived possibly in the time of the Judges, about 1215 B.C.,[2] is in the Salle Civile of the Louvre; and is published by the same author in his Étudés Égyptologiques.[3] Two others are in the Museum at Boulak, and are published by Mariette Bey in his "Monuments Divers,"[4] one of which we will give presently. Another has lately been discovered by Mr. Petrie, the eminent excavator of Egyptian monuments, in the Fayoum, and was exhibited by him in London in 1889. Lastly, an Egyptian Treatise on the game is said to exist in the Museum at Turin. Evidently therefore, it

[1] 616, *Armoire* C.

[2] The date of King Amon-mes.

[3] *Huitieme Livraison, Deuxième Partie.* 1878, p. 81, 82.

[4] 1872, pl. 51, 52.

was a very common game among the Egyptians. The game, however, is not referred to in the Ritual of the Dead, nor is it represented in any tomb-sculptures, or in hieroglyphic inscriptions. In fact, like all the Egyptian games, we have no *description* of it whatever.

Nor, as we have mentioned, have we much information except in name, of the Greek or Roman games. We are told however that they were played with dice, (κυβειας,[1] not the astragal), having numbers, 1-6, on four sides only; that the central line of the board was called the Sacred Way (ἱερὰ γραμμή),[2] that the pieces on this line were called kings, as in our game of draughts pieces are said to *queen*; and that pieces could be taken off from this Sacred Way. This is all we knew of it: indeed, so little did we know, that it was supposed that the board consisted of six lines crossing six lines, thus making twenty-five squares, or thirty-six points.

Let us then begin by studying the Egyptian board. The board has three columns. The side ones have

[1] Pollux, *Onom.* "Dice were used by the Egyptians in the reign of Rhamsinitus; that monarch, according to Herodotus, being reported to have played with the Goddess Ceres . . . . . Plutarch would lead us to believe that dice were a very early invention in Egypt, and acknowledged to be so by the Egyptians themselves, since they were introduced into one of their oldest mythological fables: Mercury being represented playing at dice with Selene (De Is s. 12) previous to the birth of Osiris, and winning from her the five days of the epact, which were added to complete the 365 days of the year." Sir Gardner Wilkinson, *Anct. Egypt* ii, 62.

Dr. Birch, however, contests this. He says,—"No dice have been found in Egypt older than the Roman period; nor have they been recognized in inscriptions and texts: nor are there any representations of playing at dice in the earlier or older sepulchres." *Notes to ditto.*

However, we have found the dice, as we shall see.

[2] Theocritus, vi, 18. *Schol.*

only four cells, and the central one twelve. This accords with all we know of the requirements of the game of the Sacred Way. It has a central line, and this central line has twelve cells; and as no other boards comply with these requirements, and as other of the Egyptian games were handed down to the Greeks and Romans, we may conclude that this also is the game which was played by those nations. All these Egyptian boards we have described—like our backgammon boards—consist of two games; and each of these games has three columns, and therefore a Sacred Way; and consequently they must be variations of the same game. The principal game, which we have already described, is the uppermost one, and is determined by the position of the drawer which contains the pieces. The lower game consists of three rows of ten cells.

In all these boards, with the exception of Dr. Abbot's, one of the side columns has four cells marked with hieroglyphics. In Queen Hatasu's board, in the British Museum, the second cell has two men marked on it; the third has three men; and the first and fourth cells are wanting.

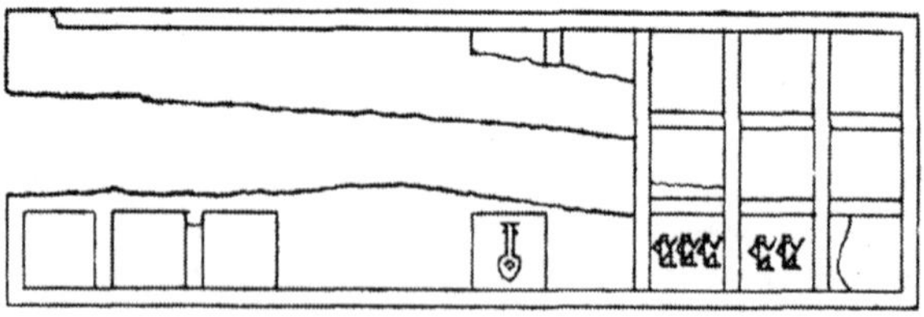

Queen Hatasu's board in the Louvre, and that of Amon-mes also, have two men in the second cell: but the third cell has three birds, forming the word Ba-a (spirits), and the fourth has the sign of water. In all the boards the fifth cell has the sign *nefer*; the two latter boards having three *nefers* instead of one. Mr. Petrie's board, however, instead of having hieroglyphics, has the simple numerals II and III on the second and third cells, and the fourth cell divided by two diagonal lines, to signify four. There can be no doubt therefore that these four cells were known as 1, 2, 3, and 4.

Queen Hatasu's board in the Louvre and that of Amon-mes and those in the Boulak Museum are further distinguished by having all the plain surfaces, and even some of the cells, filled in with hieroglyphic inscriptions, precatory and laudatory. On one side of Queen Hatasu's is her cartouche name, on the opposite her throne name, Ra-ma-Ka; and at one end is an embryo figure of Ptah. On the corresponding space of Amon-mes' board is a representation of himself playing the game, and moving one of the pieces. M. Pierret states that the first, fifth, and ninth cells of Queen Hatasu's central way are marked with hieroglyphics, which he thought had some "importance particulière:" but no doubt they are of the same nature as those on Amon-mes' board, on the fourth cell of which Mr. le Page Renouf reads "Favoured by the good God;" on the eighth, "Commanding officer of the Royal Court;" and on the twelfth, his own name, "Amon-mes;" which is also seen on the first of the right lateral row; and on the first of the left lateral the words, "*che-en-hap*," the signification of which is uncertain.

From these materials we have to construct the game. Evidently it was a game for two players, who have four pieces each, and the central column was common to both players. This was the Sacred Way, on entering which each party would strive to take up the other's pieces, and arrive at the goal. There being so few men to start with, the game would soon come to an end if the prisoners were not made use of by the victor. Accordingly they were entered in the cells 1, 2, 3 or 4, as those numbers were thrown by the four-sided dice. It is this feature which gives interest to the game. One of the players may be reduced to one piece, and the game then be considered lost: but with this piece he takes one of his opponent's, and then another, and by entering these men as his own may eventually win the game.

It will be asked why the cells 2, 3, and 4 were marked on the lower game, and not on the upper? I suppose it was because these four squares on the upper board speak for themselves. Again, why only four cells were thus distinguished on the lower game? It was probably because the earlier dice had only four numbers; and the *nefer* on the fifth cell did not mark a number, but only the termination of the series of re-entering cells.

Since this was written Professor Maspero has directed my attention to the two boards in the Boulak Museum, published by Mariette Bey, one of which has the fourth cell of lower game divided off from the remaining six cells by a broad line, thus seeming to confirm this supposition.

But not only is there this broad line of separation, but it will be observed that the cells beyond these four are divided from each other by two lines, while the four cells and all those of the central line are divided by four lines. There were two forms of pieces found in the tomb of Ak-Hor, some of the *ab* shape, and some of reel shape. Many of these, we are informed, were stolen, and sold to travellers: but no "draught"-board for the game of *Tau* or *Senat* was found. We may suppose therefore that the reel-shaped pieces stood upon the cells outside the four cells, and that these reel-shaped pieces had not the power of re-entering. This board is remarkable also for combining in itself the two games for which all other boards of this description were intended. It could be used

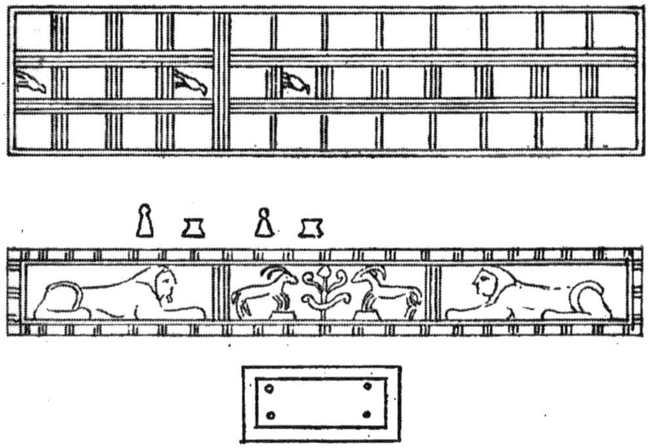

for the upper game of the usual board, and with four *ab*-shaped pieces; or it could be used for the lower game with both the *ab*-shaped and the reel-shaped pieces: but in this case there would be twelve cells instead of ten as usual. Fortunately one dice is preserved of this game, and this is highly interesting as it is of oblong form having only four numbers, as we surmised was the case, in consequence of the cells numbered 1, 2, 3 and 4.

As all games increase in interest as there is greater opportunity for the exercise of skill and reasoning and the calculation of chances, we will imagine that players were not obliged to move unless they chose.

The game would consist, not in getting out first, but in having the greater number of pieces at the end of the game, whether home or on the board, or prisoners as recruits not even entered; and the end of the game would be when one of the players has no more men to play with.

It has been surmised, but on insufficient evidence or consideration—for the word *scribo* may be equally understood to draw spaces or squares, as to draw lines—that the pieces were placed on the lines, not in the squares: for we may take it for granted that the custom in each country would be maintained throughout. Thus, in China, both the game of Chess and the game of Enclosing are played on lines. It is true that in Japan they play Chess on squares, and their game of Enclosing on lines: but the latter game was not their own, but was borrowed from China. We may therefore feel assured that the Greeks and Romans would play this game as the Egyptians played it. Now it is evident from Queen Hatasu's *Tau*-board that the game was played on the squares, and it is evident from the Roman gem at the end of the article on the game of *Senat* that that game was played on the squares; and it is evident again from the painting of the game of *Han*, that that game also was played on the squares. But independently of this analogy, it is certain that this game was played on the spaces, from all these

Egyptian boards having the hieroglyphics or numbers painted on the squares, and not on the lines; and still more conclusively by Dr. Abbot's board having the cells sunk in order to hold the pieces; and if we accept these boards as representing, and being identical with the Greek and Roman games, then all doubt is at an end; for the "duodecim" of the latter is represented by the twelve *squares* of the former.

We will now give an example of the game, which we think will show that it is a very exciting game, exhibiting great changes of fortune, and sometimes ending with one player having all the eight pieces. The unexpected way in which the pieces are often taken up, or removed from the Sacred Way, accompanied by the expression, κίνειν τὸν ἀφ' ἱερὰς,[1] *I remove this from the Sacred* (Way) passed into a proverb; just as we should speak of anyone being "removed from the stage of life."

In the score of the following game the squares on the sides 1, 2, 3 and 4 are lettered A, B, C and D; and the Sacred Way numbered from 1—12.

GAME.

Throws.	*Black.*	Takes.	Throws.	*White.*	Takes.	Throws	*Black.*	Takes.	Throws.	*White.*	Takes.
3	D—A		2	C—A		1	8— 9		2	A— 2	
1	C—B		4	A—4		4	9——	Out	2	2— 4	
2	———		1	4—5		4	B— 3		3	A— 3	3
2	———		1	D—C		4	B— 3	3	3	C	
4	A— 4		1	B—A		3	C		1	A	
3	A— 3		4	A—4	4	1	3— 4	4	3	A— 3	
1	3— 4	4	3	5—8		2	4— 6		1	3— 4	
4	4— 8	8	2	C—A		1	6— 7		4	———	

The odds now are 6 to 2 in favour of *Black*.

[1] καὶ τὸν ἀπὸ γραμμῆς κινεῖ λίθον. Theoc. *Id.* vi.

Throws.	*Black.*	Takes.	Throws.	*White.*	Takes.	Throws.	*Black.*	Takes	Throws	*White.*	Takes.
3	7—10		4	4— 8		4	2— 6		2	——	
1	10—11		1	8— 9		4	6—10		1	——	
2	11——	Out	4	9——	Out	1	10—11		1	——	
3	C		3	——		4	A— 4		4	A— 4	4
1	C—B		2	C—A		4	A— 4	4	1	A	
1	A		2	——		4	4— 8		3	A— 3	
1	A		1	——		3	B— 2		4	3— 7	
2	C—A		3	——		4	8—12		2	7— 9	
2	A— 2		3	——		3	2— 5		1	9—10	

The odds are still 6 to 2 in favour of *Black.*

1	5— 6		1	10—11	11	1	2— 3		1	12——	Out
2	6— 8		1	11—12	12	2	3— 5		3	B— 2	
1	A		2	B		2	5— 7		1	2— 3	
1	8— 9		1	12——	Out	1	7— 8		3	3— 6	
2	9—11		1	A		3	8—11		1	6— 7	
3	——		4	A— 4		4	——		3	7—10	
1	11—12		4	4— 8		1	11—12		3	C	
2	——		3	8—11		4	——		3	C— 1	
2	A— 2		1	11—12	12	2	——		2	10—12	12

Black 2 out

White 3 out
2 on board
1 prisoner
—
6

Game ends 6 to 2 in favour of *White.*

It will be seen that, owing to the uncertainty of dice, there are great fluctuations in this game; and that, like Crœsus, being successful in the beginning is no proof of being victor at the end.

Like so many other oriental games, it was a game of war. The four squares on each side represent the respective camps, and the Sacred Way the battle field, in which the pieces fight like hostile kings or heroes; and the forces consist of victors, combatants and reserves.

The game at the back, of three by ten squares.

This is merely a variety of the same game. The central line is still the Sacred Way; but as each player has ten pieces instead of four, and the game thereby lengthened, the Sacred Way is made to correspond. The difference then between the two games would be, that they chose either the short game or the long game, according as they had a shorter or a longer time to play in; or, if there was no option of playing in this game, they preferred a game more entirely of chance. And this accords with what we have seen in the game of *Senat*, and its modern name of *Seega*, in which larger or smaller boards were used, as they were disposed to give more or less time for their amusement.

The *nefer* or *nefers* merely mark, as in Queen Hatasu's *Tau*-board, or the Ludus Latrunculorum, a division in the board, and confine the entries of new men or prisoners to the squares 1 to 4.

VIII.

THE GAME OF ATEP

DACTYLON EPALLAGE (Finger-changing)—THE GREEK GAME.

MICATIO, MICARE, DIGITIS MIRARE—THE ROMAN GAME.

MORA—THE ITALIAN GAME.

This is another game invented by the Egyptians, and handed down to modern times. We have shown that the double group of Benihassan (p. 44), represents two different games, the *Senat* and the *Tau*: so here there are two varieties of the same game. One group represents two women playing the double game, in which both players throw out their fingers at the same time, and each guesses; the other represents two men playing the single game, when one throws out his fingers while the other guesses. The illustration is from Sir Gardner Wilkinson; but unfortunately, although he states it is from Thebes, he does not tell us whether he took it from any other author, or whether he copied it from the monument itself. The women will be distinguished by their hair, by their faces, by their tunics, and by their smaller stature, and more delicate bodies; the men simply wear drawers. It will be observed that the attitude of the man with folded arms is exactly similar to that of the two spectators of the game of *Han* (p. 83): thus showing that he is merely guessing, and not operating with his fingers. The vase in the middle shows that in each case they are playing for stakes; and thus confirms our conjecture relative to the game of the *Han*. We cannot say whether an inscription exists above the groups: but Champollion gives us several other groups from Beni-hassan, accompanied with inscriptions; from which we learn some fresh particulars of the game as practised by the Egyptians. In one group we have, written over the group, the words, "Let it be said": or as we might say—guess; or how many?[1]

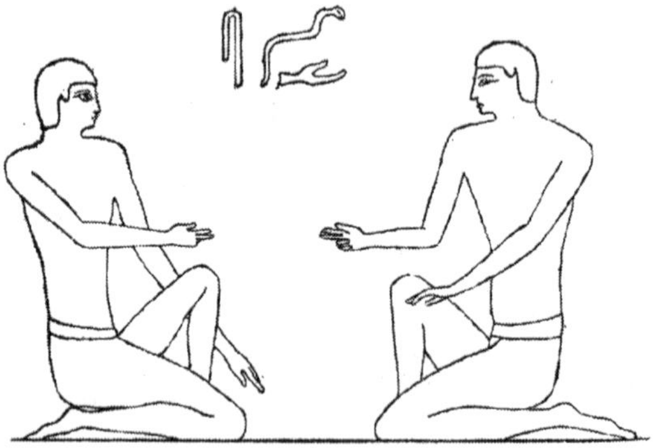

In two other groups we have the name of the game, A T P. In one a player who is operating with one hand, conceals it behind the palm of the other which he places on the forehead of the other player, to prevent his seeing how many fingers he is stretching out: and

[1] The translation of these inscriptions has been kindly given me by Mr. Renouf.

on his making a guess, withdraws his hand. The inscription is, "Putting the *Atep* on the forehead."

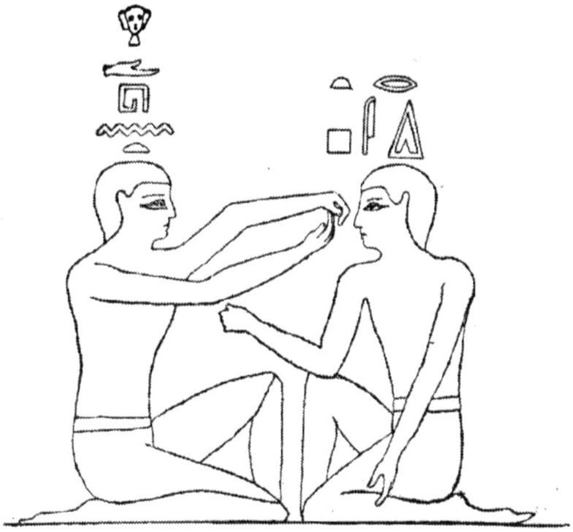

In the other the fingers are concealed as before in the palm of the other hand, and then placed on or under the opponent's hand: and the inscription is, "Putting the *Atep* on (or under) the hand." Unfortunately, the hand in this case is destroyed: so we cannot see how it was placed.

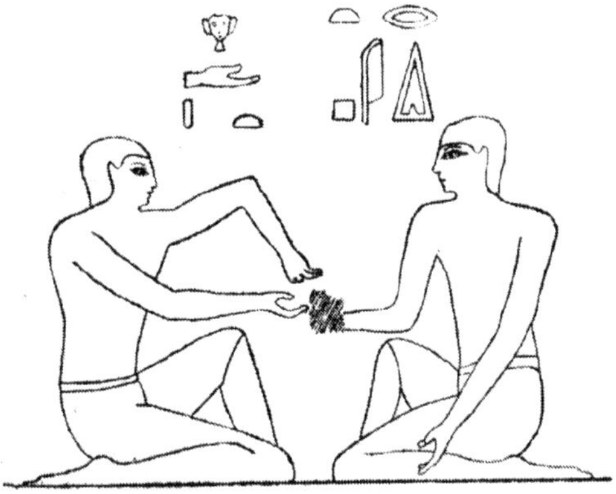

In another group we have the two players seated back to back; so that they cannot see how many fingers their opponent stretches out. In this case a third party would watch the game, and declare the odds.

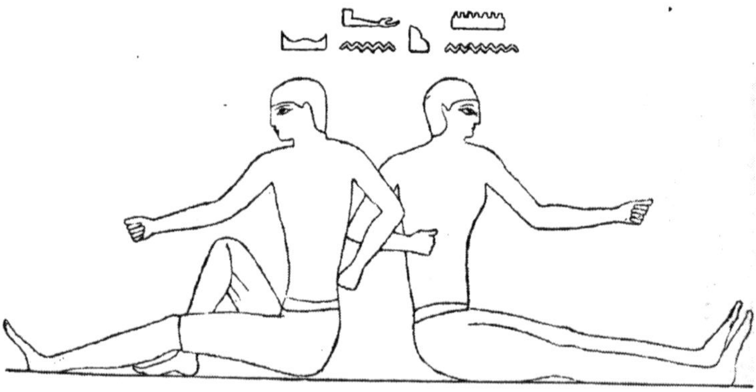

Another group exhibits a player prostrate on the ground on his hands and knees, while two other players thump him with the fleshy part of their fists. In this case the game is not played for stakes, but is played for forfeits. The prostrate figure is evidently a defeated player; for his hand is clenched with the thumb extended, exactly similar to the hands of the other players, and to those of other groups.[1]

[1] Dr. Birch, however, gave a different interpretation of this group; the inscription over which however, *ha ua em abqa*, he could not explain. He says, "Analogous to the game of Odd and Even was one in which two of the players held a number of shells or dice in their closed hands, over a third person who knelt between them, with his face towards the ground, and who was obliged to guess the combined number ere he could be released from this position; unless, indeed, it be the *Kollabismos* of the Greeks (Pollux, *Onom.* ix, 7), in which one person covered his eyes, and guessed which of the other players struck him." *Note to Sir Gard. Wilkinson*, vol. ii, 59.

It was possibly from their thinking of this last game that "The men that held Jesus blindfolded him, and struck him on the face, and blasphemously asked Him, saying, prophesy, who is it that smote Thee?" Luke xxii, 64.

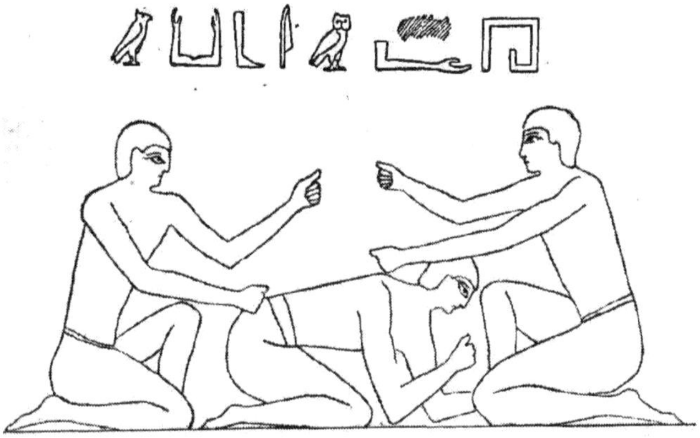

As the Thebes painting shows, the game was not confined to men. In the accompanying playful illustration

we see two young Egyptian girls enjoying the game with the greatest animation. They stand upon a vase, to denote that they are competing for a prize. The vase is chequered to show that, like the chequered boards of *Tau* and *Senat*, it is a game of pleasure; and the whole is surrounded by a purse with an outside pouch, in which to carry off the prize. It was, with the game of the Sacred Way, already described, found in the tomb of Ak-Hor.[1]

In the Greek game another feature is observable. A long rod is held by each player in the left hand, while the game is played with the right hand. It appears from the following beautiful vase painting[2] that the rod was pulled away by the winning side from the opponent's hold. Possibly the rod was numbered with divisions, and the finger was advanced or withdrawn one mark or number at each correct guess or bad guess, as the case might be. If so, the lady on the right is evidently winning: for she is seated securely on her vase, and holds the rod firmly, and has a considerable length of it behind her. A cupid floats in the air above, holding a tænia or fillet, and having his head adorned with a myrtle wreath; and a female most richly attired stands behind the winner with a corona or wreath; her rich attire showing the value of the prize. The two vases are indicative of stakes as usual; though the ladies appear to be playing for love or honour.

Another beautiful vase painting represents a lady, possibly the same lady, richly apparelled, reclining on a rustic couch. She is evidently a celebrated player in

[1] Mariette Bey, *Monts divers*, 1872, p. 51.
[2] Inst°. Archeologico di Roma, *Aunali*, 1866, p. 326.

VASE PAINTING.

EROS AND ANTEROS.

VASE PAINTING.

the game: for her hair is decorated with a chaplet, and a cupid is flying towards her about to crown her with a wreath, which is drawn in perspective so as to fit the head. In front of her is a cupid sitting on a rock, with wings extended on each side of him; and facing him is another cupid holding a wreath: while behind the lady is a group of Eros and Anteros playing the game.[1] They each hold the rod firmly with the left hand: showing that their forces are equal. Their placid and smiling faces are to teach us that as this lady played, gentleness and sweetness should always be present at games of play. They are crowned with myrtle, and are sitting on rustic seats in imitation of the feet of animals, covered with their clothes.

Another example, given in the *Annali*,[2] represents an old man playing the game with a woman. The man is standing, supporting himself with a staff; the object of the artist apparently being to show that old age, with failing eyes, dull perception, and stiff fingers, has no chance at such a game, against a woman's quick eye, or the activity of youth. All three paintings are in red on a black ground.

The Italian game of Mora is thus described by Mr. Rich: "A game of chance, combined with skill, still common in the south of Italy, where it now goes by the name of *Mora*. (Varro, *ap.* non. *s.v.* p. 547. Suet. *Aug.* 13, Calpurn. *Ecl.* ii, 26). It is played by two persons in the following manner. Both hold up their right hands with the fist closed; they then simultaneously extend a certain number of their fingers, calling out at the same time by guess-work the collective

[1] Dubois de Maisonneuve, *Introduction à l'étude des Vases*, 1817, p. xliv.
Inst. Archeol., p. 327.

number extended by the two together, and he who succeeds in hitting on the right number wins the game. . . . . If neither succeeds in guessing right, they again close their hands, cry out a number, and open the fingers, until one of them calls the right amount. What appears to be so simple is most difficult to execute with any chance of success, and requires more skill and calculation than a person, who had not himself made the experiment, would imagine. Each player has first to settle in his own mind how many fingers he will show; then to surmise how many his opponent is likely to put up, which he does by observing his usual style of play, by remembering the numbers he last called, and those he last showed; he then adds these to his own, and calls the collective numbers, thus endeavouring to make the number he calls. But as all this, which takes so much time in narrating, is actually done with the greatest rapidity, the hands, being opened and closed, and the numbers simultaneously called as fast as one can pronounce them—eight, two, six, ten—it requires great readiness of intellect, and decision of purpose, for a player to have any chance of winning; as well as a quick eye and acute observation, to see in a moment the aggregate number of fingers shown, so as not to overlook his own success; nor, on the other hand, suffer himself to be imposed upon by a more astute opponent; whence the Romans characterized a person of exceeding probity and honour, by saying that one might play at Mora with him in the dark—*dignus, quicum in tenebris mices.* Cic. Off. iii, 19."[1]

Although *Micatio*, or *Micare*, is the latin name, it

[1] Anthony Rich, Junr., B A. *The Illustrated Companion to the Latin Dictionary, and Greek Lexicon.* Lond. 1849, *s.v. Micatio.*

is evident from the accompanying gem, published by Ch. Lenormant, in his *Trésor Numismatique* de 1834,[1] that the name *Mora* was also an ancient name.[2] M. Lenormant fancied the marks on the left indicate a vase on the top of a column, in which the stakes were held.

[1] Art. Iconographie des Empereurs Romains, pl. x, med. 4.
[2] See also Calpurnius, *Eclog.* ii, 25.

INDIAN CHESS-BOARD.

CHESS.

The laws of European Chess are so well known, that it is quite unnecessary to give the rules: we will therefore proceed to describe the rules and peculiarities of several of the oriental games, such as the Chaturanga, Tamerlane's Chess, Chinese Chess, Japanese Chess, and others. But before doing so, it is necessary, in order to note the games, to give a system of notation adapted to all such games; and we think that this system, from its simplicity, must eventually succeed the one in present use.

The chess-board from which the photograph is taken, was purchased at a pawnbroker's shop, so I cannot tell where it came from. It is of a light-coloured wood, like satin wood, but being of this colour it unfortunately appears dark by photography; but nevertheless on examining it, it will be seen to be of exquisite carving, and having no two squares alike. One of the cells represents a miniature chess-board.

IX.

CHESS NOTATION.

The established system of chess notation is liable to the following objections. Each piece is distinguished according to whether it is on the King's or the Queen's side; and the squares are reckoned sometimes from your own side, and sometimes from your opponent's side. Two men may thus be in two adjoining squares, but instead of being distinguished by two consecutive numbers, one may be termed King's Bishop's 2, and the other King's Knight's 7, designations which to the uninitiated would imply no idea of propinquity. I would therefore suggest the following system.

17	27	37	47	57	67	77	87
16	26	36	46	56	66	76	86
15	25	35	45	55	65	75	85
14	24	34	44	54	64	74	84
13	23	33	43	53	63	73	83
12	22	32	42	52	62	72	82
11	21	31	41	51	61	71	81
10	**20**	**30**	**40**	**50**	**60**	**70**	**80**

The Notation to proceed from one side only. The first or back row to be distinguished by decimal numbers, as 10, 20, 30, &c. The columns in front of this row to be distinguished by units, as 1, 2, 3, &c. Thus in the ordinary chess-board, the first row would consist of numbers 10 to 80, and the columns above them of 1 to 7. According to this method the four middle squares would be described as 43, 44, 53 and 54, and so with any others, and thus, instead of scoring K's. B's. 2, and K's. Kt's. 7; we should write 61 and 71.

In order to score a game with celerity, I use the following signs or ciphers.

○ = King, as representing universal dominion, or the Sun; and indeed the Japanese sign for King.
☾ = Queen, or the Moon.
+ = Bishop, or the Cross.
2 = Knight, or horse's head,
□ = Rukh, a castle or tower.
⊥ = Pawn, a single man standing on a base.
✓ = Check.

In Tamerlane's chess we have castles of three powers.
□ = Greatest power which we will call the Rukh.
⊟ = Middle " " " Castle.
⊞ = Least " " " Vizir.

Bishops of three powers.
☾ = Pherz, the Queen, moving only one square at a time.
T = A piece we will call lame Bishop, moving or leaping always two squares at a time, as if on a *crutch.*
+ = Bishop.

And Knights of three powers.
2 = Knight, same as our Knight; his horse's head.
✱ = Chevalier, moving one diagonal and two straight squares, showing his spur.
∅ = Cavalier, moving one diagonal and any number straight, showing his lance and shield.

In Chinese chess the only extra pieces are :

⊗ = The Cannon, representing the wheels of a gun carriage.
G = Guards, or Mandarins.

In Japanese chess the names and moves of the pieces are so peculiar, that we must leave them till we come to speak of the game itself.

*** Thus it will be seen that these signs are not arbitrary or irrelevant signs, but signs significant of the pieces' movements; and thus, with these signs, we not only remember the name but the power of the piece.

X.

CHATURANGA.

INDIAN CHESS

Sir William Jones, *Asiatic Researches*, Vol. ii.	-	1788
Captain Hiram Cox, „ „ „ vii.	-	1799
Professor Duncan Forbes, *History of Chess*	- -	1860
Antonius Van der Linde, *Geschichte und Litteratur des Schachspieles*	- - - - - - -	1874

The photograph represents an Indian set, which I was fortunate to find in London. I have never met an Indian who played Chaturanga, so cannot say whether the game is still played. It will be seen that it has four kings, and boats instead of bishops. The red pieces appear black in photograghy.

The Ludus Latrunculorum, the progenitor of draughts, has been shown to have had its origin long before the time of Moses. The various games of oriental chess *pretend* to a like antiquity. The Chaturanga, the progenitor of chess, was supposed to go back to a period, according to Sir William Jones, of 3900 years, while Professor Forbes put it at "between three and four thousand years before the sixth century of our era," *i.e.*, upwards of four or five thousand years ago. Like the fables of other countries which attribute the invention of chess to a time of war, the Chaturanga is said to have been invented by the wife of Ravana, King of Ceylon, when his capital, Lanka, was besieged by Rama.

This pretended antiquity has been set aside by recent critics. The earliest[1] description of the game is found in the Bhavishya Purana: and Dr. Van der Linde asserts that some of the Puranas, though formerly considered to be extremely old, are held, in the light of modern research, to reach no further back in reality than the tenth century; while, moreover, the copies of the Bhavishya Purana which are in the British Museum and Berlin do not contain the extract relied upon by Professor Forbes.[2] Herr Van der Linde ascribes the invention of chess to the eighth century.

But admitting the judgment of Sanscrit scholars that the Bhavishya Puranas are not of the great antiquity which was supposed, and admitting, if need be, that the copy in which this description of the game is given was written later than the others, it is evident that the account must have been taken from some ancient record or tradition, and its antiquity may be greater than is now supposed. The very fact of its referring to the mythical and not historic characters of Yudhishthira and Vyasa, Mahadeva and Parvati, Draupadi, Dhritarashtra, and Shakuni—as the Egyptian game, as we have seen, is associated with Isis the wife of Osiris—would denote an antiquity beyond record. Mahadeva and Parvati are represented as "playing with dice at the ancient game of Chaturanga, when they disputed

[1] A later description by Alberuni has been recently discovered, which will be given at the end of this article. He lived in 1000 A D.

[2] "The best original account of this very ancient game to which we have yet obtained access, is to be found in the Sanskrit Encyc. *Shabda-Kalpa-Druma*, published at Calcutta within the last twenty years (*i e.* after 1840) in seven vols., 4° (in Vol. i. under art. "Chaturanga"), also in a work published at Serampore in two Vols, 8vo., 1834, entitled *Raghu-Nandana-Tatwa*, or Institutes of the Hindu Religion, &c., by Raghu-Nandana (see Vol. i, 88). Forbes, *Hist. of Chess*, p. 13. There have been later editions since.

and parted in wrath."[1] Mahadeva is the Siva of the Hindu Trinity—Brahma, Vishnu and Siva—and Parvata, or Durga, or Kali, was his wife. Dice naturally were earlier than chess, and were used by the Hindoos at a very early age, and the habit of gambling was very prevalent, and was sanctioned by the Shastra. Thus we find in the Mahabharata the story of Nala and Damayanti, beginning with the fearful gambling by which he lost his Kingdom, and everything except his wife :—

Lived of yore a Raja Nala, Virasena's mighty son,
Gifted he with every virtue, beauteous, skilled in taming steeds,
Head of all the kings of mortals, like the Monarch of the gods ;
Over, over all exalted, in his splendour like the sun ;
Holy, deep read in the Vedas, in Nishada lord of earth :
Loving dice, of truth unblemished, chieftain of a mighty host.

Who to Nala, with all virtue, rich endowed would not incline ?
He who rightly knows each duty, he who ever rightly acts,
He who reads the whole four Vedas, the Purana too, the fifth.
In his palace with pure offerings, ever are the gods adored :
Gentle to all living creatures, true in word, and strict in vow ;
Good and constant he, and generous, holy temperate, patient, pure ;
His are all those virtues ever, equal to earth guarding gods.

Then follows a description of his bride :

In her court shone Bhima's daughter, decked with every ornament,
Mid her maidens like the lightning, shone she with her faultless form ;
Like the long-eyed queen of beauty, without rival, without peer.
Never did the gods immortal, never mid the Yaksha race,
Nor 'mong men was maid so lovely, ever heard of, ever seen.
Pearl art thou among all women, Nala is the pride of men:
If the peerless wed the peerless, blessed must the union be.

[1] Lieut. Welford, *Asiatic Researches*, iii, 402.

A disappointed lover now vows vengeance:

Kali with his dark ally
Haunted they the stately palace, where Nishada's monarch ruled,
Watching still the fatal instant, in Nishada long they dwelt.
Twelve long years had passed ere Kali saw that fatal instant come,
Nala, after act unseemly, the ablution half performed,
Prayed at eve with feet unwashen.
. . . . Kali seized the fatal hour:
Into Nala straight he entered, and possessed his inmost soul.
Pushkara by Kali summoned, "come, with Nala play at dice;
"Ever in the gainful hazard, by my subtle aid thou'lt win,
"E'en the kingdom of Nishada, e'en from Nala all his realm."

. . . .

Pushkara, the hero-slayer, to King Nala standing near:—
"Play me with the dice, my brother?" thus again, again he said.
Long the lofty-minded Rajah that bold challenge might not brook.
In Vidarbha's princess' presence, seemed he now the time to play,
For his wealth, his golden treasures, for his chariots, for his robes.
These possessed by Kali, Nala in the game was worsted still.
He with love of gaming maddened, of his faithful friends not one
Might arrest the desperate frenzy of the conqueror of his foes!

. . . .

Thus of Pushkara and Nala, still went on the fatal play,
Many a weary month it lasted, and still lost the king of men.

. . . .

As by Pushkara is worsted, ever more and more the king,
More and more the fatal frenzy maddens in his heart for play.

. . . .

Scarce Varshneya had departed, still the King of men played on,
Till to Pushkara his kingdom, all that he possessed was lost.
Nala then, despoiled of kingdom, smiling Pushkara bespake:—
"Throw me yet another hazard, Nala, what is now thy stake?
"There remains thy Damayanti, all thou hast beside is mine;
"Throw we now for Damayanti, come, once more the hazard try."[1]

[1] *Story of Nala:* an episode of the Maha-bharata. By Monier Williams, Professor of Sanscrit at Haileybury, metrically translated by the Very Rev. Dean H. H. Milman. 8vo., Oxford, 1860.

The overture was rejected with disdain; and Nala and Damayanti then enter the forest, with only one garment between them, and their adventures begin, which I hope terminated happily: but I had not time to read more; so they may be still in the forest, for what I know.

The story of Yudhishthira, the hero of this game, is very similar. He loses his kingdom by dice, and last of all his wife. On their being given back to him he loses all again at chess; and they retire to the forest.

"Yudhisht'hira first lost all his estates; then in succession, all the riches in his treasury, his four brothers, and his wife Droupudee. When Droupudee was brought to be given up to Dooryodhunu, he ordered her to sit on his knee, which she refused to do; he then seized her by her clothes, but she left her clothes in his hands; and as often as he stripped her, she was miraculously clothed again. At length Dhritu-rashtru, the father of Dooryodhunu, was so pleased with Droopudee, that he told her to ask what she would, and he would grant it. She first asked for her husband's kingdom, this was granted; and she was permitted to ask for other blessings, till all that her husband had lost was restored. Yoodhisht'hiru again encounters Shukunee at chess, and again loses all. After this Droopudee and her five husbands enter the forest"[1] (her husband, and his four brothers).

All these names, whether relating to the gods, or history, or legends, are mythical. It is evident therefore that those who have described this game must have been satisfied that its origin was lost in the ages

[1] William Ward. *A View of the History, Literature, and Mythology of the Hindoos.* 4 Vols., Lond., 1820. Vol. iv, 433.

of antiquity. But if we cannot date down from the time of Yudhishthira and Vyasa, we can at least date upward from the time when the more modern game of Shatranj was played. Now we are told by Professor Forbes that Masoudi, who lived about 950 A.D., says that Shatranj was played long before his time. Abul Abbas, who lived about a century earlier, wrote a treatise on chess; and the celebrated poet Firdausi, who flourished in the tenth century, and wrote his Shahnama, or book of kings, a poem of 120,000 verses, founded on the Bastan-nama, or book of antiquity, gives an account of the introduction of the game into Persia by an ambassador of a Prince of India supposed to live about four hundred and fifty years before the time of Firdausi.[1]

Whatever its origin, whether of an earlier or later antiquity, Chaturanga was from the very beginning a game of war. The king and his ally went to battle with a hostile king and his ally. These forces were naturally placed opposite to each other, each Rajah occupied a central position, and had next to him his elephants, then his horsemen, and lastly his ships;[2] while his foot soldiers stood in front. The name Chaturanga signifies these four divisions of the army.[3] Chaturanga would also apply to the four armies, the red, the green, the yellow, and the black.

The following is the description of the game as given in the *Bhavishya Purana*, a portion of the great poem

[1] *Hist of Chess.*

[2] The ships played an important part in the conquest of Cyprus, when the game was supposed to have been invented, and Professor Forbes points out that the boat is used in the Punjab, in the plains occasionally flooded by the Ganges.

[3] In the *Amarakosha*, where *Nauka*, the ship, had given place to *Ratha*, the chariot, the game is called "Hasti-aswa-ratha-padatam," "elephant, horse, chariot, and infantry," Captain Hiram Cox. It is difficult to believe that this could be a common appellation of the game.

Mahabharata, translations of which are given by Sir William Jones, Professor Forbes, and later by Antonius Van der Linde, who in his exhaustive history and literature of the game of chess not only gives us a translation by the eminent Sanscrit scholar of Berlin, Dr. Weber, but appends the Sanscrit itself in the Roman character. It is from this German rendering that I have endeavoured to offer the following translation, making such alterations as I considered necessary from the requirements of the game, consistent with the original, and putting it in the form of poetry, so as to correspond better line by line with the original Sanscrit, and thus give it a more exact and picturesque appearance.[1] It will be observed that the numbers of the verses are not all consecutive. Whether they have been dislocated in the original it is difficult to say: but I think it will be seen that they follow naturally in the order which I have assigned them.

Yudhishthira having heard of the game of Chaturanga, applied to Vyasa for instructions concerning it.

Yudhishthira said :—

1 Explain, O supereminent in virtue, the game on the eight-times-eight board :
Tell me, O my Master, how the Chaturanga may be played.

Vyasa replied :—

2 On a board of eight squares place the red forces in front,
The green to the right, the yellow at the back, and the black to the left.

3 To the left of the Rajah, O Prince, place the Elephant, then the Horse,
Then the Ship; and then four foot-soldiers in front.

[1] I am indebted to my friend Mr. Bendall, the Professor of Sanscrit in Universal College, London, for great assistance in the more difficult passages, though it would be wrong to make him accountable for any mistakes which I may have made.

4 Opposite, place the Ship in the angle, O Son of Kunti:[1] the Horse in the second square,
The Elephant in the third, and the Rajah in the fourth.

5 In front of each place a foot-soldier. On throwing five,
Play a foot-soldier or the Rajah; if four, the Elephant:

6 If three, the Horse; if two, then, O Prince, the Ship must move.
The Rajah moves one square in any direction.

7 The foot-soldier moves one square forwards, and takes diagonally;
The Elephant can move at will—north, south, east, or west.

8 The Horse moves awry, crossing three squares at a time;[2]
The Ship moves diagonally, two squares at a time, O Yudhishthira.

10 The foot-soldier and the ship may take; or run the risk, O Yudhishthira:
The Rajah, Elephant and Horse may take; but must avoid being taken.

11 A player should guard his forces with all possible care.
The Rajah, O Prince, is the most powerful of all.

12 The most powerful may be lost, if the weaker, O son of Kunti, are not protected.
As the Rajah's chief piece is the elephant; all others must be sacrificed to save it.

36*b* Never place an elephant where it can be taken by another elephant:
For that, O Prince, would be very dangerous.

37 But if impossible to make any other move,
Then, O Prince, Gotama says it may be done.

38 If you can take both of the hostile elephants,
Take that to the left.

(The following, O Prince, are various positions and actions in the game):—

[1] He gives the mother's name Kunti, not the father's Pandu.

[2] We should call it *two* squares at a time, one diagonal and one straight or *vice versa*; but the Oriental way of looking at the move was like that of forked lightning, one forward, one horizontal, and one forward again.

It might be supposed that the three squares include that from which the piece started; but this cannot be, for in the next line the ship is said to move two squares.

9 Sinhasana, Chaturaji, Nripakrishta, Shatpada,
Kakakashtha, Vrihannauka, Naukakrishtapracaraka.

Sinhasana (A throne).

14 If a Rajah enters the square of another Rajah, O Yudhishthira,
He is said to have gained a Sinhasana.

15 If, when he gains the Sinhasana, he takes the Rajah,
He gains a double stake: otherwise a single one.

16 If a Rajah, O Prince, mounts the throne of his ally,
He gains a Sinhasana, and commands both forces.

which shows the "throne" is square upon which the King is first placed, not the upon which the latter.

17 If a Rajah, in seeking a Sinhasana, moves six squares away,
He exposes himself to danger, however secure he thinks himself.

Chaturaji (The four Rajahs).

18 If you still preserve your Rajah, and take the other Rajahs,
You obtain Chaturaji.

19 In gaining Chaturaji, and taking the other Rajahs,
You gain a double stake: otherwise, a single one.

20 If a Rajah takes the other Rajahs on their own thrones,
His stakes are fourfold.

13 To enable the Rajah to obtain Sinhasana or Chaturaji,
All other pieces, even the elephant, may be sacrificed.

21 If both a Sinhasana and a Chaturaji are obtained,
The latter only can be reckoned.

Nripakrishta (Exchange of prisoners).

22 If you have taken a Rajah, and your ally has lost one of his,
You may propose an exchange of prisoners.

23 But if you have neither of the other Rajahs, and your ally has
lost one,
You must try to take one of the other Rajahs.

24 If a Rajah has been restored, and is taken again, O Yudhishthira,
He cannot be again restored.

Shatpada (six squares' move).

25 When a foot-soldier reaches an opposite square, other than of the Rajah or Ship,
He assumes the rank of the piece corresponding to such square.

27 If the Shatpada is reached on the square of the Rajah or Ship,
It has not the privilege of a Shatpada.

28 When a foot-soldier, after many moves, gains the seventh square,
The defenceless forces on the opposite side can easily be taken.

29 O son of Kunti, if the player, however, has three foot-soldiers remaining,
He cannot take his Shatpada. So decrees Gotama.

30 But if he have only one foot-soldier and a Ship, the piece is called *Gadha*,
And he may take his Shatpada in any square he can.

26 If Chaturaji and Shatpada, O Prince, are both obtainable,
Chaturaji will have the preference.

Naukakrishta (the Ships' move):
Vrihannauka (the great Ship).

35 When three Ships come together, and the fourth Ship completes the square,
The fourth Ship takes all the other three Ships.

36 This fourth Ship is called Vrihannauka.

Kakakashtha.

31 If a Rajah has lost all his pieces before being taken, it is Kakakashtha,
So decide all the Rakshasahs. It is a drawn game.

32 If the Gadha, on gaining the Shatpada, and becoming a fifth Rajah, is taken,
It is a misfortune: for the pieces which remain will have to fight the enemy.

33 If this happens a second time,
The conqueror then sweeps off all the pieces.

34 But if, O Prince, Kakakashtha and Sinhasana occur together,
It is counted as a Sinhasana, and is not called a Kakakashtha.
That is — if the Rajah's last piece is taken on the Throne, or Rajah's Square

We cannot suppose for one moment that the use of dice, as described in verses 5 and 6, would continue to be applied to every move when the game became fully established. The game, even in the primary stage of chess, exhibited in Chaturanga, is too ingenious to be subject to a chance which would render inoperative the most brilliant conceptions, and by which the worst player, having luck on his side, might defeat the most skilful. Indeed, by being obliged to move some other piece, the player might destroy his own game. Even if we were to suppose that dice were merely used for the first move on either side, this will be found to be attended with a difficulty, a difficulty for the solution of which the description is not very clear; for we are told "If four be thrown, the Elephant must move," but the Elephant cannot move till an opening is made. But we will consider this further on, when we discuss the openings of the game, in the last paragraph of this description of Chaturanga, p. 134.

As to the stakes, we are told constantly by Oriental writers that chess was played for estates, for principalities, for petty kingdoms, and even for wives and children or other relatives; and we find examples of this gambling in the history of Yudhishthira and others. Gaming is an amusement of the most primitive races, and thus we find Mahadeva and Parvati quarrelling over their dice; we read of "dice-loving" Nala, and we see Yudhishthira himself playing with dice before he had learnt to play at chess. No wonder then that chess was at this earliest period connected with stakes on certain contingencies happening; and even when Chaturanga gave place to Shatranj a stake was still very frequently dependent on the issue of the game. As our business, however, is confined to the game itself, in order to bring it into harmony with other games of chess, we will lay aside Sinhasana, Chaturaji, and all other stake-contingencies of the game, to which so much importance is given in the poem, and proceed now with the game itself.

The Game.

Each player has a Rajah, an Elephant, a Horse, and a Ship, and four foot-soldiers; or, as we should term them, a King, a Rukh, a Knight, a Bishop, and four Pawns.

The partners' pieces occupy the opposite diagonals.

The pieces are placed in the order of Ship, Horse, Rukh, and Rajah, beginning from the left corner. In front are the four soldiers.

The players play alternately in the order of the sun, red, green, yellow, and black, as described by Vyasa; but with two sets of ivory and box-wood chessmen the colours would be red, buff, black and white; the red and black against buff and white. My Indian chessmen are seen in the photograph, and are remarkable as having ships or boats. Although the allied forces are not distinguished from each other in colour, they are known, like the Japanese chessmen, by the direction in which they face.

The Rajah, the Elephant, and the Horse move as in modern chess, the Ship always two squares diagonally, hopping over an intermediate piece if necessary.

The Rajah was not checkmated in this early game; but is taken like any other piece. The Rajah may remain in check, or may place himself in check, but at his peril; and before dying or being taken prisoner, may slay any piece he can, either personally, or by any of his men.

When the Rajah is slain or taken prisoner, all his forces, being leaderless, may be taken by the enemy, or even by his ally if they stand in his way.

When a Rajah sees that his ally's forces are not properly handled, or that the allied Rajah is about to be taken by the enemy, he may, if he can, take his ally, either personally or by any of his men, and so obtain sole direction of both armies. This power of taking a partner's Rajah has been misunderstood, and supposed to indicate a selfish Ishmaelitish principle, whereby each player would look at all the other three players as equally his enemy, and his lawful prey; but it will be seen from the above that it results from consideration of the common interest, just as in military and naval action it is expedient and necessary that the united forces should be under one control.

When a Rajah on each side has been taken prisoner, such Rajahs may, by the consent of both parties, be restored, each Rajah being restored in the order of his turn, and each Rajah choosing any unoccupied square, such restoration to count as a move.[1] This exchange of prisoners can only happen once.

If all the Rajah's pieces are taken, the Rajah

[1] In the original this power seems to be given only to the last victor, and to be compulsory; but independently of the unfairness of the second victor being entitled to a greater privilege than the first, and of an obligation to restore the Rajahs, when one has lost all his forces, and the other none—we must remember that the game represented real war: consequently, an exchange of prisoners would only be by mutual consent. This exchange of prisoners has a slight resemblance to the enrolling of prisoners in Japanese chess, for in each case the chances of the game may be materially altered by the sudden irruption of an unexpected force.

remaining alone, he retires with all the honours of war. It is a drawn game.

The Elephant being the most powerful piece, and being so blocked in, it is expedient to get it out as soon as possible, and to prevent the opponents getting out theirs.

The Ships, operating on different squares, can neither attack nor support each other: but should the four Ships come together, the last Ship takes the rival Ships.

The Foot-soldier moves and takes as our Pawn. When two Foot-soldiers are taken, either of the remaining may become an Elephant or a Horse, on reaching the opposite side, according as it reaches the square opposite the Elephant or Horse, or the Horse's or the Elephant's square of the ally's quarters. But if only one Foot-soldier remains, and a Ship, he is called a *Gadha*, and is entitled to become a Rajah, an Elephant, a Horse, or a Ship, according to the square he reaches.

The game must naturally, at first sight, strike everyone as being very similar to the modern Double Chess. But the resemblance is only outward; there being only half the number of men, the board being of only half the number of squares, there being no Queen, and the Bishop being lame, all this constitutes a great difference in starting. But in addition to this, the genius of Double Chess is to attack the last player, hoping that the partner will follow up the attack, and thus assist in the capture of a piece; but in Chaturanga the chief attention is given to the next player, to paralyze his action. Agreeably with this is the precept of Vyasa, v. 38, which, looked at by a player of Double Chess, would seem to be a mistake.

It is a good game, and superior to Double Chess in its being more convenient for two players, owing to its smaller size, and being a shorter game through having only half the number of pieces; but, like it, requiring constantly a calculation of four moves in advance. It will therefore naturally be regarded as a new game, although older than any other game of chess. Unless played by experts, when played by four the partners on each side should be permitted to consult together, although by so doing they reveal their plans: as otherwise the best player would find himself beaten, and his pieces lost, through his partner not understanding his tactics. More especially should it be so in this game, it being a game of war, when the allied forces would naturally consult and act together.

It will be seen at starting that the Rajah is in a place of danger, while the Elephant is shut in and powerless. The first thing to do, therefore, is to get out the Elephant, and to put the Rajah in a place of safety. Two ways of accomplishing this present themselves. One is to bring out, say, the Red Rajah, diagonally from 14 to 23, and at next move to bring out the Elephant behind it from 15 to 13; and taking the Rajah back again at next move to 14. But White may prevent this, if not otherwise engaged, by moving out his Foot-soldier 21 to 22, which would drive back Red's Elephant before his Rajah could get behind it. The other way is by moving the Foot-soldier from 25 to 35, and at next move to 45, when the Elephant could come out. Two other openings, however, may be made. One by Ship's Foot-soldier 27, being moved to

37, which will prevent Buff's Rajah coming out; or the Ship itself might come out and check Buff's Rajah: but this is not advisable, as it should be regarded as a Reserved Force, to be used only at a critical moment. The other by Horse's Pawn being moved from 26 to 36, and then bringing out the Horse; or the Horse itself might be moved first.

As, therefore, there are four openings, it is probable that the throws of the dice on starting meant one of the principal pieces, *or its pawn,* and this seems supported by the Rajah and its Pawn being mentioned together for the first throw, v. 5. If this be so, we should not only have a variety of openings in the game at starting, but we should get over the difficulty of the Elephant not being able to move when four is thrown.

Game I.

Red.	*Buff.*	*Black.*	*White.*
○ 14—23	○ 57—46	2 81—62	⊥ 31—32 ✓
— 23—34	□ 67—47	— 62—54 ✓	— 11—12
□ 15—13	○ 46—57	+ 80—62 ✓	— 40—31
+ 17—35 ✓	— 57—67	⊥ 70—60	⊥ 41—42
□ 13—63	⊥ 66—65	+ 62—44	— 42—43 ✓
○ 34—33	2 77—85	□ 82—80	— 43—54 2
⊥ 24—34	⊥ 76—75	○ 83—82	— 12—13
+ 35—53 ✓	○ 67—76	— 82—81	○ 31—40
2 16—35	⊥ 75—74	⊥ 71—61	2 20—41 ✓
○ 33—42	□ 47—44 + ✓	— 61—51 ✓	○ 40—50
— 42—52	2 85—73 ⊥ ✓ ✓	○ 81—82	2 41—33 ✓
— 52—62	⊥ 74—63 □	— 82—73 2	⊥ 54—55
2 35—56 ⊥	□ 44—54	— 73—63 ⊥	2 33—41 ✓
○ 62—52	— 54—53 + ✓ ✓	— 63—64	⊥ 32—33
— 52—42	⊥ 86—85	⊥ 72—62	□ 30—32 ✓
— 42—32 □	□ 53—54 ✓	○ 64—63	+ 10—32 ○
	⊥ 65—64	□ 80—84	○ 50—61
	○ 76—75	— 84—81 ✓	— 61—50
	□ 54—44	— 81—71 ✓	2 41—60 ⊥
	○ 75—65	⊥ 51—41	⊥ 13—14
	□ 44—43 ✓		
	Game.		

In this game the danger is shown of neglecting the counsel of Vyasa, v. 17—not to move the Rajah too far from its base.

Game II.

+ 17—35 ✓	○ 57—46	○ 83—74	○ 40—51
○ 14—23	— 46—55	□ 82—84	2 20—12
□ 15—13	⊥ 86—85 ✓	○ 74—83	□ 30—70 ⊥
○ 23—14	□ 67—47	+ 80—62	— 70—71 ⊥
□ 13—53 ✓ ✓	○ 55—65	□ 84—64 ✓	○ 51—42
⊥ 26—36	— 65—75	2 81—60	+ 10—30 ✓
○ 14—13	□ 47—43 ✓	□ 64—44	

The Red and Black Elephants form a very strong position: each Elephant being defended by its own Ship, and after Red's next move the White Rajah seems in a hopeless condition: but though relieved by his Elephant, the Red Ship nearly robs him of his victory.

Red.	*Buff.*	*Black.*	*White.*
			□ 71—81 ✓
□ 53—43 □✓	+ 87—65 ✓	2 70—81 □	○ 42—43 □
+ 35—57 ✓	— 65—83 ○	————	○ 44—53 +

The Red Rajah now surrenders in despair.

A well-fought game.

This game shows the advantage of not checking the Rajah prematurely with the Ship, but of keeping the power of check for the right moment, as a Reserve Force.

GAME III.

Red.	*Buff.*	*Black.*	*White.*
○ 14—23	⊥ 66—65	⊥ 72—62	⊥ 21—22
□ 15—11 ⊥	— 65—64	— 73—63	2 20—32
— 11—12	□ 67—65	○ 83—72	— 32—44 ✓
○ 23—14	— 65—75 ✓	— 72—61	+ 10—32 ✓
— 14—15	2 77—65	⊥ 62—52	2 44—23 ✓
+ 17—35 ✓	— 65—73 ✓	○ 61—50	

A bold play—all four Rajahs being checked in four successive moves—and each attacking, instead of guarding against its own danger.

			2 23—15 ○
——	2 53—61	○ 50—61 2	□ 30—20
	+ 87—65	— 61—60	○ 40—30
	□ 75—85	□ 82—85 □	⊥ 41—52 ⊥
	⊥ 76—85 □	⊥ 63—52 ⊥	+ 32—54
	+ 65—83	○ 60—51	○ 30—21
	⊥ 64—63	⊥ 70—60	+ 54—32
	— 63—52 ⊥	○ 51—52 ⊥	□ 20—50 ✓

Red.	*Buff.*	*Black.*	*White.*
	— 56—55	— 52—62	2 15—34
	— 55—54	— 62—72	□ 50—53
	— 85—84	2 81—62	— 53—73 ✓
	— 54—53	○ 72—82	2 34—42
	— 53—62 2	+ 80—62 ⊥	— 42—63 ✓
	○ 57—56	○ 82—81	□ 73—71 ⊥ ✓

Black's pawn is now a *Gadha*, but can do nothing.

	— 56—55	— 81—80	— 71—41
	— 55—64	— 80—70	2 63—42
	— 64—73	⊥ 60—50	□ 41—51
	— 73—82	○ 70—80	— 51—71
	— 82—72	+ 62—84 ⊥	2 42—61 ✓
			Game.

This game shows the power of opening by Elephant's pawn and Horse's pawn.

Game IV.

Red.	*Buff.*	*Black.*	*White.*
+ 17—25 ✓	○ 57—46	○ 83—74	○ 40—51
2 16—37	⊥ 86—85 ✓	— 74—64	□ 30—70 ⊥
○ 14—23	— 56—55 ✓	— 64—63	⊥ 11—12 ✓
— 23—34	— 55—54 ✓	— 63—54 ⊥	+ 10—32 ✓
— 34—45 ✓	○ 46—45 ○	— 54—45 ○	⊥ 21—22

Nripakrishta, or an exchange of captive Rajahs is here made.

○ ——16	○ ——86	⊥ 72—62 ✓	○ 51—52
+ 35—53	□ 67—47 ✓	○ 45—36	+ 32—54 ✓
— 53—31 ⊥	+ 87—65	— 36—35	⊥ 22—23
⊥ 24—34	— 65—87	□ 82—84	□ 70—30
+ 31—53	⊥ 66—65	2 81—60 ✓	○ 52—42
⊥ 26—36	□ 47—37 2	○ 35—46	⊥ 23—34 ⊥
— 25—34 ⊥	— 37—67	⊥ 73—63	□ 30—34 ⊥
□ 15—45 ✓	⊥ 76—75	□ 84—83	○ 42—33
— 45—25	— 75—74	— 83—82	□ 34—44 ✓
— 25—20 2	— 65—64	○ 46—35	○ 33—43
— 20—40	□ 67—65 ✓	— 35—26	□ 44—14 ✓

The Red and Black Rajahs being in contiguous squares, Black might take his ally's Rajah and so gain *Sinhasana*, and have command of both forces; but it is not expedient to do so, as both would be lost.

Red.	*Buff*	*Black.*	*White.*
— 40—41 ⊥ ✓	2 77—56	⊥ 63—54 + ✓	○ 43—54 ⊥
+ 53—35	— 56—35 + ✓	2 60—52	□ 14—16 ○ ✓
	⊥ 64—63	○ 26—25	— 16—17
	2 35—47 ✓	— 25—24	— 17—27 ⊥ ✓
	□ 65—35	— 24—14	○ 54—45
	— 35—36 ⊥	— 14—15	— 45—54
	2 47—35	2 52—33 ✓	— 54—55
	□ 36—16 ✓		
	Game.		

Alberuni's description of Chaturanga.

Alberuni's name was Abu-Raihan Muhammad. He was born at Khiva (Khwarizm or Chorasmia) in 973, and lived in Hyrcania, on the southern shore of the Caspian Sea; and dedicated his Description of India, from which book[1] this account is taken, about the year 1000, to the Prince of that country. He died in 1048.

"In playing chess, they move the Elephant straight on, not to the other sides, one square at a time, like the pawn, and to the four corners also one square at a time, like the Queen (firzan). They say that these five squares—*i.e.* the one straight forward, and the others at the corners—are the places occupied by the trunk and four feet of the Elephant."

This does not in the least agree with the foregoing description, and indeed seems to have been taken from the Japanese game; for Alberuni travelled about everywhere, and indeed the move he describes is that of the Japanese *Ghin*. Evidently therefore he was not a chess-player, and this seems implied by what he himself says immediately: "I will explain *what I know of it.*" It is probable however that many of his accounts were collected from other travellers, and so became mixed together.

[1] *Alberuni's India*, By Edward C. Sachau, Prof. R. Univ., Berlin, 2 vols. 8°, 1888. Trübner's *Oriental Series*.

"They play chess, four persons at a time, with a pair of dice. Their arrangement of the figures on the chess-board is the following[1]:—

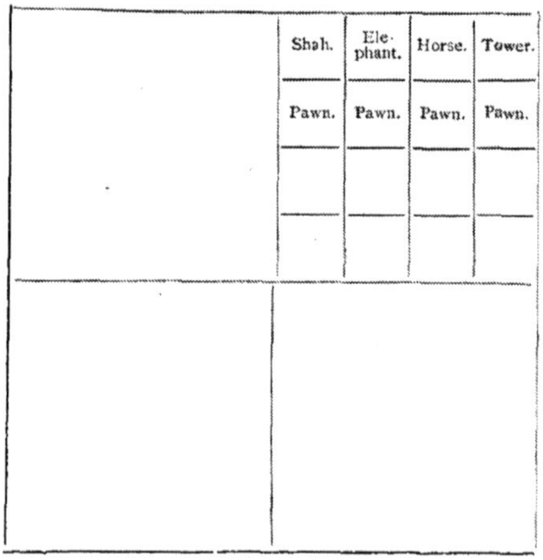

"As this kind of chess is not known to us, I shall here explain what I know of it.

"The four persons playing together sit so as to form a square round a chess-board, and throw the two dice alternately. Of the numbers of the dice the five and six are blank. In that case, if the dice show five or six, the player takes one instead of five, and four instead of six, because the figures of these two numerals are drawn in the following manner:

6			5
4	3	2	1

so as to exhibit a certain likeness of form to four and one in the Indian signs.

"The name *Shâh* or *King* applies here to the Queen.[2]

[1] In the German or English translation the diagram is reversed by mistake, probably by taking it from a tracing.

[2] What does the good man mean? — Probably that the two ... Kings were reduced to Prime Ministers when ...anga was played by two players (as it must have ... often enough) and they thus became the pieces we now

"Each number of the dice causes a move of one of the figures.

"The *one* moves either the Pawn or the King. Their moves are the same as in the common chess. The King may be taken, but is not required to leave his place.

"The *two* moves the Tower. It moves to the third square in the direction of the diagonal, as the Elephant moves in our chess.

"The *three* moves the Horse. Its move is the generally known one, to the third square in oblique direction.

"The *four* moves the Elephant. It moves in a straight line, as the Tower does in our chess, unless it be prevented from moving on. If this be the case, as sometimes happens, one of the dice removes the obstacle, and enables it to move on. Its smallest move is one square, the greatest fifteen squares, because the dice sometimes show two fours, or two sixes, or a four and a six. In consequence of one of these numbers, the Elephant moves along the whole side on the margin of the chess-board; in consequence of the other number it moves along the other side, on the other margin of the board, in case there is no impediment in its way. In consequence of these two numbers, the Elephant, in the course of his moves, occupies the two ends of the diagonal.

"The pieces have certain values, according to which the player gets his share of the stakes; for the pieces are taken, and pass into the hands of the player. The value of the King is five, that of the Elephant four, of the Horse three, of the Tower two, and of the Pawn one. He who takes a King gets five, for two Kings he gets ten, for three Kings fifteen, if the winner is no longer in possession of his own King. But if he has still his own King, and takes all three Kings, he gets fifty-four, a number which represents a progression based on general consent, not on an algebraic principle." [1]

This account is interesting from being the only other description of the game handed down to us, but it is wholly unintelligible. The King is said to be the Queen! The Elephant is first described as moving like the Ghin in Japanese chess  and as representing the four feet and trunk of the Elephant: afterwards as having the move of our Rukh. Again, the "Tower" or "Rukh" has the move of the Oriental Elephant (our Bishop), but moving always two squares only; and finally, although stakes are mentioned in both descriptions, the accounts of them do not agree. He evidently makes a mistake both in the names and the powers of the pieces. The confusion arises from Alberuni not understanding the game. But whether he saw the game played, or whether it was described to him by somebody who played the game, the description he has given us shows if such were the case, that about the year 1000 A.D. the moves were directed by dice, and the game was played for money; unless indeed, as is more probable, he borrowed the account from the Purana, but did not thoroughly understand it.

[1] 1, 183—185.

CHINESE CHESS-BOARD.

XI.

CHINESE CHESS.

Triganthius, De Christiana Expeditione apud Sinas	-	1616
Purchas, His Pilgrimes	-	1625
Samedo, Relatione della grand Monarchia della China		1643
De la Loubere, Relatione du Royaume de Siam	-	1693
Hyde, De Shahiludio Chinensium	-	1694
Eyles Irwin, Trans. Roy. Irish Academy	-	1793
Hiram Cox, Asiatic Researches	-	1801
Silberschmidt, Lehrbuch des Schachspieles	-	1845

The Chinese game of Chess is said to have had its origin about two hundred years before the time of our Lord.[1] The usual story is given of the game being invented during a state of siege. In this case the honour is given to Hong Cochu, king of Kiangnan, who is said to have sent an army to invade the Shense country. On the approach of winter his general Han-Sing invented the game in order to amuse his soldiers and keep them together. When operations were renewed in the spring the King of Shense was defeated, and he killed himself in despair.

From one of its names, Choke choo-hong-ki—game of the science of war—it is considered to have had its origin in an imitation of actual war: and thus we find in this game not only elephants, cavalry, infantry, and war-chariots, but a fortress in which the king and his counsellors are intrenched, and from which they direct operations; a fortress belonging to the enemy, which they have to storm, and a wide river between the two

[1] "Two hundred and seventy-nine years after the time of Confucius."

armies, which can only be crossed with difficulty. The elephants, being supposed to be unable to cross, are left behind to protect the field against any of the enemy who might get across; and we see them moving slowly and heavily up and down with measured tread. And lastly, we have the introduction of artillery, in the shape of a gun and a catapult, which send their missiles over the heads of intervening forces and indeed across the river. The military character of the game is further seen by the king taking the command of his forces, and calling himself general or governor, and his two councillors acting as his lieutenants or guards. Next to these, on either side, are the elephants, then the cavalry and the war-chariots in the wings, while the artillery and infantry are placed in advance. The river dividing the two forces is called *Kia-ho*, the dividing river, and is supposed to be the Hoang-ho, or the Yellow River, one of the great rivers of China, which flows into the Yellow Sea, dividing China proper from Manchouria and the Corea, a tributary of which has its source in Shense.

The Chinese chess-board is only a paper board, which can be folded up and carried with the chess-men, or a new one can always be bought and thrown away when the game is over. The Chinese game of Enclosing is also commonly played on a paper board, with a margin attached at top for making notes. One chess-board in my possession has an inscription on the river—Fung-chang-tso-ching: Ku-seu-po-Whei: which may be translated—"An amusing game for friendly meeting: Touch a piece, move it."[1] The chess-board consists of two halves, each of eight squares by four, which are

[1] Prof. Douglas, British Museum.

separated from each other by a river, the width of which is equal to one square, thus forming one move for the pawn, and half a move for the knight. The pieces are placed, not in the centre of the squares, but on the intersection of the lines: so there are nine men in a row instead of eight. In the centre of each side, 50, is the King or General, with a Guard on each side, 40 and 60. They occupy the fortress, a square of nine points, having diagonal lines running through it, the King moving along the perpendicular and horizontal lines, and his Guards along the diagonal lines. They never quit the fortress, but other pieces may enter, or pass through it. Next to the Guards are the Elephants, 30 and 70, then the Horse, 20 and 80, and in the corners the Chariots, 10 and 90. In front of the Horse are the Guns, on the third line, 22 and 82; and on the fourth line are five Soldiers, 13, 33, 53, 73 and 93.

The men are circular in form, and flat, like draughtmen, and have their names engraved on each side. I have an ivory set, and a wooden one; in each case the engraving of one player's men is filled with blue, and that of the other's in red, but the colours cannot be shown in the photograph. The red writing appears black, and the blue inscription disappearing altogether had to be filled in again with ink and re-photographed. Some of the corresponding pieces of the opposite players have different names. Thus the General of the blue becomes the Governor of the red: the Elephant of the blue the Assistant of the red; the Catapult of the blue the Cannon of the red; and the Soldiers or pawns of the different colours are written differently, though pronounced alike. The following are the names of the pieces:—

			Name.	Equivalent.	Sign.
	將	Tsiang	General	King	○
	士	Ssu	Mandarin Officer Guard	Guard	G
	象	Sang	Elephant	Bishop	+
	馬	Ma	Horse	Knight	2
	車	Tche	Chariot	Castle	□
	砲	Pao	Catapult	Cannon	⊗
	兵	Ping	Footsoldier	Pawn	⊥

The red pieces have the following distinctions:—

	師	Seu	Governor (General)
	相	Sang	Assistant (Elephant)
	炮	Pao	Cannon (Catapult)
	卒	Tsu	Footsoldier

The King's moves we have already described. The game is won when the king is checkmated. Wo-té is check, and Tsumda is checkmate.

The Elephants have the move of the ship in Chaturanga—two squares diagonally: but they cannot jump over an intermediate piece, neither can they cross the river.

The Horse has the move of our knight, but may not jump over an intermediate piece; it may cross the river, the river forming one half of the knight's move.

The Chariot moves as our rukh, and may cross the river.

The Catapult and Cannon move like the Chariot, except that they cannot move without jumping over one piece; but they cannot jump over two.

The Soldiers move and take one point at a time in a forward direction; they can cross the river, the river itself being one move; when across they can move and take either in a forward or a lateral direction; on reaching the opposite end they can move and take only laterally.

The Kings may not face each other without intervening pieces. He who moves away his only intervening piece between the two kings, would place his own King in check by so doing.

The most characteristic piece of the game is evidently the Catapult or Cannon; and as its move is so complicated it is at the same time most dangerous in its attack, and yet constantly liable to capture. It should never be left without support, for if then attacked it has no means of escape. For this reason great caution is requisite in moving into the enemy's field, relying solely on some one of his pieces over which to vault at the next move: for if this piece be moved the Cannon's escape is cut off, and its capture is inevitable.

On the other hand, the King should be very watchful against its attack: for when the Cannon is opposed to it, without any other piece intervening, it is latent check, and so cannot put any piece between.

The prettiest checkmate is with two Cannons in a line, in which case the second Cannon gives the checkmate; and if the enemy insert another piece, the first Cannon would checkmate, should the King not be able to move away.

This hidden power of the Cannons, and the character they give to the game, makes them dangerous pieces in the hands of a lady whose quick eye and ready wit would enable her to take advantage of their power of sudden and unexpected attack, and of the means of obviating it. Indeed owing to the lightness and brilliancy which distinguish this game as compared with the solidity and deep-thinking of ordinary Chess, it might with great propriety be designated Ladies' Chess.

GAME. I.

Red.	*White.*
⊗ 27—97	⊗ 82—12
2 89—68	2 20—32
⊗ 97—37	⊗ 12—14
+ 39—17	⊥ 33—34
⊥ 16—15	⊗ 14—54 ✓
G 49—58	— 54—51
⊗ 37—34 ⊥	⊥ 53—54
— 34—37	2 32—53
□ 99—97	⊥ 54—55
⊥ 56—55 ⊥	⊗ 51—55 ⊥ ✓
G 58—49	2 53—32
⊗ 37—32 2	⊗ 22—52 *Mate.*

Checkmate by the two Cannons in one line.

GAME II.

⊗ 27—99	2 80—72
— 99—37	— 20—32
— 37—33 ⊥	⊗ 82—52
— 33—73 ⊥	— 52—54 ✓
G 49—58	— 54—51
⊗ 73—77	— 51—56 ⊥ ✓
G 58—49	— 22—52
2 29—37	— 52—55 *Mate.*

Checkmate by the two Cannons in one line.

GAME III.

Red.	*White.*
⊗ 27—97	⊗ 22—92
— 97—37	— 92—72
— 37—33 ⊥	— 82—52
— 33—73 ⊥	2 80—92
— 73—33	⊗ 52—56 ⊥
2 29—48	— 56—51 ✓
G 49—58	— 51—54 ✓
2 48—56	— 72—79 + *Mate.*

Checkmate from elephant's square.

GAME IV.

2 29—48	□ 90—91
⊗ 87—80 2	⊗ 82—12
□ 99—98	□ 91—81
⊗ 80—88	— 81—87
2 89—68	— 87—57 ✓
G 69—58	⊥ 53—54
2 68—89	□ 57—87
— 89—68	— 87—85
G 58—47	⊥ 54—55
⊥ 56—55 ⊥	⊗ 12—52 ✓
G 49—58	□ 85—55 ⊥
□ 98—97	— 55—65 ✓
○ 50—60	⊗ 22—62
□ 97—67	— 52—82
— 67—65 □	— 82—89 *Mate.*

GAME V.

⊗ 27—97	⊗ 82—12
2 89—68	2 20—32
⊗ 97—37	⊗ 12—14
+ 89—17	⊥ 33—34
⊥ 16—15	⊗ 14—54 ✓
G 49—58	— 54—57 ✓
— 58—49	— 22—52
○ 59—58	— 57—54 ✓
— 58—48	— 52—12

Red.	*White*
⊥ 56—55	— 54—52
+ 17—39	— 12—42
⊗ 37—34 ⊥	— 52—55 ⊥
— 34—37	— 55—52
2 68—56	— 52—54
⊗ 37—97	2 32—44 ✓
— 97—47	— 44—56 2 ✓ ✓ *Mate.*

All moves, except four, by the cannon.

GAME VI.

⊗ 27—97	⊗ 22—92
— 97—37	— 92—52
— 37—33 ⊥	2 80—61
— 33—37	+ 30—12
2 89—77	⊗ 82—32
+ 39—57	□ 90—80
□ 99—89	⊗ 32—72
⊥ 76—75	⊥ 53—54
2 29—48	— 54—55
□ 19—29	— 73—74
[1] — 29—21	2 61—42
— 21—71	⊗ 52—22
— 71—21	⊥ 74—75 ⊥
⊥ 56—55 ⊥	— 75—76
2 77—65	□ 80—82
— 48—56	⊗ 22—52
— 56—68	— 52—57 +
— 68—76 ⊥	— 57—52 ✓
G 49—58	□ 82—87 ⊗
□ 69—87 □	⊗ 72—79 + *Mate.*

GAME VII.

⊗ 87—17	⊗ 22—92
2 29—48	— 92—72
— 89—97	— 82—52
⊗ 17—37	2 20—41
— 27—77	⊗ 72—74

[1] Attacks 2 61; and ⊗ 37 threatens 30 ✓ and then taking □ 10.

Game VII—*Continued.*

Red.	*White.*
2 97—85	2 80—72
— 85—73 ⊥	⊗ 74—77 ⊗
— 73—52 ⊗	+ 70—52 2
□ 99—97	⊗ 77—73
— 97—47	— 73—79 + ✓
G 69—58	□ 90—80
□ 47—77	— 80—89
2 48—67	⊗ 79—49 G ✓
G 58—69	— 49—19 □ ✓
+ 39—57	— 19—69 G
□ 77—79	— 69—19
⊥ 16—15	□ 10—20
○ 59—58	— 20—28 ✓
— 58—59	28—29 ✓
— 59—58	⊗ 19—79 □
+ 57—79 ⊗	□ 89—99
⊗ 27—97	— 99—98 ✓
○ 58—57	— 29—27 *Mate.*

Game VIII.

⊗ 27—97	⊗ 82—12
— 97—37	2 20—41
2 29—48	□ 10—20
— 48—27	2 80—72
⊥ 16—15	⊗ 22—92
2 89—77	[1] — 92—94
+ 79—97	⊥ 73—74
⊗ 87—57	2 72—64
— 57—55 ✓	G 60—51
⊥ 76—75	⊥ 74—75 ⊥
□ 99—89	2 64—76
⊥ 96—95	⊗ 94—92
⊗ 55—58	— 92—95 ⊥
+ 97—75 ⊥	2 76—68
[2] 2 27—35	⊗ 95—35 2
⊗ 58—55	— 25—27 ⊗

[1] □ 20—27 2

[2] To guard 47 from checkmate.

Red.	*White.*
○ 59—58	2 68—47
□ 19—18	— 47—39 + ✓
○ 58—57	□ 20—27
— 57—67	⊗ 37—77 2 ✓
— 67—68	2 39—18 □
□ 89—87	□ 28—27 ✓
⊗ 55—58	— 27—28
— 58—98	— 90—92
— 98—18 2	— 92—62 ✓
○ 68—58	— 27—28 ✓
⊗ 19—48	⊗ 12—72
+ 75—97	□ 28—27
⊗ 48—98	— 62—67
+ 97—79	⊗ 72—79 +
⊥ 36—35	□ 27—57 ✓
○ 58—48	— 57—47 ✓
— 48—58	— 67—57 ✓
— 58—68	— 47—48 ✓
	Game.

GAME IX.

⊗ 27—97	2 80—72
⊥ 56—55	⊗ 82—52
⊗ 97—95	□ 90—80
2 89—68	⊥ 93—94
⊗ 95—35	+ 30—12
— 35—75	⊥ 53—54
□ 19—17	⊗ 52—55 ⊥
⊗ 75—72 2	— 55—52 ✓
+ 39—57	— 22—72 ⊗
2 29—48	⊥ 73—74
□ 99—97	— 74—75
— 17—27	— 75—76 ⊥
2 68—76 ⊥	⊗ 72—77
⊗ 87—67	— 77—72
□ 27—21	— 72—79 + ✓
G 69—58	— 79—72
2 76—64	□ 80—89 ✓
— 48—69	⊗ 52—57 + ✓

GAME IX—*Continued.*

Red.	*White.*
G 58—47	— 57—97 □
2 64—72 ⊗	— 97—47 G
⊗ 67—17	2 20—32
□ 21—22	[1] □ 10—30
— 22—12 +	2 32—44
⊗ 17—57 ✓	+ 70—52
— 57—53 ✓	G 40—51
G 49—58	⊗ 47—43
□ 12—42	□ 30—40
— 42—12	⊗ 43—23
⊗ 53—57	□ 89—85
2 69—77	— 85—55
— 77—69	2 44—65
2 72—84	— 65—57 ⊗
— 69—57 2	□ 55—57 2
[2] — 84—92	— 40—42
□ 12—13 ⊥	⊗ 23—53
— 13—33 ⊥	□ 57—58 G ✓
○ 59—69	— 42—49 *Mate.*

[1] 2 32—44.

[2] Next move checkmate.

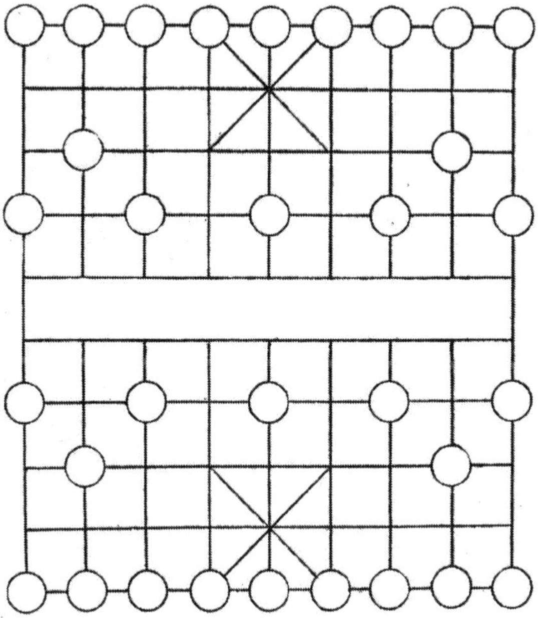

CHINESE CHESS-BOARD.

JAPANESE CHESS-BOARD.

XII.

JAPANESE CHESS.

SHIO-GHI—THE GENERAL'S GAME.

Chinese Repository	-	-	-	1840
Games with Natives	-	-	-	1872-1888

Shio-ghi is played chiefly by the intellectual classes; Go is the popular game, and Sugorochu, or Double-six, a game of chance, is the favourite of the lower orders.

Japanese Chess differs from all other games of chess in having the men all of one colour, and thus the same pieces serve for the player and his adversary. The pieces are punt-shaped pieces of wood of different sizes, lying flat upon the board, not upright, and slightly inclined towards the front; the direction of the point determining to whom the piece belongs. Any piece taken up may be entered by the adversary in any vacant place he chooses, and at any time he thinks it desirable to enter it, such entry constituting his move. The consequence is that the loss of any piece is a double loss: for not only do you lose a piece, but your adversary gains one whenever he is disposed to make use of it. And another consequence is that the game can never be judged of by the appearance of the board; for fresh pieces can be entered in at any moment—if you have taken prisoners—which may change the whole character of the game. Another peculiarity is that the pieces gain increased power on arriving at a certain portion of the board, or if a piece be a conquered piece, and re-entered in this portion of the board, it acquires this increased power after it has made one move. Consequently a conquered piece frequently becomes more formidable than it was before. Another peculiarity of the game consists in the board being constantly covered with men: for as soon as any are taken off they can be replaced on the board. But a still stranger peculiarity, if possible, is exhibited in the fact that while the game is begun with one set of men, it may be finished with another set. Indeed, it is possible that while beginning with a King, a Hisha, a Kaku, two Kins, two Gins, two Kas, two Yaris, and nine pawns, it may finish with a King, a Nari-Hisha, a Nari-Kaku, and seventeen Kins on each side.

Like all other games of chess, it has a military character; it is called the Game of War. The King General has at his side a gold commander, and a silver commander, he has infantry and cavalry, and lancers or spearmen, he has swift chariots, and reserved forces: for the prisoners are compelled to fight for their conqueror. In one respect it resembles war more than any other game of chess, for the general has not merely to calculate the chances of the armies in the field, but the contingency of other forces coming up.

The board consists of a square of nine, or 81 cells, which are of a slightly oblong form for the greater convenience of placing the pieces. The pieces are placed in the cells, not on the intersections as in Chinese chess. The cells are all of one colour. The portion of board containing the nine central cells has a dot at the four corners, the use of which is to mark the seventh, eighth, and ninth rows of squares which form that portion of the board on which pieces on arriving acquire their increased power.

The following are the names and positions of the pieces. It will be observed that the Yari and Hio or Fu are narrower in shape than the other pieces, to distinguish their perpendicular movement.

Names of the pieces.

	In print.		Pronunciation.		Translation.		Equivalent.	Sign.	
First. Second.	First.	Second.	First.	Second.	First.	Second.		First.	Second.
 [1]	王將		O or Sho		King General		King	○	
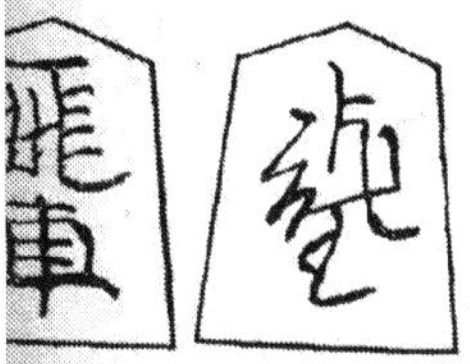 [2]	飛車	龍王	Hisha	Nari Hisha	Flying Chariot	Dragon King	Castle	□	$\underline{\square}$
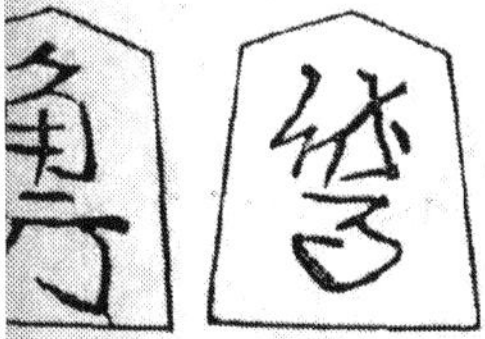	角行	龍馬	Kaku	Nari Kaku	Diagonal Moving	Dragon Horse	Bishop	+	$\underline{+}$
	金將		Kin		Gold General		Kin	K	

[1] The maker's name is often written at the bottom of the King. In this set it is Shei-Sei.
[2] The chariot in Chinese chess also, *Tche*, is the castle.

		In print.		Pronunciation.		Translation.		Equivalent.	S
First.	Second	First.	Second.	First.	Second.	First.	Second.		First.
		銀將	金	Ghin	Kin	Silver General	Kin	Ghin	G
		桂馬	金	Ka Ma	Kin	Horse	Kin	Knight	
		香車	金	Yari or Kioshia	Kin	Spear. Fragrant Chariot	Kin	Yari	Y
		步兵	金	Fu or Hio	Kin	Foot Soldier	Kin	Pawn	

These names are written differently by different writers, and at different times, so the writing does not always agree. I have three sets, but only one table, which is shown in the photograph, and this suits the smallest set. This table is only $5\frac{3}{4}$ by $6\frac{1}{2}$ ins. square, and $3\frac{1}{4}$ high; my largest set has only a yellow paper with the squares printed on it, measuring $10\frac{1}{4}$ by $12\frac{1}{4}$; for the squares are somewhat elongated in order to contain the pieces. The pieces here represented are of the middle size, and they also had originally only a folded paper board inside the box. The nine squares in the centre are distinguished by round points at the four angles, so as to mark the line of increased power.

O, the King, written king general, stands in the centre of first row. He moves one square in any direction; and loses the game when checkmated. Check is called O-té, check to the king; and checkmate is Tsumu, or Tsumda, finished.

Kin, written Kin-sho, gold general, stands on either side of the King, and moves one square in any direction, except the two back diagonals.

Gin (pronounced *Ghin*), written Gin-sho, silver general, stands on each side next to the Kin, and moves one square in every direction, except sideways and backwards.

Ka-Ma,[1] a horse, stands next to the Gin, and has a knight's move, but only forwards.

Yari, spearman, occupies the extreme ends, and moves any number of squares, perpendicularly only.

Hisha, flying chariot, stands in front of the right-hand Ka, and has the move of our rook.

Kaku, diagonal-moving, stands in front of the left-hand Ka, and has the move of our bishop.

Hio, or *Fu*, soldier. These, nine in number, occupy the third row, and move and take one square forwards only.

The King, and the Gold General hold their full honours, but all the other pieces look forward to promotion immediately on entering the enemy's camp, which comprises the three furthest lines of squares.

The Gin, the Ka-Ma, the Yari, and the Hio or Fu, can all attain the rank of Kin.

The Hisha, now called Nari-Hisha, dragon-king, has

[1] Ma is a horse, both in Japanese and Chinese. In Burmese it is Mhee.

increased rank, and the privilege, in addition to his former power, of moving one square diagonally like the Kaku.

The Kaku, now called Nari-Kaku, dragon-horse, has increased rank, and the privilege, in addition to his former power, of moving one square forward, sideways, or backwards, like the Hisha.

Prisoners are forced to enter the army, but are not obliged to begin from the ranks. They may be placed in any open square, even if desired, in the enemy's camp; but, if placed within the enemy's lines they do not get their promotion till they have held their position sufficiently long to make one move; but when re-entered go back to their original power. Thus, though the Gin, the Ka, the Yari, or the Fu may have acquired the rank of Kin before being taken, they are re-entered only according to their original power. In like manner the conquered Nari-Hisha, or Nari-Kaku, becomes a simple Hisha, or Kaku.

A captive pawn may not be entered in a perpendicular line with another pawn.

The Gin, the Ka-Ma, the Yari, and the Hio or Fu, on becoming Kins, have the name Kin on the other side written in a more or less negligent way, according to the original value of the piece. The Kin itself is 金, the Gin is written rapidly 金, the Ka [illegible], the Yari [illegible], and the Hio or Fu と or |, thus enabling a player to perceive the original power of a piece should it be turned over.

We fear that this account of Japanese chess, interesting though it may be, will appear too confused and intricate to be made available for our use, and will be given up as hopeless: so we will endeavour to simplify it by calling the pieces by names we can understand, and by changing the punt-shaped pieces, with their, to us, unintelligible writing, to an arrangement of ordinary chessmen. To do this we must make use of parts of three sets of chessmen, two of ivory—a medium and a smaller set—and one of box-wood of larger size. The pieces and their signs will now be:—

		Ivory Chessmen *Small size.*	Ivory Chessmen *Medium size*	Box-wood Chessmen *Large size.*
○	King ...	...	... ○	
□	*Hisha* (Castle)	..	... □	
+	*Kaku* (Bishop)	...	... +	
K	*Kin* ...	...	...	. ⊥
G	*Ghin* ...	+ on becoming a *Kin*		... ⊥
2	Knight ...	2 „	„	... ⊥
Y	*Yari* ...	□ „	„	.. ⊥
⊥	Pawn ...	⊥ „	„	... ⊥
□̲	*Nari-Hisha*...	...	...	... □
±̲	*Nari-Kaku* ...	..	...	... +

But on using a wooden pawn for the kin, it will not be known whether the piece was originally of lower value; and as it has to return to that lower value when taken, it is necessary when a piece becomes a Kin, to put a small piece of paper under the Kin, or a label over it, giving the name of the original piece, Gin, Ka, Yari or Hio; the Nari-Hisha and Nari-Kaku will not require it, as they would go back to their original ivory.

A pawn is used by the Japanese to determine the first move, and in throwing for it you ask your opponent whether it is a Hio or a Kin? just as we say heads or tails; or, as in tennis, rough or smooth?

In opening the game the first thing to be done is to clear the way for the Hisha and the Kaku; but as the opponent will naturally do the same on his side, care must be taken to prevent the opposite Hisha's attack on the left: but a defensive game is not a safe game; and victory will generally follow the first success. If the Hisha and the Kaku are prevented from operating by the defences of the enemy, the Gin and the Ka can be brought out to break the outposts, and form a breach for the entry of the superior pieces, thus, at the end of Game I, although *White* had two Hishas, it was unable to pierce the intrenchment, till the Gin came up in six moves and did so. The Ka would reach the intrenchment in three moves, and the Hio in four. As the Hios have only half the taking power of our Pawns, and cannot support each other, their use is not so much to force the intrenchment, as to support other pieces in doing so.

As in war victory often follows the unexpected entry of fresh troops, so in Japanese chess, the great danger to be constantly kept in view is the entry of captive pieces, forming the reserved forces. The eye must be ever fixed on the captives in the possession of the enemy, and on what points they may possibly enter. An example of this occurs in Game I, in *White's* moves 17, 18 and 20. Two captive Gins are suddenly brought in, in two successive moves, thus causing the loss of a Hisha; and this Hisha is as unexpectedly entered in the innermost line of the enemy's intrenchment, giving check to the king, and at the next move becoming a Nari-Hisha, and soon giving a checkmate. In like manner in Game II, the Hisha is lost by the entrance in two successive moves of the Yari and Kama, and checkmate follows in four moves afterwards. The loss of a piece therefore is not merely the loss of such piece, but, as we have said, the conqueror thus gains an extra piece of the same value. Nor is this all: for this extra piece, instead of being placed where such piece would stand in the beginning of a game, can be placed anywhere on the board, and, if placed within the enemy's line, will gain its increased power at the next move—a result resembling that of an Indian game of cards, *Shataro* (seventeen), in which after every deal, the winners take at chance as many cards from the hand of the loser as they have won tricks, and give back to him in return as many of the worst cards they have in their own hands; and thus at every deal he is worse off, till he is happily out of the game. For this reason, when two pieces are *en prise*, it is advisable to examine carefully whether, if the pieces are exchanged, the new piece can be entered in a more commanding position, or whether the opponent can improve his position; and in either case to be the first to exchange, so as to be the first to enter the new piece, and then perhaps obtain another piece, or even lead to a checkmate; and thus give no opportunity for the opponent to enter his piece. This also is seen in Game I. In his seventh move *Red* opened a way for his Kaku, and *White* opened his Kaku five moves afterwards. *Red* should have immediately exchanged Kakus: but neglecting to do so, *White* made the exchange, and thus at the next move entered a new Kaku, forking the Hisha and Gin, taking two Gins, and, as we have already seen, with these two new Gins taking the Hisha.

Owing to the necessity of carefully and continually watching the number and powers of the captive pieces belonging to the enemy, and how they may affect the game; and of not neglecting to make use of one's own captive pieces as occasion offers; it is advisable that they should be placed carefully on each side, so as to be seen by both players. When each player has taken a piece of the same value, the prisoners should be exchanged, so as to enter the right colour on each side.

This is a very intricate game, indeed the most so of all varieties of chess, owing to the complicated nature of the moves, the unexpected importation of new pieces, and the constant changing of the power of the pieces: but for this very reason, and from the fact of its being so peculiar, it becomes a game of great interest. The game requires great practice, before a novice however experienced in European chess, can recollect the powers of the several pieces, present or prospective; and can grasp at a glance the effect produced by the advent of new pieces, and understand where to place them. The result in each such case must be a lamentable and disgraceful defeat. This circumstance therefore proves that Japanese chess is no weak variety of ordinary chess; but that it is a game of great originality, and of high intellect.

The examples of games which follow were played by different Japanese of various degrees of efficiency, but however weak the play in some instances, they all show the nature of the game. The men being all alike, except in size, and not having any difference in colour, as in the Chinese, it must be very difficult, even for the Japanese, to distinguish one man from another merely by the writing; and even this writing though it is upright for one's own men, is upside down for one's opponent's; and of course it is as necessary, or even more so, to distinguish the adversary's men than one's own, for though it takes a long time to make a successful attack, a single adverse move by one's own may be fatal. Owing to this difficulty, although Japanese, and indeed all Orientals, unlike European chess players, play very rapidly, from their quicker preception,[1] they occasionally make mistakes or oversights relative to the pieces; and it is astonishing that such mistakes are not more frequent. If anyone doubt this, let him write the names of the pieces in English on flat counters, and see what he would make of it.

From the games which I have seen played, they do not always observe the rule—"Touch a piece, move it." On the contrary, I have seen them touch one piece, and then another, and then go back perhaps to their first move. The pieces were turned over also on entering the seventh line of squares, without directing attention to the fact by saying Kin, Nari-Hisha, or Nari-Kaku; taking it for granted that the opponent would perceive that it was all right; and in like manner new pieces would be entered without comment. Some players did not even call out O té, check, when checking the King; and I have seen a game finished without saying Tsumu, or Tsumda, checkmate, or finished: so that I had to ask whether it was checkmate.

Game IV, notwithstanding its mistakes, is interesting as exhibiting a well-fought game. It is curious

[1] In a chess tournament played recently, I see it was provided that fifteen moves be made in the hour. Game iv. occupied one hour exactly, and there were 109 moves: so the Japanese play was more than seven times as rapid.

to see how *Red*, in 95, had won the game if he had played the right piece; and how a second time he had the chance of doing so in 99, in two moves, but failed to see it, and how by not doing so, and making a false move through the temptation of taking a Kin, he thus allowed *White* to get the move, which being skilfully followed up by entering his reserved forces unexpectedly, ended in checkmate.

Owing to the intricacy and length of Game IV, and the mistakes which arose from errors in following the score, which obliged me to begin several times all over again, I found it necessary to take account of the game from time to time, as bankers cast their balance every day, to prevent having to go back. The result will be seen in the score of the game, and will show how available the notation I employ is for noting down the condition of a game from time to time throughout the game. This repeated record of the score will also be found of use to the reader who wishes to learn the game by playing it out according to the score: for if at any of these breaks he finds his game does not accord with the score, he will be obliged either to begin again, or to start afresh from one of these scores.

The following announcement in the *Times* will be read with pleasure by chess players:—

"The *Japan Mail*, referring to attempts now being made to revive chess in Japan, says that during the long peace enjoyed by that country under the rule of the Shoguns the game of chess flourished. Once every year, on the seventeenth day of the eleventh month, the masters of the game met in Yedo and fought a grand tourney in an appointed place within the precincts of the palace. Judges, umpires, strict rules, and all things necessary to the combat were provided, and after the fight was over the ranks of the various combatants were officially fixed. The number of ranks was seven in all, the seventh being the highest.[1] Rarely did any player attain the distinction of reaching this, but the sixth generally had one or two representatives. There appears to have been a certain element of heredity in the game as played in Japan, for certain families took the lead for many generations, and the contests between their champions were a salient feature of every tourney. To this time-honoured custom, as to many another of even greater merit, the Revolution of 1867 put a stop. A long era of neglect ensued for chess players; but it did not fall into disuse because Court patronage was wanting. Its votaries still studied their gambits and elaborated their variations, and now once more the science promises to resume its place of importance. In October last a grand meeting of all the principal chess-players in Japan was organized in Tokio. Over 200 players assembled, all boasting greater or less degrees of skill, from the first up to the sixth. Count Todo, the former Daimio of Tsu, who has the honour of belonging to the sixth rank, is among the chief promoters of the revival. Another meeting took place on the 18th of January, when a ceremonial in honour of the revival of chess was performed. There appears to be a considerable chess literature in Japan: one

[1] The early Arab and Persian chess players were divided into five classes. The first were called *'Aliyat*, or grandees. Frequently it consisted of only one player, seldom of more than three. A grandee gave a pawn to a member of the second class, a Queen or Ferz to the third class, a Knight to the fourth class, and a Rook to the fifth class. Forbes, *Hist. of Chess.*

leading work contains problems, the solution of which is said to make the player worthy to be placed in the sixth rank."[1]

GAME I.

	Red.	*White.*
1	⊥ 26—25	K 40—31
2	— 25—24	⊥ 82—83
3	K 68—77	— 83—84
4	⊥ 24—23	— 22—23 ⊥
5	□ 27—23 ⊥	⊥ 22
6	— 23—25	⊥ 12—13
7	⊥ 76—75	— 84—85
8	— 86—85 ⊥	□ 81—85 ⊥
9	⊥ 86	— 85—81
10	G 78—67	G 70—71
11	⊥ 56—55	⊥ 32—33
12	G 67—56	+ 21—87 +
13	K 77—87 +	+ 34
14	□ 25—35	— 34—56 G
15	K 48—57	— 56—38 G (Nari-Kaku)
16	□ 35—25	K 31—32
17	+ 47	G 34
18	— 25—26	— 25
19	+ 47—38 +̲	G 25—26 □
20	+ 54	□ 78 ✓
21	○ 58—47	□ 78—75 ⊥ (Nari-Hisha)
22	⊥ 76	□̲ 75—55 ⊥
23	+ 54—65	G̅ 71—82
24	K 57—56	□̲ 55—64
25	⊥ 76—75	G̅ 82—73
26	K 87—76	— 73—84
27	⊥ 86—85	— 84—85 ⊥
28	K 76—77	— 85—86 (Kin)
29	— 77—78	□̲ 64—75 ⊥
30	— 78—68	K̅ 86—77

[1] *Times*, 10th April, 1890.

19 *White's* Nari-Kaku captured by *Red* is entered in the following move, but being a captive, goes back to its first estate, viz., a Kaku.

	Red.	*White.*
31	○ 47—58	— 77—68 K
32	— 58—68 K	□ 81—88 2 √(Nari-Hisha)
33	— 68—57	□ 75—77
34	G 67	— 88—68
35	— 57—47	— 77—67 K *Mate.*

In move 12 *Red* ought to have exchanged Kakus first, 87—21. Neglecting to do so *White* had the first exchange 21—87, and entered his prisoner in the following move, which took two Gins in the two following moves, and became a Nari-Kaku. *Red* entered his Kaku in move 17, which took *White's* Nari-Kaku in move 19, but in the same move *White* immediately took *Red's* Hisha, which he entered in the following move, and which eventually gave the checkmate.

32 In like manner *White's* Kin taken by *Red* is entered in 34 as a Gin.

GAME II.

	White.	*Red.*
1	⊥ 32—33	K 68—77
2	K 40—31	G 78—67
3	⊥ 82—83	⊥ 26—25
4	— 83—84	— 25—24
5	— 84—85	— 86—85 ⊥
6	□ 81—85 ⊥	⊥ 86
7	— 85—83	— 24—23
8	⊥ 22—23 ⊥	— 96—95
9	K 31—22	G 38—37
10	⊥ 72—73	— 37—26
11	G 70—61	— 26—35
12	⊥ 52—53	○ 58—57

2 *Red* G should have stopped to protect +

8 *Red* □ 27—23 ⊥

GAME II—*Continued.*

	White.	*Red.*
13	G 61—52	⊥ 66—65
14	○ 50—61	K 77—66
15	⊥ 85	⊥ 86—85 ⊥
16	□ 83—85 ⊥	+ 87—96
17	— 85—88 2 (Nari-Hisha)	⊥ 24
18	⊥ 23—24 ⊥	G 35—24 ⊥
19	+ 21—43	— 24—33 ⊥
20	⊥ 26	□ 27—26 ⊥
21	⊥ 25	— 26—27
22	K 22—23 G	⊥ 26—35
23	G 26	□ 27—47
24	G 26—35 ⊥ becomes K	⊥ 46—45
25	⊥ 25—26 becomes K	— 45—44
26	+ 43—25	— 44—43
27	⊥ 42—43 ⊥	⊥ 36
28	K 26—36 ⊥	2 28—36 K
29	G 35—36 2 becomes K	□ 47—45
30	+ 25—34	— 45—15
31	K 33—24	— 15—55
32	□ 88—98 Y	⊥ 65—64
33	— 98—96 +	□ 55—75
34	Y 74	— 75—65
35	2 45 ✓	— 65—45 2
36	+ 34—45 □	2 37
37	+ 35 ✓	○ 57—58
38	□ 96—98 ✓	G 67—78
39	— 98—78 G *Mate.*	

13 *Red* blocks up his own +

18 *Red* □ 27—24 ⊥

20 Good play.

25 This is a mistake. The ⊥ must make another move, being a captive piece, before it becomes a K.

26 G 67—78 as □ 88 could not take 98 without being ultimately taken, and if it moved to 86, + would move to 87, and so drive it away.

34 Courting capture, in order to draw away □ 75.

GAME III.

Red.	*White.*
K 40—31	⊥ 76—75
□ 81—41	— 26—25
50—61	— 25—24
⊥ 32—33	+ 87—21 +
G 30—21 +	⊥ 24—23
⊥ 22—23 ⊥	□ 27—23 ⊥
⊥ 22	— 23—27
— 42—43	K 68—77
— 43—44	G 78—67
K 31—32	— 38—37
⊥ 44—45	⊥ 46—45 ⊥
□ 41—45 ⊥	⊥ 46
— 45—75 ⊥	— 76
— 75—73	+ 64
— 73—63	+ 64—20 2 (Nari-Kaku)
⊥ 22—23	+ 20—21 G
K 32—42	□ 27—23 ⊥
— 42—53	— 23—22 (Nari-Hisha)
⊥ 72—73	+ 21—10 Y
G 70—71	□ 22—21 ✓
○ 61—72	2 75
□ 63—64	□ 21—41
⊥ 82—83	⊥ 66—65
□ 64—65 ⊥	Y 66
— 65—25	□ 41—42
K 53—63	Y 66—63 K
⊥ 62—63 Y	+ 10—54
□ 25—27	— 54—63 ⊥ ✓
○ 72—82	□ 42—52 ⊥ ✓
— 82—91	2 75—83 ⊥ *Checkmate.*

The Japanese who played *Red* was evidently only a beginner, who "knew the moves, but that was all:" for when once the game was fairly opened every move he made was a bad one. But *White's* play shows some new points, especially in the power of the Kaku, and the skill in bringing in new pieces; whereas *Red* never used his captive Kaku, and only brought in a ⊥, and even in the last move he might have avoided checkmate by entering his Kaku at 72, or placing his 2 there; and instead of using his Hisha, he placed it out of the way where it could be of no use.

GAME IV.

	White.	*Red.*
1	K 40—31	⊥ 76—75
2	⊥ 82—83	K 68—77
3	— 83—84	G 78—67
4	— 84—85	⊥ 86—85 ⊥
5	□ 81—85 ⊥	G 67—76
6	— 85—81	⊥ 86
7	G 70—71	⊥ 26—25
8	○ 50—51	○ 68—57
9	G 71—82	⊥ 96—95
10	⊥ 92—93	— 25—24
11	— 12—13	— 16—15
12	G 82—83	G 76—85
13	K 60—61	⊥ 24—23
14	⊥ 22—23 ⊥	□ 27—23 ⊥
15	⊥ 22	— 23—24
16	G 30—41	K 48—47
17	⊥ 52—53	G 38—37
18	G 41—52	— 37—26
19	K 61—71	— 26—25
20	⊥ 32—33	⊥ 23
21	+ 21—87 +	K 77—87 +
22	⊥ 22—23 ⊥	□ 24—23 ⊥
23	⊥ 22	— 23—33 ⊥
24	⊥ 32	— 33—35
25	+ 44	— 35—65
26	+ 44—26 (Nari-Kaku)	G 25—16
27	⊥ 72—73	+ 45
28	G 83—72	⊥ 75—74
29	⊥ 73—74 ⊥	G 85—74 ⊥

	White.	*Red.*
30	□ 81—84	— 74—73
31	G 72—63	— 73—84 □
32	— 53—54	+ 45—54 G
33	⊥ 53—54	□ 65—75
34	⊥ 72	G 84—83
35	± 26—53	□ 75—78
36	⊥̄ 54—55	⊥ 56—55 ⊥
37	+ 43	G 54
38	⊥ 43—54 G	⊥ 55—54 +
39	± 53—54 ⊥	⊥ 76
40	⊥ 55	□ 84
41	G 52—63	G 83—82
42	G 73	□ 84—54 ± (+)
43	G 63—54 □	G 82—71 K (K)

Condition of the game as at present.

White, ○ 51 : K 31 : G 54.73 : 2 20.80 : Y 10.90 : ⊥ 13.22.32 42.55.62.72.93.

Red, ○ 57 : □ 78 : K 47.71.87 : G 16 : 2 28.88 : Y 18.98 : ⊥ 15.36.46.66.76.86.95.

Prisoners or Reserved Forces.

White, □. *Red,* ++. K. ⊥⊥⊥.

Red has the best of the game by ++. KKK: ⊥⊥: including Reserved Forces.

Continuation.

	White.	*Red.*
44	G 73—64	+ 60 ✓
45	○ 51—52	+ 70 ✓
46	— 52—53	+ 60—51 (Nari-Kaku)
47	G 54—63	K 71—61
48	— 64—73	⊥ 76—75
49	⊥ 42—43	— 75—74
50	G 63—74 ⊥	□ 78—74 G
51	— 73—74 □	K 61—62 ⊥
52	○ 53—64	+ 70—43 ⊥ (Nari-Kaku)

31 An oversight. G 72—73 G.

	White.	*Red.*
53	□ 78	G 65 ✓
54	○ 64—75	G 65—76 ✓
55	— 75—64	⊥ 66—65 ✓
56	— 64—73	K 62—63 ✓✓
57	— 73—82	+̲ 51—61
58	□ 58 ✓	○̲ 57—66
59	□ 78—68 ✓ (Nari-Hisha)	K 67
60	G 74—63 K (G)	K 67—68 □̲ (□)
61	□ 58—68 K ✓(Nari-Hisha)	G 76—57
62	G 54	+̲ 61—60 ✓
63	○ 82—73	— 43—70
64	⊥ 75	○ 66—75 ⊥
65	G 63—74	— 75—66

Condition of the game as at present.

White, ○ 73 □̲ 68 : K 31 · G 54.74 . 2 20.80 Y 10.90 : ⊥ 13 22.32.55.72.93

Red, ○ 66 +̲ 60.70 K 47.87 G 16.67 . 2 28.88 : Y 18.98 : ⊥ 15.36.46.65.86.95.

Prisoners or Reserved Forces.

White, K *Red*, □ ⊥ ⊥ ⊥ ⊥ ⊥ ⊥

Relative Value.

White, □̲ *Red*, □ +̲ +̲ ⊥ ⊥ ⊥ ⊥ ⊥ ⊥ ⊥ . so still has the best of the game.

Continuation.

	White	*Red.*
66	G 74—65 ⊥ ✓	○ 66—75
67	□̲ 68—67 G	⊥ 95—94

Here *White* might have won the game at the next move by playing G 66—75 checkmate.

68	○ 73—63	⊥ 64 ✓
69	— 63—53	+̲ 60—71 ✓
70	G 62	□ 52 ✓
71	○ 53—44	+̲ 71—62 G ✓
72	— 44—33	□̲ 52—53 ✓ (Nari-hisha)
73	K 43	+̲ 62—51 ✓

	White.	*Red.*
74	○ 33—23	± 70—43 K
75	□̲ 67—66 ✓	Ō 75—85
76	G 54—43 ± (+)	□̲ 53—43 G ✓
77	○ 23—12	± 51—40
78	⊥ 42	□̲ 43—53
79	+ 58 ✓	G 76
80	G 65—76 G ✓	○ 85—74
81	□̲ 66—65 ✓	— 74—63
82	G 30	⊥ 15—14
83	○ 12—21	— 14—13 ⊥
84	+ 58—47 K (Nari-Kaku)	G 16—25
85	± 47—56	□̲ 53—51
86	K 41	K̄ 87—76 G
87	K 41—51 □̲ (□)	± 40—51 K
88	□̄ 65—68	G 12 ✓
89	Ȳ 10—12 G	⊥ 13—12 Y
90	2 20—12 ⊥	Y 18—12 2
91	± 56—12 Y	2 24
92	— 12—23	⊥ 12 ✓
93	— 23—12 ⊥	2 24—12 ± (+)
94	○ 21—12 2	Y 14 ✓

Condition of the game as at present.

White, ○ 12 · □̲ 68 · K 31 · G 30 · 2 80 : Y 90 . ⊥ 22.32.42 55.72.93.

Red, ○ 63 : ± 51 : K 76 : G 25 : 2 28.88 : Y 14.98 : ⊥ 36.46 64.86.94.

Prisoners or Reserved Forces.

White, □ G 2 Y ⊥ ⊥ *Red,* + K K G ⊥ ⊥ ⊥ ⊥ ⊥

Relative Value.

White, □̲ □ *Red,* ± + K K ⊥ ⊥ ⊥

At this period of the game each player made several mistakes. In 95 *White* went into a trap, but *Red* neglected to checkmate him. In 96 *White* should have opened an escape. In 99 *White* should have opened another escape, by taking Nari-Kaku 52; and *Red* should have moved up ⊥ to become a K, and given check, and at next move entered K at 22, and given checkmate.

Conclusion.

	White.	*Red.*
95	○ 12—21	⊥ 12
96	K 31—41	G 10 ✓
97	○ 21—31	K 21 ✓
98	G 30—21 K	G 10—21 G
99	○ 31—21 G	+̲ 51—41 K
100	□ 61 ✓	○ 63—52
101	K 62 ✓	— 52—42 ⊥
102	G 53 ✓	— 42—43
103	□ 61—41 +̲ ✓ goes back to +	— 43—34
104	— 41—44 ✓	— 34—35
105	□̲ 68—28 2	G 45
106	— 44—64 ⊥	K 44
107	+ 26 ✓	○ 35—34
108	G 23 ✓	— 34—43
109	⊥ 42 *Checkmate.*	

95 *White* ○ 12—23 . *Red* K 11 checkmate next move.

96 *White* ⊥ 22—23.

97 *White* ○ 21 could not take G 10, for ⊥ 12 would move to 11 and become K, and give checkmate.

99 *White* K 41—51 + : *Red* ⊥ 12—11 and become K ✓, and entering K 21 checkmate.

BURMESE CHESS-BOARD.

XIII.

BURMESE CHESS.

CHIT-THAREEN, or the General's game.

Major Symes, Embassy to the Kingdom of Ava 1800
Capt. Hiram Cox, Trans. Bengal Asiatic Soc. 1801
Shway Yoe (James George Scott), The Burman. His life and notions 1882

Professor Forbes thought this game common to the regions situated between India and China, viz., Tibet, Burmah, Siam, and Cochin China.

The names of the pieces are, according to Captain Cox :—

Mong—The King, or General,	which	we will call	King,	○
Chekoy—Lieutenant General,	,,	,,	Queen,	☾
Ratha—War Chariots,	,,	,,	Rukhs,	□
Chein—Elephants,	,,	,,	Bishops,	+
Mhee—Cavalry,	,,	,,	Knights,	2
Yein—Foot Soldiers,	,,	,,	Pawns,	⊥

The King has the same move as with us.

The Queen moves diagonally only, but only one square at a time.

The Rukhs have the same move as with us.

The Bishops move one square diagonally, but are able to move, but not to take, one square forward, being thus able to change their colour. They are therefore like the Japanese Ghin, except that this latter is able to take, as well as to move, one square forward.

The Knights move as our Knights.

The Pawns also move and take as our Pawns, and queen on arriving at the diagonal line.

The Board is a square of eight cells, and has a line, or is supposed to have a line running diagonally from top of right side to bottom of left side.

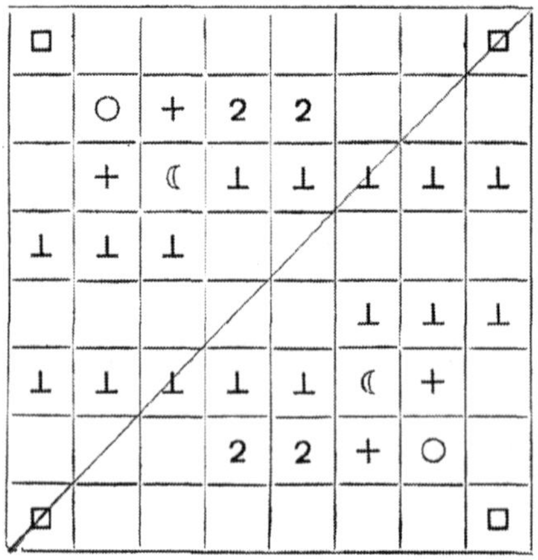

Although this is the ordinary disposition of the men, either party may adopt another line of battle; but the pawns must not be altered. The board is very large, and stands high, for the convenience of the players, who sit upon the ground; as will be seen from the photograph which Mr. Scott of St. John's College, Cambridge, obligingly allowed me to take of the table and men in his possession.

It will be seen on examining this game that there is only one line of squares dividing the combatants, and that the battle must begin immediately. Further, that as the diagonal line shows the line of queening, the pawns would soon queen were they not opposed by hostile pawns. The power of queening is confined to the three[1] advanced pawns on right hand side; and thus the first pawn queens in four moves, the second in three, and the third in two moves. But we will speak of this presently.

As the game is peculiar in the pawns being put in fighting position, and in strike of each other: so the defensive position of the King is equally remarkable. The King stands in a strong intrenchment. He fights as it were "with his back to the wall," being close to a corner, and thus protected on one side and the rear, while he has guards to protect him on the other side and the front. Of these guards the Elephants, being of the same colour, defend each other, and three diagonal points each, the Queen protects three diagonal points, and the King protects all those in the rear, besides giving support to his guards. Thus all the surounding squares are protected from attack.

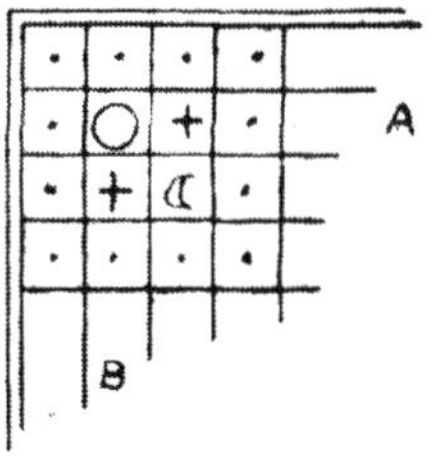

[1] Captain Cox gives the privilege of queening to the *five* right hand pawns: but this is a mistake. Were it so, each player would be enabled to queen at his first move, if placed originally as in diagram; for if all five were to be in the advanced line, one would be already on the line. This, therefore, is evidently a mistake, in writing five for three.

Mr. Scott—who, of course, is a great authority—says that the *four* pawns to the right may queen, but this seems unlikely, as the fourth pawn would be at striking distance if placed in the advanced row, and so might as well not be placed on the board.

As all these pieces move only one square at a time, they often remain in much the same position all through the game, unless the King, in the ardour of battle, thinks more of attacking his opponent than of defending himself.

Owing to this strong position there is no sudden checkmate at an early period of the game, or so long as most of the pieces are in the field; and when the principal pieces are much reduced, it becomes very difficult, unless an additional piece can be obtained by queening a pawn, to get a checkmate.

A good way of getting into the fortress is to place a Castle opposite each Bishop, at A and B, and then taking one of the Bishops with some other piece. This move will be seen in Game I, move A, where 2 takes ☾ 35, being protected by □ 30; and + 46 being prevented from moving by □ 66.

Other peculiarities of the game are exhibited in the power of the Bishops of changing their colour; and in the facility with which the Castles are enabled to support each other, and to force a passage.

The distinctive peculiarity of the early queening of the pawn would invest this game with interest, if the pawns on reaching the diagonal could exchange as in other games for one of the superior pieces: but not only is the increased power limited to that of the Chekoy, or *Queen*; but after all the difficulties of obtaining this position have been overcome, they cannot acquire even this privilege, unless the Queen has been previously taken; but have to wait, at constant risk of capture, till such event occurs. Mr. Scott, indeed, gives a still further limitation of privilege: for he says—" he must be placed on one of the eight squares around the King," but he does not state whether these squares are those around the original position of the King, or whether they must be in a square contiguous to the King, wherever he may be.

It cannot be supposed that a game like this—where the King is so securely intrenched behind his guards; where the Castles and Knights, and these matched against others of their like, are the only formidable pieces—can be a very brilliant one. Indeed, where the players are pretty equal, it must be a heavy, wearisome, uninteresting game. Even the queening of the pawns is of such trifling advantage, being allowed only when the Queen is taken, that it scarcely enters into consideration. We give, however, two examples:—

Game I.

Red.	*White.*
⊥ 65—64	⊥ 73—74
— 85—84	— 52—53
— 64—53 ⊥	— 42—53 ⊥
— 45—44	— 12—13
— 44—53 ⊥	2 41—53 ⊥
2 56—64	⊥ 13—24 ⊥
☾ 35—24 ⊥	□ 10—50
— 24—35	2 53—65
2 46—65 2	⊥ 74—65 2
□ 17—47	☾ 62—53
2 64—85	⊥ 22—23
⊥ 34—23 ⊥	2 51—43
— 23—32 ⊥	— 43—62
— 32—31	□ 40—30
2 85—73	2 62—54
+ 36—45	— 54—66
□ 47—57	— 66—45 +✓
○ 26—36	— 45—57 □✓
□ 87—57 2	□ 80—50
2 73—65 ⊥	+ 61—62

Red.	*White.*
⊥ 14—13	□ 30—31 ⊥
○ 36—26	+ 72—61
⊥ 13—12	□ 31—41
+ 25—24	⊥ 63—64
⊥ 75—64 ⊥	☾ 53—64 ⊥
⊥ 55—64 ☾	□ 41—45
□ 57—67	— 50—55
2 65—44	— 55—85
— 44—63 ✓	○ 71—72
— 63—44	□ 85—86 ✓
○ 26—25	— 86—85
⊥ 64—63 ✓	○ 72—71
□ 67—77 ✓	— 71—81
— 77—37	□ 45—44 2
○ 25—26	— 85—86 ✓
— 26—25	— 86—85
⊥ 12—11	— 44—40
□ 37—36	+ 62—53
○ 25—14	□ 40—30
— 14—25	— 85—84 ⊥
— 25—14	+ 53—44
⊥ 63—62	— 44—35 ☾
□ 36—35 +	□ 30—35 □
⊥ 11—10 becomes ☾	— 35—34
○ 14—23	— 34—24 + ✓
— 23—32	— 84—44
— 32—33	— 24—34 ✓
— 33—22	— 44—43
— 22—11	— 43—23
☾ 10—21	— 34—14 ✓
— 21—12	— 23—13
○ 11—21	-- 13—12 ☾
— 21—31	— 14—44
— 31—21	— 12—17
— 21—22	— 44—46

and soon wins the game

Game II.

Red.	*White.*
⊥ 55—54	⊥ 63—64
— 75—64 ⊥	— 73—64 ⊥
2 56—64 ⊥	+ 72—73
□ 17—77	— 61—72
2 64—52 ⊥ ✓	○ 71—61
— 52—73 + ✓	☾ 62—73 2
□ 77—73 ☾	⊥ 83—84
⊥ 65—64	— 42—43
— 54—43 ⊥	— 32—33
— 24—33 ⊥	— 22—33 ⊥
2 46—54	2 51—63
□ 87—77	□ 80—82
⊥ 45—44	⊥ 33—44 ⊥
☾ 35—46	— 44—45
+ 36—45 ⊥	2 63—44
2 54—66	— 41—33
+ 45—36	— 44—65
— 25—24	— 65—77 □
□ 73—77 2	— 33—14 ⊥ ✓
○ 26—25	— 14—22
+ 36—45	□ 82—83
2 66—74	— 83—63
— 74—53 ✓	○ 61—62
— 53—72 +	□ 10—70
☾ 46—55 [1]	— 70—72 2
□ 77—17	2 22—41
— 17—12 ⊥ ✓	○ 62—61
— 12—11	— 61—50
+ 45—54	□ 63—62
⊥ 64—63	— 72—75
□ 11—10 ✓	○ 50—61
⊥ 34—33 [2]	□ 75—55 ☾ ✓
○ 25—36	2 41—33 ⊥
+ 24—33 2	□ 55—54 +
□ 10—11 ✓	○ 61—70
— 11—15	□ 62—63 ⊥
+ 33—32	— 63—66 ✓
○ 36—25	— 66—65 ✓
— 25—26	— 54—56 ✓
— 26—37	— 65—67 *Checkmate.*

[1] + 45—54.

[2] Would "queen" next move.

BURMESE CHESS,

No. II.

The following variety of the game agrees better with other games of Chess, where the Pawn in queening takes the power of one of the superior pieces, which the Queen in Oriental chess never is. The only difference in this game is that it allows the three right hand Pawns to become Castles when they reach the diagonal line: and the game becomes one of some interest. Every attention has now to be given to these three Pawns: for when one of them reaches the diagonal, the player has immediately three Castles to his opponent's two, and can then afford to exchange Castles, indeed, it is to his interest to do so, for by such exchange the proportion of strength in Castles becomes 2 : 1, instead of 3 : 2.

The following are examples of this game .—

Game I.

Red.	*White.*
⊥ 55—54	⊥ 12—13
— 24—23	— 32—23 ⊥
— 34—23 ⊥	— 63—64
— 75—64 ⊥	— 73—64 ⊥
□ 17—77	☾ 62—53
— 77—73	⊥ 83—84
⊥ 45—44	+ 61—62 [1]
□ 73—76	— 72—73
⊥ 44—53 ☾	⊥ 42—53 ⊥
□ 87—77	□ 80—82
2 46—34	— 10—20
☾ 35—46	○ 71—72
2 34—42	2 41—33

[1] ☾ 53—62 would have been better.

Red.	*White.*
— 42—34	□ 20—21
— 34—53 ⊥ ✓	+ 62—53 2
□ 76—73 + ✓	○ 72—62
+ 36—35	[1] 2 33—54 ⊥
⊥ 65—54 2	⊥ 64—65 becomes □
+ 35—44	+ 53—64
□ 73—74	⊥ 52—53
+ 41—35	□ 65—85 ⊥
[2] 2 56—64 +	⊥ 53—64 2
□ 74—64 ⊥ ✓	○ 62—52
— 77—67	□ 85—86
— 64—66	— 86—66 □
— 67—66 □	⊥ 84—85
— 66—86	2 51—72
○ 26—36	— 72—53
☾ 46—55	— 53—74
□ 86—87	⊥ 85—86
☾ 55—44	□ 82—62
⊥ 54—53	— 62—66 ✓
+ 35—46	○ 52—43
☾ 44—35	□ 21—81
□ 87—57	⊥ 86—87 becomes □
— 57—87 □	□ 81—87 □
⊥ 53—52	— 87—80
— 52—51	— 80—30
— 51—50	2 74—62
○ 36—26	— 62—54
— 26—36	[3] — 54—35 ☾
— 36—45	□ 66—65 ✓
— 45—36	2 35—14 ⊥ ✓
— 36—27	□ 65—25 + ✓
— 27—16	— 25—24
— 16—15	— 30—34
— 15—16	— 34—84
— 16—15	— 84—87
— 15—16	— 87—47
— 16—15	— 47—17 *Checkmate.*

[1] A good move. [2] A bad exchange, though followed up by a check.
[3] See introductory remarks.

In this game *White* "queens" two pawns.

GAME II

Red.	*White.*
⊥ 55—54	⊥ 42—43
— 54—63 ⊥	— 52—63 ⊥
— 85—84	— 73—84 ⊥
— 75—84 ⊥	— 43—34 ⊥
— 45—34 ⊥	— 32—33
— 24—23	— 12—23 ⊥
— 14—23 ⊥	+ 61—52
2 56—64	— 52—61
□ 87—77	2 41—53
— 17—12	□ 10—12 □
⊥ 23—12 □	[1] 2 51—32
2 64—43	— 53—41
+ 25—14	□ 80—10
2 43—31	— 10—11
+ 14—23	2 32—51
2 31—43	○ 71—82
□ 77—57	2 51—43 2
⊥ 34—43 2	☾ 62—71
— 65—64	2 41—62
□ 57—53	— 62—50
2 46—65	⊥ 33—34
— 65—46	2 50—42
— 46—34 ⊥	[2] — 42—34 2
+ 23—34 2	□ 11—12 ⊥
⊥ 43—42	⊥ 22—23
+ 34—23 ⊥	□ 12—42 ⊥
— 23—24	— 42—52
— 34—43	— 52—42
☾ 35—44	+ 61—62
— 44—33	— 62—53 □
— 33—42 □	— 53—42 ☾
○ 26—35	☾ 71—62
+ 36—45	+ 42—51
○ 35—44	— 51—42
— 44—55	[3] ☾ 62—53

[1] To prevent ⊥ 12 "queening."

[2] To draw away + 23 from defending ⊥ 12 which is about to "queen."

[3] The object was to get rid of ⊥ ⊥ 64 and 84, and so to "queen" with ⊥ 83.

Red.	*White.*
⊥ 64—53 ☾	+ 42—53 ⊥
○ 55—66	⊥ 63—64
+ 45—54	○ 82—71
○ 66—65	— 71—62
+ 54—45	— 62—63
— 45—54 ✓	— 63—62
○ 65—66	+ 72—63
+ 54—63 +	○ 62—63 +
○ 66—65	+ 53—62
+ 43—54 ✓	○ 63—53
— 54—45	+ 62—63
○ 65—66	— 63—74
+ 45—56	— 74—75 ✓
○ 66—65	— 75—84 ⊥
+ 56—67	— 84—73
— 67—76	⊥ 83—84
○ 65—66	○ 53—63
— 66—65	+ 73—82
— 65—66	○ 63—74
— 66—67	⊥ 64—65
+ 76—87	○ 74—75
○ 67—57	⊥ 84—85
— 57—67	+ 82—71
— 67—57	○ 75—86
— 57—66	— 86—87 +
— 66—65 ⊥	⊥ 85—86
— 65—66	+ 71—72
— 66—67	— 72—73
— 67—66	— 73—74
— 66—67	— 74—75
— 67—56	○ 87—77
— 56—65	+ 75—76
— 65—74	⊥ 86—87 becomes □

and Checkmate easily follows.

A see-saw game.

GAME III.

White.	*Red.*
⊥ 83—84	⊥ 75—84 ⊥
□ 80—84 ⊥	— 55—54
⊥ 63—64	[1] — 54—53
— 42—53 ⊥	2 46—54
2 51—63	⊥ 45—44
⊥ 53—44 ⊥	2 54—62 ☾
○ 71—62 2	— 56—44 ⊥
2 41—53	□ 17—57
— 63—44 2	☾ 35—44 2
— 53—65 ⊥	□ 57—54
⊥ 52—53	☾ 44—35
— 73—74	□ 87—47
— 74—75	— 47—42 √
○ 62—63	— 54—56
2 65—77	56—57
⊥ 75—76 becomes □	— 42—32 ⊥
— 22—53	— 32—33
+ 61—62	— 57—47
⊥ 23—34 ⊥	□ 33—34 ⊥
□ 84—85 ⊥	— 34—32
+ 72—73	— 47—41
⊥ 64—65 becomes □	— 41—61
2 77—56	— 61—31
— 56—35 ☾	— 32—35 2
□ 10—40	⊥ 24—23
⊥ 12—23 ⊥	— 14—23 ⊥
□ 40—45	+ 25—24
— 45—35 □	— 24—35 □
— 65—66	○ 26—25
— 66—36 +	[2] ⊥ 23—22
— 36—26 √	○ 25—14
— 26—22 ⊥	+ 35—24
— 76—16 √	— 24—15
— 85—15 + *Checkmate.*	

This game was begun by *White* in order to "queen" by pawn 63, first getting rid of pawn 75. *White* subsequently "queened" both pawns 63 and 73; thus having four castles on the board at the same time.

[1] To bring out 2

[2] "Queens" next move.

Game IV.

Red.	*White.*
+ 55—54	⊥ 42—43
— 54—63 ⊥	+ 72—63 ⊥
— 34—43 ⊥	⊥ 32—43 ⊥
2 56—44	— 52—53
— 44—56	— 53—54
⊥ 45—54 ⊥	— 43—54 ⊥
— 65—54 ⊥	[1] + 63—64
— 75—64 +	⊥ 73—74
□ 87—77	[1] ☾ 62—73
⊥ 64—73 ☾	2 41—53
□ 77—75	— 51—72
2 46—67	⊥ 83—84
□ 75—76	— 74—85 ⊥
2 67—55	[2] 2 53—65
□ 76—66	— 72—53
⊥ 73—72	+ 61—72 ⊥
2 56—64	⊥ 85—86
□ 66—76	— 84—85
— 76—75	□ 10—60
2 64—43	2 65—77
☾ 35—44	⊥ 86—87 becomes □
— 44—53 2	2 77—56
□ 75—73	□ 87—17 □
○ 26—17 □	⊥ 85—86
2 55—63 ✓	○ 71—61
+ 36—45	⊥ 86—87 becomes □ ✓
○ 17—26	□ 87—83
□ 73—76	+ 72—63 2
— 76—56 2	— 63—52
2 43—22 ⊥	□ 83—53 ☾
— 22—34	-- 53—83
□ 56—76	— 83—86
2 34—53 ✓	○ 61—50
□ 76—86 □	□ 80—86 □ ✓
○ 26—35	— 86—83
2 53—32	○ 50—61

[1] *White* sacrifices + and ☾, in order to "queen" a ⊥.
[2] ⊥ 85—76 □ better.

Red.	*White.*
⊥ 14—13	□ 60—30
— 24—23	⊥ 12—23 ⊥
— 13—12	□ 30—32 2 ✓
+ 25—34	— 32—12 ⊥
— 34—25	— 83—33 ✓
○ 35—44	— 33—83
+ 25—36	— 12—14 ✓
○ 44—35	— 83—33 ✓
— 35—46	— 14—15
— 46—47	— 33—83
— 47—37	— 83—87 ✓
— 37—26	⊥ 23—24
+ 36—25	□ 87—86 ✓
— 45—36	+ 52—53
○ 26—27	□ 86—87 ✓
— 27—26	+ 53—44
+ 36—27	— 44—35 ✓
○ 26—36	□ 87—86 ✓
— 36—45	— 15—25 +
— 45—34	— 25—27 +

Gives up the game.

XIV.

SIAMESE CHESS.

The following particulars of this game have been procured for me from Prince Devawongse, Minister of Foreign Affairs of H.M. the King of Siam, through the kindness of E. B. Gould, Esq., H.B.M.'s Consul at Bangkok, August, 1889.

"British Legation,
Bangkok,
Oct. 22, 1889.

"Dear Sir,

I took an opportunity to make enquiries of Prince Devawongse, the King of Siam's Minister for Foreign Affairs, and a keen chess player, both at the native game, and our European one, on the subject of your letter of the 23rd of April. I left your letter with the Prince, who appeared to take much interest in the subject, and promised to supply me with a record of a game played by good Siamese chess players. This he ultimately did, and I now forward a copy of the rough record the Prince gave me.

Yours faithfully,
E. B. Gould."

Names of the pieces.

King— *Khun* (Lord).
Queen— *Met*, no meaning.
Bishop— *Khōn*, no meaning.
Knight—*Ma* (Horse).
Castle— *Rua* (Boat).
Pawn— *Bia* (Cowrie shell) generally used for the Pawns.

The King moves one square in any direction: but in his first move he can move as a Knight.

The Queen has the usual Oriental move of one square diagonally: but in her first move she can take two squares, if desirable. The Queen is placed on the right hand of the King.

The Bishop has the move of the Kin in the Japanese game: one square diagonally every way, and one straight forward.

The Knight's move is the same as ours.

The Castle's move, also, is the same as ours.

The Pawns stand on the third row, and "queen" on the sixth.

Siam, being a maritime country, appears to have taken the game partly from India and Burmah, and partly from Japan. From India she adopted the name of *boat*; and from Burmah and Japan the Bishop's move; the only difference between the two being that in the Burmese game the Bishop only moves in the straightforward line, whereas in the Japanese game it both moves and takes. The Pawns stand on the third row, as in the Japanese game. The name of the Bishop, *Khōn* in Siamese, seems a corruption of the Burmese *Chein*, and the Chinese *Sang*: while the name of the Knight, *Ma*, a horse, is taken from the Chinese and Japanese.

In the following game Chong Kwa and Coy took the *white* pieces, and Nai Chang took the *black*. The game is played upon our chess-board, and the numbers refer to those given in our chess notation, p. 116.

White.				*Black.*		
⊥	52—53		1	⊥	55—54	
—	62—63		2	+	67—66	
2	70—62		3	—	66—55	
—	20—41		4	⊥	65—64	
☾	50—61		5	2	77—65	
—	61—52		6	+	37—36	
+	60—61		7	□	87—77	
○	40—51		8	⊥	35—34	
+	30—31		9	○	57—66	
□	10—60		10	+	36—35	
⊥	12—13		11	2	27—46	
—	22—23		12	☾	47—36	
+	31—22		13	○	66—56	
□	60—70		14	⊥	25—24	
⊥	13—14		15	—	64—53	⊥
—	42—53	⊥	16	—	34—33	
+	22—31		17	□	17—37	
⊥	72—73		18	⊥	75—74	
—	63—74	⊥	19	—	85—74	⊥
—	82—83		20	—	45—44	
2	62—74	⊥	21	—	44—53	⊥
—	41—53	⊥	22	2	65—53	2
—	74—53	2	23	+	35—44	
—	53—41		24	☾	36—45	
+	61—62		25	□	37—67	
⊥	83—84		26	○	56—47	
—	73—74		27	+	55—64	
—	74—75	*Queens*	28	⊥	54—53	
☾	75—64	+	29	□	77—70	□
□	80—70	□	30	⊥	53—62	+ *Queens*
2	41—62	☾	31	□	67—64	☾
⊥	84—85	*Queens*	32	○	47—36	
☾	85—74		33	+	44—53	
2	62—43		34	□	64—54	

White.		*Black.*
☾ 74—63	35	□ 54—56
□ 70—75	36	+ 53—44
2 43—64	37	□ 56—55
□ 75—76 ✗	38	○ 36—47
○ 51—41	39	□ 55—65
2 64—72	40	— 65—85
+ 31—40	41	— 85—55
— 40—51	42	+ 44—53
☾ 52—43	43	○ 47—37
□ 76—74	44	— 37—36
☾ 63—54	45	+ 53—44
— 54—45 ☾ ✓	46	○ 36—45 ☾
+ 51—52	47	— 45—35
□ 74—76	48	□ 55—65
○ 41—51	49	— 65—55
— 51—62	50	— 55—65 ✓
+ 52—63	51	— 65—55
— 63—64	52	— 55—50
□ 76—75 ✓	53	○ 35—26
— 75—45	54	+ 44—35
+ 64—53	55	○ 26—36
□ 45—85	56	— 36—26
○ 62—63	57	□ 50—70
2 72—64	58	— 70—60 ✓
○ 63—52	59	○ 26—36
2 64—72	60	□ 60—65
□ 85—86	61	○ 36—47
☾ 43—54	62	□ 65—55
○ 52—63	63	○ 47—37
2 72—64	64	— 37—47
— 64—43	65	□ 55—75
○ 63—64	66	— 75—72
2 43—35 + ✓	67	○ 47—37
☾ 54—43	68	□ 72—70
+ 53—44	69	— 70—60 ✓
○ 64—74	70	— 60—70 ✓
— 74—63	71	2 46—65
2 35—56 ✓	72	○ 37—46
□ 86—66	73	□ 70—60 ✓

White.				*Black.*		
○	63—74		74	2	65—53	✓ [1]
+	44—53	2	75	□	60—66	□
2	56—64		76	○	46—55	
☾	43—54		77	□	66—86	
2	64—43	✓	78	○	55—46	
—	43—51		79	□	86—82	
☾	54—43		80	○	46—45	
+	53—44	✓	81	—	45—46	
2	51—63		82	□	82—87	
—	63—75		83	—	87—80	
—	75—83		84	○	46—56	
—	83—75	✓	85	—	56—46	
—	75—54	✓	86	—	46—36	
○	74—65		87	□	80—85	✓
—	65—56		88	—	85—86	✓
2	54—66		89	—	86—76	
☾	43—34		90	—	76—86	
—	34—25	✓	91	○	36—26	
○	56—55		92	□	86—82	
2	66—45	✓	93	○	26—17	
+	44—35		94	□	82—86	
☾	25—36		95	○	17—16	
2	45—64		96	□	86—82	
○	55—46		97	—	82—87	
☾	36—25	✓	98	○	16—17	
2	64—56		99	□	87—67	
☾	25—34		100	○	17—16	
○	46—36		101	□	67—27	
☾	34—25	✓	102	○	16—17	
2	56—44		103	□	27—57	
○	36—46		104	—	57—77	
2	44—36	✓	105	○	17—27	
—	36—15	⊥ ✓	106	—	27—17	
—	15—36	✓	107	—	17—27	
—	36—44		108	□	77—75	
⊥	14—15	*Queens*	109	—	75—76	✓
2	44—56		110	—	76—56	2 ✓
○	46—56	□	111	○	27—37	
+	35—36	*Mate*	112			

[1] Good move.

XV.

TURKISH CHESS.

The Turks generally make their "board" of cloth, embroidered over to form the cells, several of which, and sometimes all, as in this example, have ornaments or flowers in the centre. Such a chess-cloth with the men can easily be carried about in a bag, and so be always ready to be placed on the divan or carpet. The photograph represents such a board in my possession with the ivory men, the powers of which will be seen by the order in which they stand.

The King is placed on the right of the Queen, and can take one Knight's move at any time of the game, but only one.

The pawns move one square at a time.

In castling, the King can be placed on the Rukh's square, or on any other within that distance.

The other rules are the same as those of the European game.

This is the game as played by the author in Asia Minor in 1845. The variations from our game are unimportant, and not sufficient to rank Turkish chess as a distinct game, like several other Oriental games of chess, but is interesting only from the form of the pieces, and from its embroidered cloth.

TURKISH CHESS-CLOTH.

XVI.

TAMERLANE'S CHESS

OR

GREAT CHESS.

MS. 260—Royal Asiatic Society,		
Hyde—De ludis Orientalibus	- -	1694
Bland—Persian Chess	- - -	1850
Forbes—The History of Chess	- -	1860

As we are indebted chiefly to the poem of Saleius Bassus for the Ludus Latrunculorum; and to the Bhavishya Purana solely for the Indian game of Chaturanga; so for the knowledge of Tamerlane's chess we are indebted exclusively to the anonymous author of the Persian MS. 260 belonging to the Royal Asiatic Society. Professor Forbes, who gives us a most detailed translation of this, gives us also the following extract from the preface of this MS., in which we see that the author believed that his work would give him the reward of Paradise, and that God himself assisted him in his play. Another celebrated chess player, Alau el Din of Tabriz, called Ali the chess player, declared that he once saw Mahomet in a vision, who presented him with a bag of chess-men, by using which afterwards he was ever victorious. All these chess players write in a very vain-glorious style. This anonymous author says :—

"Many a one has experienced a relief from sorrow and affliction in consequence of this magic recreation; and this same fact has been asserted by the celebrated physician Muhammad Zakaria Razi in his book entitled 'The Essences of Things,' and such is likewise the opinion of the physician Ali Bin Firdaus, as I shall notice more fully towards the end of the present work, for the composing of which I am in the hope of receiving my reward from God, who is Most High, and Most Glorious.

"I have passed my life since the age of fifteen years among all the masters of chess living in my time: and since that period till now when I have arrived at middle age, I have travelled through Irak-Arab and Irak-Ajam, and Khurasan, and the regions of Mawara-al-Nahr, and I have there met with many a master in this art, and I have played with each of them, and through the favour of Him who is Adorable and Most High, I have come off victorious.

"Likewise, in playing without seeing the board, I have overcome most opponents, nor had they the power to cope with me. I, the humble sinner now addressing you, have frequently played with one opponent over the board, and at the same time I have carried on four different games with as many adversaries without seeing the board, whilst I conversed freely with my friends all along, and through the Divine favour I conquered them all. Also in the Great Chess I have invented sundry positions, as well as several openings, which no one else ever imagined or contrived.

"There are a great number of ingenious positions that have occurred to me in the course of my experience, in the common game as practised at the present day; and many positions given as won by elder masters, I have either proved to be capable of defence, or I have made the necessary corrections in them, so that they now stand for what they were originally intended to be. I have also improved and rendered more complete all the rare and cunning stratagems hitherto recorded or invented by the first masters of chess. In short I have laid before the reader all that I have myself discovered from experience, as well as whatever I found to be rare and excellent in the labours of my predecessors."[1]

The author's description of the game is rather prolix, so we will give it in other words:—

The game played by Timur the Tartar, called afterwards, when wounded in the leg, Timur lenk, lame Timur, and, as corrupted by us, Tamerlane the Great, consisted of a board of eleven squares by ten, with two outlying squares,[2] making a total of 112 squares.

In this game the principal pieces occupy the second row. In the middle is the *Shah*, 1, having on his right his *Vizir*, 2, and on his left his *Ferz*, or General, 3. Next to these on either side is a *Zarafah*, Giraffe, 4; then a *Taliah*, advanced picket, 5; then an *Asp*, Horse or Cavalry, 6; and lastly the *Rukh*, Chariot, 7. Behind the Rukh is a *Pil*, or *Phil*, Elephant, 8; behind the advanced picket is a *Jamal*, Camel, 9;

[1] Forbes, *History of Chess*, p. 80, 81. [2] Outside of squares, 18 and 111.

and behind the Vizir and Ferz are *Dabbabahs*, war engines, 10. These occupy the first line, a *Piyade*, Pawn, occupies each square of the third line.

The Ferz, and each of the pieces on the right of the Shah, has its proper Pawn, 15; but the left hand Giraffe has an Elephant's Pawn, 14, in front; the Picket has a Camel's Pawn, 13; the Horse has a War engine's Pawn, 12; and the left hand Rukh has the Pawn of pawns, 11.

As these names and the respective powers of the pieces are very difficult to be remembered, I adopt names which are more intelligible to Western ears, so that the name shall at once enable us to determine the power of the piece.

The principal pieces are divided into three classes, according to their moves, which are the Straight, the Diagonal, and the Mixed.

Of the Straight moves are the Vizir, the Dabbabah, and the Rukh. As the moves of the pieces are all analogous, and varying only in power, we will change the names to others which will better remind us of their moves; and call them the *Vizir*, moving only one square forwards, backwards, or sideways; the Dabbabah we will change to the *Castle*, moving always two squares in the same directions, and hopping over the first if covered; and the *Rukh*, moving any number of squares, as our Rook, but without jumping. For the Castle I employ an ivory Castle of the ordinary size; for the Vizir one of smaller size; and for the Rukh a boxwood one of larger size.

Of the Diagonal moves are the Ferz, the Pil, and the Taliah. In like manner, and for the same reason, we will retain the name of the *Ferz*, moving only one square diagonally; but will change the Pil to *Lame Bishop*, moving always two squares, and leaping over the first when occupied; and the Taliah to *Bishop*, having the full power of our Bishop, but which has not the move of the Ferz, nor the privilege of leaping. For the Lame Bishop I employ an ivory Bishop of the ordinary size; for the Ferz one of a smaller size; and for the Bishop a box wood one of a larger size.

Of the Mixed moves are the Asp, the Jamal, and the Zarafah. The Asp we change to the *Knight*, having the same move as our Knight, one diagonal and one straight; the Jamal or Camel to the *Chevalier*, having one diagonal and two straight; both these have the privilege of vaulting; and Zarafah or Giraffe to the *Cavalier*, having one diagonal and any number straight, or any number straight and one diagonal; but without the moves of the Knight or Chevalier, or the privilege of vaulting. For the Chevalier I employ an ivory Knight of the ordinary size; for the Knight one of a smaller size; and for the Cavalier a box wood one of a larger size.

It will be seen from the above that the privilege of leaping is confined to the pieces in the first or back row, all of which move two squares at a time, and to the Knights; and that by using box wood for the principal superior pieces in the second row the eye will at once be able to distinguish them.

We will now place the men in their proper position according to their new names :—

11	12	13	14	15	15	15	15	15	15	15
7	6	5	4	3	1	2	4	5	6	7
8		9		10		10		9		8

First Row.		Second Row.		Third Row.	
8	Lame Bishop	7	RUKH	11	Pawn of pawns.
		6	Knight	12	Castle's pawn.
9	Chevalier	5	BISHOP	13	Chevalier's ,,
		4	CAVALIER	14	Lame Bishop's ,,
10	Castle	3	Ferz	15	Ferz's ,,
		1	The Shah	—	Shah's ,,
10	Castle	2	Vizir	—	Vizir's ,,
		4	CAVALIER	—	Cavalier's ,,
9	Chevalier	5	BISHOP	—	Bishop's ,,
		6	Knight	—	Knight's ,,
8	Lame Bishop	7	RUKH	—	Rukh's ,,

It will thus be seen that there is a Pawn representing each superior piece whether of the first or second line, and capable of becoming a piece of such power, on the loss of the piece itself, on reaching the opposite end. There is, moreover, one extra Pawn, called the Pawn of pawns, which has peculiar privileges. All the Pawns move and take as in our chess; but the Pawn of pawns on reaching the further end can be transferred, at will, to any (vacant) square of the board, and on reaching the further end a second time may be transferred again; and on reaching the further end a third time it acquires the moves of the Shah, and like the Shah's pawn may replace the Shah when slain.

We have yet to speak of the Shah. This piece moves one square at a time in any direction. When in distress the Shah may make his way to the opposite outlying space, where he is safe from any attack; and can be driven out of it only by a stale-mate. But it also has the privilege of exchanging positions with any other of his pieces: but this can only be done once.

These privileges, however, of the Shah and of the Pawn of pawns are so peculiar, and the opportunity of availing ourselves of them occurs so seldom—not once, indeed, in any of the games which we have played—that in giving the rules of this ancient game we may suppose them to have never existed. Their introduction would appear to have been merely to spin out the game, and thus by omitting them we bring the game more in unison with other games of chess.

The most formidable piece in this game is the Cavalier. The power of this piece for sweeping across the board is about equal to that of the Rukh; but having two lines in every direction instead of one, and its attack being more insidious, this piece becomes much more dangerous. Like the Knight, its chief power consists in its being able to fork two pieces: but while with the Knight these pieces are contiguous, with the Cavalier they are at a considerable distance; consequently the difficulty of evading it is greatly increased. As it requires half the width of the board to be able to make a move, so its power of acting is only developed when the board becomes more and more cleared. Another advantage of the Cavalier is that if it can place itself on the same line with the hostile Shah, and the Shah is not supported by other pieces in its vicinity, it cannot move to the right or left without going into check, in which case it becomes easy to follow up the advantage with another piece, and so procure a checkmate. This piece therefore is by far the most powerful on the board when once it has a free motion: for while it commands almost as many squares as the Rukh, the Rukh commanding nineteen, and the Cavalier from fourteen to twenty-two, according to its position, being an average of eighteen, its power of forking makes it a most fearful engine in the hands of a skilful player: for while the Rukh threatens in only four directions, the Cavalier threatens in eight.

The Cavalier being thus powerful, it is evidently to the interest of a player to bring out his own Cavaliers, and to prevent his adversary from moving his. In the one case, he advances his Bishop's pawn sufficiently far, if not stopped, to enable him to bring out his piece; in the other he advances his Cavalier's pawn one square, which will then command the only two squares to which his adversary's Cavalier could move if the way were open, and will thus make him a prisoner. But he must not be content with making him a prisoner, he must endeavour to capture him while he is thus blocked up. This is best effected by means of the Knights, moving one from 21 to 13, 34, 15, and 27; and the other from 101 to 113, 94, 115 and 107. Examples of these moves will be found in the games which follow.

On turning our attention to the Shah's position, we find him surrounded by seven pieces which mutually defend each other while protecting the Shah, thus forming an impregnable fortress around his person. In front are three Pawns, the centre one of which is defended by the Shah and Ferz: that on one side is defended by the Shah, Vizir, and Castle; that on the other by the Shah and Castle; while the Castles mutually protect each other. As one's own Pawns are required to protect one's own Shah, it follows that the enemy's fortress can only be forced by the sacrifice of two or more superior pieces.

Our first attempts at playing the game were to leave the Shah unmolested, and to bring out the superior pieces to attack those of the enemy. The result in every case, owing to the number of pieces and their formidable character, was a terrific fight, which lasted till, from mutual losses, neither party was strong enough to force the position of the enemy and obtain a checkmate.

It is of the first importance therefore in this game, so soon as the side pieces are prepared for action, to force the centre. Even when this is attended with considerable sacrifice an easy victory can be achieved, if only the side pieces follow up the advantage which is obtained without delay. The pieces which can be best sacrificed for this work are the lame Bishops. Their moves are 10, 32, 54, 76, which either bring out the Pawn 67, or capture the Vizir 58; and 110, 92, 74, 56, which either bring out the same Pawn 67, or capture the Ferz; but if these fail, it is advisable to sacrifice even the Bishop or Chevalier, if necessary, either to break the opposite centre, or to make way for the play of the Cavaliers.

The two prettiest checkmates are by the Cavalier and Rukh in one line.

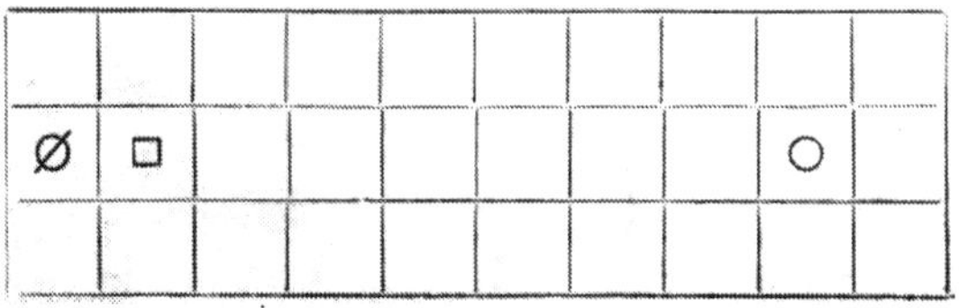

Or the two Cavaliers side by side.

Ø									
Ø								○	

The pinning in accomplished by a single Cavalier, when the checkmate can be given by any other piece.

Ø								○	

GAME I.

	Red.			*White.*	
2	28—16		⊥	32—33	
⊥	37—36		—	33—34	
2	108—96		—	34—35	
T	19—37		—	42—43	
2	16—24		—	43—44	
—	24—45		—	82—83	
T	37—15		2	101—113	
⊥	27—26		⊥	35—26	⊥
—	17—26	⊥	2	113—94	
—	36—35		⊥	44—35	⊥
—	26—35	⊥	2	21—13	
□	18—28		—	13—34	
T	15—33		⊥	22—33	T
2	45—33	⊥	Ø	41—55	
□	28—24		2	34—15	
⊥	47—46		Ø	55—114	
—	35—34		2	15—36	
[1] □	24—22		—	36—48	Ø
⊞	58—48	2	⊥	83—84	
⊥	107—106		Ø	114—33	2
+	38—16		⊥	84—85	

[1] Useless move.

	Red.				*White.*	
2	96—115		[1]	2	94— 75	
⊥	46— 45			Ø	33—114	
—	45— 44			2	75— 56	✓
—	67— 56	2		Ø	114— 73	✓
☾	78— 67			—	73— 22	□
+	16— 49			—	81— 75	
⊥	87— 86			—	75—114	
—	34— 33			—	22— 19	
+	49— 16			—	19— 20	
—	16— 38			✱	30— 43	
[2] ⊥	77— 76			⊥	85— 76	⊥
+	98— 76	⊥		□	11— 21	
—	38— 16			—	21— 28	
⊥	106—105			—	28— 48	⊞ ✓
☾	67— 58			Ø	114— 73	✓
O	68— 78			—	20— 16	+
—	78— 89			✱	43— 56	⊥
⊥	44— 43			—	56— 63	
2	115— 94			—	63— 76	+ ✓
O	89— 78			□	48— 58	☾ ✓
—	78— 87			✱	76— 83	✓ ✓
—	87— 98			□	58— 88	Ø ✓
—	98—109			✱	83— 96	*Mate.*

In this game the object of *White* was to bring out his Cavaliers as early as possible by making an opening in front of them, while the Knight 21 advanced rapidly to capture the hostile Cavalier 48, before it had a possibility of moving. The *Red* lost the game, in addition to other bad play, by opening his centre; the Vizir 58 taking Knight at 48, the Pawn 67 taking Knight at 56, and advancing Pawn 77 to 76, when it was immediately captured, thus forming a breach in his own lines. It thus became easy for the *White* Cavaliers to check the Shah, which was uncovered, and

[1] Refuses to take 2 115, in order to attack centre.
[2] Wrong to open centre.

so lead to the checkmate. The *White* Cavalier's move from 114 to 73, forking Shah at 68, and Rukh at 22, shows the great power of these pieces. The Chevalier's move 76 to 83 was pretty, giving double check by revelation with the two Cavaliers.

GAME II.

	Red.			*White.*	
⊥	47— 46 [1]		⊥	42— 43	
—	87— 86		—	82— 83	
2	28— 36		—	32— 33	
⊥	17— 16		—	33— 34	
—	27— 26		2	21— 33	
—	16— 15		—	33— 45	
□	18— 17		✱	30— 23	
2	36— 44		—	23— 54	
+	98— 54	✱	⊥	43— 54	+
—	38— 16		—	22— 23	
⊥	15— 14		—	23— 14	⊥
+	16— 34	⊥	2	101—113	
□	17— 14	⊥	—	113— 94	
+	34— 12	⊥	—	94—115	
2	44— 23		□	11— 21	
—	23— 35		2	45— 33	
□	14— 44		+	31— 13	
2	35— 54	⊥	2	33— 12	+
—	54— 62	⊥	☾	51— 62	2
□	44—104		⊥	102—103	
—	104—105		—	103—104	
—	105—104	⊥	—	112—113	
—	104—100		✱	90—103	
2	108— 87		2	115—107	⊥
—	87— 95		—	107— 88	Ø
—	95—103	✱	⊥	92—103	2
□	118— 88	2	2	12— 24	
—	100—103	⊥	—	24— 36	
⊥	26— 25		—	36— 48	Ø
⊞	58— 48	2	+	13— 40	

[1] To prevent opposite Cavaliers from coming out.

Red.	*White.*
□ 103—105	+ 40— 22
— 105— 75	T 110— 92
✱ 39— 26	— 92— 74
□ 75— 76	+ 22— 77 ⊥
— 76— 77 +	T 74— 56
⊥ 37— 36	+ 91— 46 ⊥
T 19— 37	— 46— 82
✱ 26— 55	Ø 41— 37 T
— 55— 62 ☾	○ 61— 62 ✱
○ 68— 69	+ 82— 55
⊥ 67— 66	— 55— 33
✱ 99— 68	Ø 37— 43
□ 77— 73	T 56— 78 ☾
— 88— 78 T	Ø 43—114
— 73— 77	□ 21— 61
⊥ 97— 96	○ 62— 51
— 96— 95	+ 33— 66 ⊥
— 57— 66 +	□ 61— 66 ⊥
□ 77— 17	Ø 114— 53 ✓
⊞ 48— 58	⊖ 50— 30
□ 78— 73	Ø 53—114
— 17— 11 ✓	○ 51— 42
⊥ 95— 94	⊥ 83— 94 ⊥
□ 11— 12 ✓	○ 42— 31
— 73— 93	[1] Ø 114—108 ✓
○ 69— 78	— 108— 93 □
□ 12— 11 ✓	○ 31— 20
— 11— 71 ⊞	⊖ 30— 50
✱ 68— 97	□ 66— 86 ⊥
□ 71— 61	Ø 93— 12
— 61— 64	□ 86— 66 ✓
○ 78— 89	Ø 12— 73 *Mate.*

In this game *White* sacrifices both his Bishops, two of his principal pieces, in breaking the enemy's centre and his Knights take each of *Red's* Cavaliers; while each side breaks the opposite centre. The checkmate is given by two Cavaliers, one of which has never moved.

[1] This move shows the power of the Ø

Game III.

	Red.			*White.*	
⊥	47— 46		2	21— 13	
2	28— 16		—	101—113	
⊥	97— 96		⊥	32— 33	
—	107—106		✱	90—103	
—	117—116		2	113— 94	
T	119— 97		⊥	42— 43	
⊥	87— 86		T	10— 32	
—	106—105		2	94— 73	
✱	99—106		T	32— 54	
⊥	37— 36		2	13— 34	
—	27— 26		T	54— 36	⊥
□	18— 28		—	36— 58	⊞
○	68— 58	T	⊥	82— 83	
2	16— 35		—	22— 23	
+	38— 65		✱	103— 74	
□	28— 38		—	74— 45	✓
○	58— 49		—	45— 38	□
—	49— 38	✱	2	73— 54	
⊥	46— 45		—	54— 35	2
—	26— 35	2	—	34— 55	
○	38— 37		—	55— 67	⊥ ✓
—	37— 47		—	67— 88	Ø
⊥	35— 34		⊥	43— 34	⊥
—	45— 34	⊥	—	23— 24	
✱	39— 26		☾	51— 42	
+	65— 32		—	42— 51	
—	32— 14		Ø	41— 35	
—	98— 65		2	88— 76	
T	97— 75		Ø	35— 40	
☾	78— 87		2	76— 68	*Mate.*

In this game *White's* lame Bishop breaks the centre at 58, and the *Red* King leaving its centre, the Cavalier 40 pins in the King, and the Knight coming up at 68, gives it the *coup de grace.* In not one of these games has *Red* been able to bring out his Cavaliers.

GAME IV.

	Red.			*White.*	
⊥	47— 46		2	101—113	
—	97— 96		✱	90—103	
—	87— 86		2	113— 94	
—	37— 36		—	94—115	
T	19— 37		—	115—107	⊥
⊥	86— 85		—	107— 88	Ø
T	37— 55		⊥	82— 83	
✱	99— 86		2	88—107	
⊥	85— 84		—	107— 86	✱
T	55— 73		✱	103— 74	
+	38— 74	✱	⊥	83— 74	+
⊥	77— 86	2	—	42— 43	
T	73— 91	+	□	111— 91	T
⊥	46— 45		+	31— 86	⊥ ✓
⊟	79— 77		—	86—113	
✱	39— 46		2	21— 42	
⊥	36— 35		—	42— 63	
2	28— 36		—	63— 84	⊥
✱	46— 75		—	84— 63	
—	75— 62	⊥	☾	51— 62	✱
⊥	35— 34		2	63— 75	
2	36— 55		+	113— 77	⊟
⊥	34— 43	⊥	—	77— 55	2
—	43— 52	⊥ ✓	⊟	50— 52	⊥
2	108— 89		Ø	41— 35	
□	18— 38		—	35— 96	⊥
⊥	45— 44		+	55— 82	
—	44— 43		—	82—104	✓
○	68— 69		✱	30— 43	⊥
+	98— 43	✱	⊥	32— 43	+
□	118— 88		T	10— 32	
—	88— 84		+	104— 59	⊟
○	69— 59	+	2	75— 67	⊥ ✓
☾	78— 67	2	⊥	92— 93	
□	84— 74	⊥	Ø	81— 98	✓
—	74— 78		—	96— 80	
—	78— 88		[1] □	91— 81	

[1] Oversight.

Red.			*White.*		
□	88— 98	Ø	□	81— 89	2 ✓
○	59— 68		Ø	80— 98	□
Ø	48— 89	□	—	98—104	
□	38— 36		—	104—119	T ✓
○	68— 69		T	32— 54	
□	36—106		□	11— 31	
☾	67— 78		—	31— 39	✓
⊞	58— 59		—	39— 37	
□	106—109		Ø	119—104	
—	109—107		□	37— 39	
⊥	117—116		Ø	104— 53	✓
○	69— 58		□	39— 38	*Mate.*

A well-fought game, and *Red* would not have lost it if three moves before the end □ 109 had taken Ø 104. and it might then have possibly won the game.

GAME V.

Red.			*White.*		
⊥	47— 46		⊥	42— 43	
—	87— 86		—	82— 83	
2	28— 16		—	43— 44	
⊥	37— 36		—	44— 45	
—	36— 45	⊥	—	22— 23	
+	38— 65		—	92— 93	
T	19— 37		T	110— 92	
+	65— 38		+	31— 13	
⊥	97— 96		—	13— 46	⊥
✱	39— 46	+	—	91— 46	✱
T	119— 97		—	46— 73	
—	37— 15		Ø	41— 55	
—	15— 33		2	21— 33	T
Ø	48— 33	2	□	11— 41	
⊥	86— 85		⊥	12— 13	
✱	99— 86		Ø	55—104	
Ø	33—104	Ø	⊥	93—104	Ø
✱	86— 73	+	—	62— 73	✱

[1] To open centre, but overlooked that ✱ 39 could take it.

	Red.			*White.*	
2	16— 37		□	41— 44	
+	98— 54		⊥	23— 24	
⊥	17— 16		✱	30— 23	
—	16— 15		[1] ⊥	24— 25	
2	37— 25	⊥	□	44— 45	⊥
—	25— 33		—	45— 43	
—	33— 52	⊥	⊟	50— 52	2
+	54— 98		□	43— 47	
2	108—116		⊥	112—113	
⊥	85— 84		—	73— 84	⊥
+	98— 65		□	47— 27	⊥
⊥	107—106		T	92— 74	
+	65—109		□	27— 47	
⊥	96— 95		T	74— 56	
—	15— 14		✱	23— 36	
□	18— 16		—	36— 49	
—	16— 46		□	47— 46	□
⊥	57— 46	□	T	56— 38	+
—	95— 94		—	38— 56	
—	94— 83	⊥	✱	90— 83	⊥
∅	88— 94		—	49— 78	☾
—	94— 55	✓	☾	51— 62	
□	118—108		⊥	104—105	
⊥	67— 56	T	✱	78— 47	
□	108-- 88		⊥	105—116	2
—	88— 84	⊥	∅	81— 97	T
⊞	58— 57		✱	47— 18	
∅	55—116	⊥	—	83—112	
□	84— 44		—	112—105	
—	44— 45		⊥	113—114	
⊟	79— 99		∅	97— 80	
—	99— 79		□	111—113	
⊥	77— 76		∅	80— 94	
□	45— 42		□	113— 63	∨
∅	116— 67		∅	94—109	+ ✓
○	68— 78		✱	18— 49	✓
—	78— 69		—	105— 76	⊥ *Mate.*

[1] ✱ 23—54 + better.

The *Red* ○ might go into 89 instead of 69, in which case the game would end thus:—

Red.	*White.*
○ 78— 89	∅ 109— 90 ✓
— 89— 99	□ 63— 83
□ 42— 52 ⊟	— 83— 89 *Mate.*

In this game each side brings out its Cavaliers, and each side breaks the opposite centre. The *mate* is obtained by a Cavalier and two Chevaliers.

GAME VI.

Red.	*White.*
⊥ 97— 96	⊥ 42— 43
— 47— 46	— 32— 33
— 37— 36	— 33— 34
— 36— 35	T 10— 32
2 28— 16	2 21— 13
T 19— 37	⊥ 82— 83
— 37— 55	✱ 30— 23
2 16— 24	— 23— 30
⊥ 87— 86	2 101—113
T 119— 97	— 113— 94
— 97— 75	— 94—115
2 24— 32 T	— 13— 32 2
+ 98— 43 ⊥	✱ 30— 43 +
— 38— 65	— 43— 56
— 65— 32 2	2 115—107 ⊥
⊥ 46— 45	⊥ 34— 45 ⊥
— 67— 56 ✱	∅ 41— 55 T
2 108— 87	2 107— 88 ∅
□ 118— 88 2	∅ 55—114
⊥ 35— 34	⊥ 92— 93
— 56— 45 ⊥	∅ 114— 45 ⊥
2 87— 66	— 45—114
+ 32— 54	⊥ 83— 84
⊥ 34— 33	— 22— 23
2 66— 74	— 84— 75 T
✱ 39— 26	— 75— 76
⊥ 86— 85	∅ 114— 73 ✓

	Red.			*White.*	
2	74— 66		+	31— 97	
+	54— 76	⊥	Ø	81— 95	
☾	78— 67		—	95— 44	
✱	99— 86		—	73—114	
2	66— 74		T	110— 92	
—	74— 62	⊥	☾	51— 62	
Ø	48— 54		✱	90— 83	
—	54— 49		□	11— 41	
□	18— 48		☾	62— 53	
⊥	33— 32		□	41— 51	
○	68— 69		✱	83— 76	+ ✓
☾	67— 76	✱	Ø	44— 30	
□	88— 68	✓	☾	53— 62	
—	48— 42		□	51— 31	
✱	26— 33		○	61— 51	

At this point *Red* was within one move of giving checkmate, but did not see it:—

	Red.			*White.*
□	42—52	⊥ ✓ ✓	○	51—61
—	68—62	☾ *Mate.*		

—	33— 62	☾	—	51— 42	□
—	62— 31	□	+	97— 79	⊟
⊟	59— 79	+	—	91— 46	
⊥	57— 46	+	○	42— 31	✱
—	96— 95		Ø	30— 45	
—	95— 94		—	114—109	
○	69— 78		⊥	102—103	
□	68— 64		—	103— 94	⊥
—	64— 44		Ø	45— 39	
—	44— 41	✓	○	31— 30	
—	41— 11		□	111—101	
—	11— 10	✓	○	30— 31	
—	10— 12	⊥	Ø	39— 25	
✱	86— 73		□	101—108	✓
○	78— 87		—	108— 58	⊞
✱	73— 60	✓	○	31— 20	
⊥	17— 16		Ø	25— 39	
—	32— 31	✓	○	20— 21	
□	12— 32		□	58— 38	

Red.	*White.*
□ 32— 42	⊥ 94— 85 ⊥
☾ 76— 67	— 85— 86
○ 87— 86 ⊥	Ø 109— 90 ✓
— 86— 96	⊥ 93— 94
□ 42— 41	— 23— 24
— 41— 44	□ 38— 48
Ø 49— 33	— 48— 98 *Mate.*

In this game each side breaks the opposite centre, and *Red* was on the point of winning. The close of the game exhibits a striking form of checkmate, the Cavalier 90 and the Rukh 98 being opposite each other, and having the Shah and two other pieces between them.

*** We have not availed ourselves in these games of the privilege which the Shah possesses of exchanging his position with one of his pieces when in danger of being checkmated. Such power might be exercised in playing the game, but it was considered unnecessary and tedious to exhibit it in these examples.

XVII.

GAME OF THE MAHARAJAH AND THE SEPOYS.

In this game the King or Maharajah is invested with the powers of all the other pieces: it has the combined powers of the Rukh, the Bishop, and the Knight; and plays against all the pieces of the opposite colour. At first sight it would appear that, being alone, it would be impossible for it to checkmate its adversary: but not only can it do this by a sudden checkmate when its adversary is blocked up by his own pieces, but when the board is clear it has even less difficulty in giving a checkmate. But though it has the power of checkmating its adversary, it has very little chance of so doing against a cautious player: for all that the latter has to do is to advance his pieces gradually in a solid line, so as to hem in the Maharajah, and prevent his breaking through, and never to advance a piece without a support. Although success is thus certain on the side of the cautious player, the Maharajah is by no means an adversary to be despised. It is a good game of surprise to be played against a good chess-player for the first time, before he has learnt the caution necessary to be observed. As the Maharajah stands alone, he is evidently at a great disadvantage: for he has no pieces with which to conceal his own movements, but every move he takes is narrowly watched, while every weak point is strengthened to prevent his making a surprise. When he breaks through therefore, it is not due so much to his own cunning, as to the negligence and incaution of his opponent; moreover, even after a long fight, when he has taken several of his opponent's pieces, say his Queen and two Castles, he cannot win the game if the enemy gathers his remaining pieces round the King, so as to prevent the Maharajah giving check; and it thus becomes a drawn game.

The Pawns may move one or two squares on starting, but do not queen on reaching the opposite end.

Owing to the quickness of moving in this game, mistakes frequently occur.

In the two following games the Maharajah wins easily from his opponent's inexperience of his power.

GAME I.

Maharajah.	*The Sepoys.*	*Maharajah.*	*The Sepoys.*
52	⊥ 25	34	☾ 45 ✓
43	— 85	43	⊥ 54 ✓
53	— 35	41	— 64
43	— 24	61	☾ 34 ✓
53	— 44	83	2 65
43	— 14	75 ✓	○ 47
34	— 13	66 *Checkmate.*	
43	□ 15		

Game II.

Maharajah.	*The Sepoys.*	*Maharajah.*	*The Sepoys.*
50	⊥ 55	42	2 53--34 ✓✓
10	☾ 65 ✓	32	⊥ 74
11	⊥ 45	51	— 73
71	+ 46	81	+ 67
31	— 35	21	□ 74
11	⊥ 75	32	— 84
14	○ 46	21	— 82
22	2 15	10	+ 85
72	+ 85	70	☾ 53
82	☾ 64 ✓	61	□ 80
32	2 65	65 ✓	○ 37
21	□ 87—77	56 ✓	— 27
32	2 53 ✓	47 *Mate.*	

The two following are hard-fought games, but won by the Maharajah.

Game III.

53	⊥ 44 ✓	54	☾ 45 ✓
13 ✓	— 35	52	2 15
34	— 25	25 ⊥	☾ 47 ✓
32	— 14	52	⊥ 55

There would have been a stalemate had the Maharajah taken □ 17, and the ☾ moved to 36.

62	⊥ 65	40	+ 63
84 ✓	— 75	70	2 11
40	☾ 45	82	⊥ 33
31	⊥ 34	70	— 74
22	+ 46	25	☾ 27
14 ⊥	☾ 36 ✓	61	+ 54
41	+ 85 ✓	41	⊥ 85
61	☾ 54	62	— 73 ✓
73	⊥ 64 ✓	41	2 23
83	2 23	60	□ 12
50	□ 13	80	⊥ 84

Should have been 15, to guard ⊥ 34.
Should have been ⊥ 34. An oversight.

Maharajah.	*The Sepoys.*	*Maharajah.*	*The Sepoys.*
83	+ 65 ✓	25 ✓	☾ 36 ✓
75 ✓	○ 47	70	— 72 ✓
67 ✓	— 36 ✓	34	— 36 ✓
34 ✓	— 47	67 ✓	+ 57
61	☾ 72 ✓	55 ⊥ *Mate.*	

GAME IV.

50	⊥ 45	16	○ 46
10	+ 46	27 ✓	— 55
80	— 35	36 ⊥ ✓	— 54
10	2 15	25	☾ 22 ✓
20	— 85	47	— 82
70	⊥ 75	57	— 46 ✓
10	□ 70	76 ✓	⊥ 65
30	2 64	75 ⊥ ✓	○ 55
74	— 34	76 ✓	— 54
86 ⊥	— 85	67	+ 85 ✓
74	+ 76	75 ✓	○ 55
52	□ 87	73 ✓	2 64
12	2 64	77 ✓	○ 54
30	□ 83	75 ✓	— 53
74	— 43	73 ✓	— 42
30	+ 85 ✓	75	□ 71 ✓
70	— 44	86	— 76 ✓
60	☾ 46	67	☾ 55
10	— 13 ✓	17	— 77 ✓
50	— 40 ✓	15 ⊥	□ 73
32	○ 46	24 ✓	— 33
82	□ 87	21 ✓	○ 53
32	○ 47	61 ✓	— 54
21	+ 74	51 ✓	□ 53 ✓
61	☾ 62 ✓	62 ✓	○ 55
21	□ 80	80 □	☾ 72
24	— 13	84	— 77
21	☾ 22 ✓	40	□ 63
61	— 62 ✓	51 ✓	— 53
21	□ 11 ✓	24	○ 54
23	⊥ 14 ✓	32 ✓	□ 43
24	2 43 ✓	51 ✓	+ 52

Maharajah.	*The Sepoys.*	*Maharajah.*	*The Sepoys.*
84	☾ 74 ✓	56 ⊥	⊥ 64 ✓
81 ✓	○ 55	50	☾ 53 ✓
21	☾ 71 ✓	40 ✓	□ 73
25	— 41	45 ⊥	☾ 52
47 ✓	○ 54	67	○ 83
87	□ 83 ✓	64 ⊥ ✓	— 82
75 ✓	○ 53	60 ✓	□ 71
57	☾ 11	80 ✓	— 81
24	— 13	60 ✓	— 71
32 ✓	○ 63	33	○ 72
44 + ✓	— 74	45 ✓	— 62
62 ✓	— 75	64 ✓	— 51
71 ✓	+ 74	31 ✓	— 62 ✓
44	☾ 43 ✓	23	□ 73 ✓
77 ✓	○ 84	44 ✓	○ 61
17	☾ 13 ✓	64 ✓	☾ 63 ✓
25	○ 73	34 2 ✓	○ 72
21	☾ 22 ✓	70 ✓	— 83 ✓
61 ✓	○ 84	80 ✓	☾ 81 ✓
64 2	☾ 42 ✓	81 ☾ *Mate.*	

The two following games show that the Maharajah must be defeated without losing a man, if the enemy is brought up in close formation.

Game V.

57	⊥ 13	15	☾ 24 ✓
77	— 83	16	□ 37
27	□ 12	66	⊥ 22
57	— 82	75	□ 84
37	— 82—52	66	— 85
27	⊥ 72	76	— 65
17	2 62	56	— 45
87	+ 82	66	☾ 46 ✓
65	□ 54	84	— 64 ✓
35	⊥ 42	76	— 54 ✓
25	2 32	66	+ 46
16	— 53	86	⊥ 73
66	☾ 23	66	2 74 *Mate.*
16	□ 32		

Game VI.

Maharajah.	*The Sepoys.*	*Maharajah.*	*The Sepoys.*
57	⊥ 42	56	□ 72
65	— 62	36	— 73
54	☾ 72 ✓	76	⊥ 72
34	2 32	56	— 22
14	— 82	76	2 32—53
25	☾ 74	87	+ 82
16	⊥ 13	47	□ 63
43	□ 12	17	— 65
25	☾ 24 ✓	16	☾ 34 ✓
36	□ 22	76	+ 73
16	— 23	77	□ 23—25
86	2 74 ✓	76	— 66 ✓
56	⊥ 83	57	— 35
36	□ 82	47	— 37 *Mate.*

Game VII.

The following game is won by two Rukhs supported by a line of pawns, every one of which is protected by a Knight or Bishop, the King and Queen directing all their movements from their two thrones.

57	⊥ 13	45	+ 42
17	— 83	25	⊥ 23
27	□ 12	55	— 33
23	— 82	36	2 41
45	— 12—32	56	— 22
25	⊥ 22	66	⊥ 53
44	□ 37	45	— 54 ✓
55	— 82—32	66	— 74
73	⊥ 72	55	2 51
46	□ 87	35	⊥ 63
76	— 37	62	+ 31
16	⊥ 52	35	⊥ 34
26	— 42	55	2 72
66	— 73	73 ✓	— 51
44	— 62	55	⊥ 84
55	□ 17	36	— 64
65	⊥ 43	26	+ 42

Maharajah.	*The Sepoys.*	*Maharajah.*	*The Sepoys.*
44	+ 31	16	⊥ 24
66	2 14	36	+ 33
36	□ 47	56	— 63
66	2 72	36	□ 87—57
56	⊥ 44	26	— 45
36	2 22	36	— 55
15	⊥ 14	46	— 56 *Mate.*
26	+ 42		

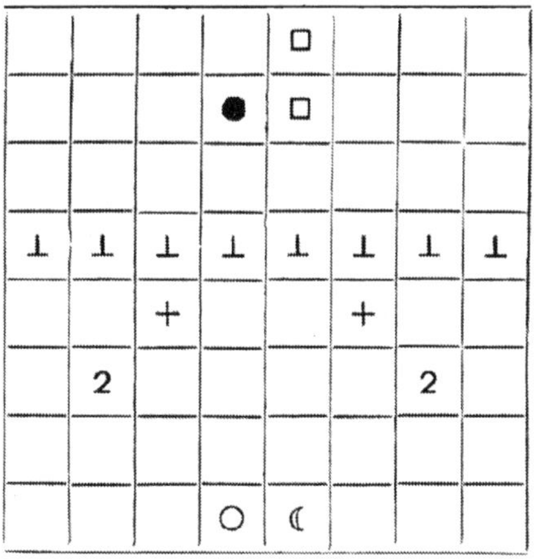

GAME VIII.

In this game the Maharajah is checkmated by the Pawns advancing in close line to the sixth row of squares, with all the principal pieces behind them.

Maharajah.	*The Sepoys.*	*Maharajah.*	*The Sepoys.*
57	⊥ 12	34	— 73
77	— 22	44	— 13
87	□ 11	77	□ 12
54	⊥ 83	55	⊥ 33
24	+ 21	75	— 42
64	⊥ 62	45	— 14
34	— 72	67	— 23
44	— 52	46	— 43

Maharajah.	*The Sepoys.*	*Maharajah.*	*The Sepoys.*
86	— 53	67	+ 43
46	— 84	37	⊥ 75
55	☾ 72	56	— 65 ✓
67	+ 32	77	— 55
85	⊥ 63	27	— 45
45	+ 42	37	+ 64
55	⊥ 15	16	2 32
36	— 85	27	☾ 44
46	— 24	16	⊥ 25 ✓
67	— 34	27	— 35
75	— 74	37	— 76
56	— 64	47	— 36 ✓
67	— 54	57	— 16
77	☾ 71	77	— 56
66	⊥ 44	57	— 46 *Mate.*

But it is not necessary to bring up the Pawns in this solid manner as shown in the last two games; on the contrary, the game is easily won by bringing out the principal pieces, taking care that they always support each other, and at the same time defend the pawns behind them. Our purpose has been in the above games, not to show how the Sepoys take the Maharajah, but how the Maharajah, though alone, and without assistance, may sometimes defeat them.

XVIII.

DOUBLE CHESS.

The most modern game of Chess bears a resemblance to the most ancient, the Chaturanga; being a game adapted for four players. It is looked upon with some degree of contempt by frequenters of Chess clubs: but unjustly so, for it is a game requiring great attention, and affording great exercise of skill and combination. Indeed, the head often aches after playing it. It may be played either by two persons, by three, or by four, thus forming a more social occupation than ordinary chess. Its scientific capabilities are seen to most advantage when played by two persons, as the same mind then directs the two allied forces: but when four players sit down together the game becomes more uncertain. If experienced players are engaged, the game of course is a silent one: but if some of the players are not very skilful, then it is necessary for the superior player to tell his partner what to do, as, if unsupported by his partner, the best player must inevitably lose his pieces, and perhaps his temper, and become checkmated. Nor is it unfair to do so: for the advantage gained by telling one's partner what to play is lost by the opponents being informed of the plot against them. But it necessarily injures the game; as the interest in playing is lost if all the plots and surprises are frustrated by being divulged, and so prevented. On the other hand it may frequently happen, even with good players, that one may not discover his partner's tactics : and thus it is a choice of evils. Where there are two superior players, and each has an inferior partner, and the superior player directs his partner what to move, especially if he does not always tell him the motive, it virtually becomes a game of two ; and a very good game it is.[1]

I. All the Queens stand upon a *white* square.

II. The Rook's pawns can move only one square at a time: but all the other pawns may move two squares at the first move.

III. Writers are not agreed about the Pawns queening. Looking at the length of the board, and the hopelessness of getting there, they make the Pawns queen at the sides; but they permit such Pawns as reach the opposite end of the board to return back again, like their partners' pawns, and on reaching home, to start again, as on first setting out, like so many "wandering Jews." As if it were possible to do such a thing! Neither is it at all probable that a Pawn could ever succeed in queening at the sides, when they could only do so by successive captures, while the central Pawns could never queen.

It is more reasonable therefore to let the Pawns queen, if they can, on reaching the opposite side. But as the probability is that they will never reach either the opposite or the side squares, we need not trouble ourselves in the matter; but may let them queen either at the sides, or opposite line, if they can.

[1] It seldom happens however that in ordinary society four chess players can be found: while in clubs the interest would always be exercised in ordinary chess.

IV. When Pawns meet their partner's Pawns they may jump over them.

V. When one of the players is checkmated, such checkmate is not final: but it lasts only so long as the opponents' pieces continue to give checkmate. The party is, as it were, shut in, or blockaded; and the blockade is raised as soon as the allies make their appearance.

VI. Such blockaded forces in this game are generally made free from capture, but as all games of chess are supposed to be imitations of war, it is more reasonable to allow the pieces to be taken by the adversary when he can; and to be removed or taken by the partner when they block up his way: otherwise they often interfere with the game.

The game is a game of combinations: combinations of assault by your opponents, combinations of counter-attack and defence on the part of yourself and partner.

After watching your right-hand opponent's move to see how it affects yourself, pay particular attention to see how it affects your partner; and if you find the attack is made on him, do all in your power to assist him: otherwise your left-hand opponent will follow up his partner's attack, and your partner will be powerless to resist it.

When no attack is made by your right-hand opponent, either on your partner or yourself, then see whether you can attack him: for if you do it is possible that your partner may be able to follow up the attack before it is his turn to move, and you may thus win a piece. When your partner moves, see therefore whether he is attacking your left-hand opponent, and means you to follow up the attack.

Avoid also, for the same reason, to put any one of your principal pieces in a position where it can be attacked by your left-hand opponent, when your partner will not be able to assist you, and when your right-hand opponent is able to put you in check, or to attack another unguarded piece: for in this case you must lose one of your men.

Should one of your opponents have lost his principal pieces, while the other has all his men, the attack should naturally be directed against the latter, as the former would be powerless to assist him.

If these rules are fully observed, the game should be a silent one, but where a skilful player sits down for the first time with one who scarcely knows his moves, he ought, as we have said, to take the command of the two forces, and tell his partner, as a general would tell his lieutenant, what to do: otherwise he has the mortification of letting onlookers suppose that he loses the game through his own incompetency.[1]

[1] It will be said that the partners in whist are not allowed to tell each other. But the case is different; as the cards are not seen, the game would be spoilt by an unfair disclosure to the partner: moreover, whist is a game of chance as well as skill, and therefore there is no disgrace in losing a game, or indeed several at one sitting. whereas chess is a game of skill, and occupies a whole sitting, and consequently, losing a game denotes an inferiority of skill.

XIX.

CHESS PROBLEMS.

There is in the King's Library in the British Museum a beautifully written MS.[1] of the fourteenth century, in Norman French, and therefore rather difficult to understand: but we venture to give what we conceive to be its rendering. It gives fifty-five positions in chess, or rather fifty-five solutions of forty-four positions. Each of these positions has a distinctive heading,[2] and each position has its separate plan, and each plan has the following system of notation.

a	*b*	*c*	*d*	*e*	*f*	*g*	*h*	
								i
								k
								l
								m
								n
								o
								p
								q

[1] Roy. Lib. 13, A. xviij—(14, i.)

[2] These headings are given by Strutt in his *Sports and Pastimes*, 4°, Lond., 1801, but without translations.

The solutions are described in verse, and the MS. is so remarkable that we wonder it has not been translated by some of the writers on chess, or by the chess clubs. The following are the headings of the different problems, with what we suppose to be their meaning.

Guy de Chivaler	(3 ways)	The Knight's game
Guy de Dames		The ladies' game
Le Guy de Damoyseles		The damsels' game
Le Guy de Alfins	(2 ways)	The bishops' game
Le Guy de Anel		The game of the ring
Le Guy de Covenaunt		The game of agreement
Guy de propre Confusioun	(3 ways)	Game of self-confusion
Mal assis		Ill at ease (Ill-placed)
Guy Cotidian	(2 ways)	The ordinary game (Day-by-day game)
Le Poynt estraunge	(2 ways)	The strange situation
Ky perde sey salve		Who loses, saves himself
Ky ne doune ceo ke il eyme, ne prent ke desire		He who gives not what he prizes, shall not get what he desires
Bien troue		Well placed (Well found)
Beal petis		Little beauty "Well done little one"?
Meut vaut engyn ke force		Skill beats strength
Ky est larges, est sages		Who is generous, is wise
Ky doune, ganye		Who gives, gains
Le Guy de Enginous e ly Coveytous		The game of the skilful and the ambitious
Covenaunt fet Ley		Agreement makes law
De pres sen joyst Ky de loyns veyt		He knows how to play, who has considered it beforehand (He sees near, who sees afar off)
Meschief fet hom penser		Misfortune makes a man think
La chace de Chivaler		The Knight's chase
La chace de Ferce et de Chivaler		The Queen and the Knight's chase
Bien fort		Very strong
Fol si prent		A fool, if he takes
Ly Envoyous		The ambassadors
Le seon sey envoye		His own ambassador

Le veyl conu		The old one found out
Le haut Enprise		The bold adventure
Le Guy de Cundut		A leading game?
Ky put, se prenge		He takes, who can
La Batalie saunz aray		The confused scrimmage
Le tret emble	(2 ways)	The ambling move? The game or plot advances? The unexpected move?
Ly desperes		The hopeless struggle
Ly mervelious	(2 ways)	A brilliant game?
De poun Ferce home fet		His pawn queens
Muse vyleyn		A villainous design?
Le Guy de dames et de damoyceles		The game of the ladies and the damsels
Fol si fie	(2 ways)	A fool, if he trusts
Mal veysyn	(2 ways)	A bad neighbour
Le mat de ferces		The Queen's mate
Flour de guys		The game of games
Le batalie de rokes		Battle of the Rooks
Duble Eschec		Double check.

No doubt the proper way of finding out the meaning of some of these headings would be by studying the games: but this could only be done by having a printed copy of the MS. with a plan of each problem.

END OF CHESS.

DRAUGHTS.

XX.

DRAUGHTS.

The game is played with three rows of four on each side, placed upon the *white* squares of a board of eight squares, having the double square at the bottom of right hand corner. The men move diagonally, one square at a time, and take diagonally by hopping over. On arriving at the opposite end they become Kings at their next move. The Kings move and take backwards as well as forwards. The first move is taken alternately.

When a player has it in his power to take a piece or pieces, but omits to do so, he may be *huffed* (lose his piece) or compelled to take the piece or pieces, at his opponent's discretion.

This power remains in force whenever it is the opponent's turn to move, however many moves may have elapsed since the piece first became *en prise*. But if he can take in two directions, he is at liberty to choose whichever direction he pleases, even though he may take fewer men one way than the other.

These are the rules: but the last three do not accord, like the rules of chess, with the usages of war, in which each side acts as he sees fit, and the opposite side has to calculate the probability of his taking one action or another.

XXI.

POLISH DRAUGHTS.

LE JEU DES DAMES.

The rules of this game are the same as those of our game, except that it is played on a different board, and with the following alterations·—

The board is a board of ten squares instead of eight; having four rows of five pieces on either side, *i.e.*, twenty pieces instead of twelve.

All the pieces have the power of moving backward as well as forward: but the Queens, as they are called in this game, have the power, whether in moving or taking, of passing over any number of squares in a straight line.

A player must always take the greatest number of pieces he can. This rule applies equally when he can take in two directions, even though the fewer number may consist of more valuable pieces. When the pieces in each direction are equal in number, he must then take that direction in which they are of more value, failing to do so, he may be *huffed,* or compelled to take in the opposite direction at his opponent's discretion.

A piece may not touch or pass over a square occupied by a piece more than once in the same coup: or, in other words he must remove each piece as he takes it.

*** This is a much more lively game than common draughts.

XXII.

TURKISH DRAUGHTS.

The Author—As he played it in Asia Minor 1845

The board is the ordinary draught-board.

The game is played with sixteen men on each side, which are placed on the second and third rows.

The pieces move and take forwards or sideways, not diagonally; and the piece is placed in the square immediately beyond that of the piece taken.

On reaching the further side they become Queens, and can then move from one part of the board to the other, forwards, sideways or backwards; and the Queen in taking can place itself in any vacant square beyond the piece taken.

This is an excellent game, as the players have the power of concentrating their forces; of bringing them all to the right if that side be attacked, or to the left if the adversary appear weak on that side, or if it be thought desirable to force a passage. Another advantage is that a player can always gain time by moving to and fro laterally, till he sees his opponent make a false move.

The author once saw a set game played, in which a skilful player after forcing his adversary to take several of his pieces, at length got a Queen with which he took all his adversary's men at one move: but having no idea then of writing on these games, he took no note of it.

XXIII.

THE GAME OF ENCLOSING.

Chinese	*Japanese*
WEI-KI.	GO.

T'ao hua ch'üan ("The book of Peach flower"), in 8 vols.	Quoted by Mr. Giles.	
Hsien chi wu k'u - - -		
Trigantius—De Christiana Expeditione apud Sinas -		1616
Semedo—Relatione della Grande Monachia della China -		1643
Hyde—De Ludis Orientalibus - - -		1694
Giles (Herbert A.)—Wei-ch'i, or the Chinese game of war[1]		1877
Playing with Chinese and Japanese gentlemen		1865, 1872, 1889

Mr. Giles, our Consul in China, who is a proficient player, and an enthusiast in the game, informs us that "several voluminous works have been entirely devoted to elucidating its principles, and many shorter treatises on the subject have appeared in collections of miscellaneous writings. Most of these are adorned with cuts showing advantageous positions, and giving problems to be worked out by the student."

He tells us that the game, like all other Oriental games, boasts of great antiquity. It is said to have been invented by the great and excellent Emperor Yao,[2] 2300 B.C., but the earliest record of the game is in 300 B.C.

[1] Published in "Temple Bar," Vol xlix, No. 194.

[2] K'ang Hsi's Dictionary.

Like all other games, it is said to be, as Mr. Giles describes it in his title, a game of war. Here we have not merely typical representatives of the various arms, but the armies themselves, some 200 men on each side: they form encampments, and furnish them with defences; and they slay not merely a single man, as in other games, but frequently hosts of men. The eye of the general is supposed to be all over the field at the same moment, watching not only the points of attack against the enemy, but the weak places of his own defence.

The game is played on a board of eighteen squares each way, forming 361 points: for the pieces are placed on the points, not in the squares. The pieces are not moved when once placed down, but they are supposed to move, and therefore have their connection one with another along the lines, but not diagonally. The pieces are called *Tze* in Chinese, and *Ishi* in Japanese. They are rounded at top, and flat at bottom , and are made of glass, marble, or composition, and generally are of *black* and *white* colours. Each player has about 200 of these pips, though perhaps not 150 are played, but the others are used to assist in counting, as we shall presently see. Being so many, the pips are placed in bowls of wood or china, which are always seen in paintings representing this game. When a player is in doubt as to playing a piece, or he wishes to show why he played in a certain manner, he reverses any of the pips he transposes, to show that they have been moved and must be replaced in their proper position.

The Chinese board has the central points 63, 75, 189, 303 and 315 marked out with four angles, and the four side points, 9, 180, 198 and 369 with two such angles. The Japanese board has the points 63, 69, 75, 183, 189, 195, 303, 309 and 315 distinguished by dots. Such boards are, in China, printed on paper, with the printer's name attached, so as to be ready either for playing the game, or for scoring a game: and there is a margin at the top for writing remarks, such as noting a point from which a pip of one colour has been taken up, and into which a pip of the other colour has subsequently been played, as 94 and 283 in the accompanying game, in each of which a *black* pip was played first, and a *white* pip afterwards.

The game is begun by placing two pips of one colour on the points 63 and 315, and two pips of the opposite colour on 75 and 303. But should the players not be of equal skill, all these, or even the whole of the marked points may be given to the weaker player. The players then place pieces alternately, one by one, placing some few pieces on intermediate points all round the board: after which the fight begins.

A player now endeavours to fence off or enclose a field or camp, *Kwei* in Chinese, *Shini-ishi* in Japanese, in any portion of the board, but while so doing he finds his opponent is surrounding him on the outside. He must therefore take care to preserve some open space behind him, called an *eye*, into which the enemy cannot enter, such as we see in No. IV in the accompanying game. This camp may be regarded as a fortress having a court-yard for the exercise of the troops. By entering a fresh piece at 78 or 98 he could make two *eyes* or court-yards. No. III has two *eyes*, 378, and the other a very large one.[1] No. II has two small *eyes*, one

[1] 336, 337 and 357 are not an *eye*, but were occupied by the enemy.

of one point, and one of two points. No. V has three small *eyes* of only one point, 11, 30 and 69, and No. I has one small *eye* and one larger one. Now if the enemy were to fill in this larger one he would take off sixteen of *Black's* men, for they would be penned in all round, but *Black* would not allow him to do so; but when *White* had filled in five of the points, *Black* would fill in the sixth and then take off *White's* five pieces. Suppose that this attempt were repeated by *White* four more times, *Black* entering a fresh piece every time, there would at length be only one vacant point remaining; and then *Black* would have two small *eyes*, 0 and 2, into neither of which could *White* enter. But if *Black* were inadvertently to enter a piece at 2, he would then leave only one up, 0, and *White* would enter there and take off all *Black's* men in that camp. For it will be understood that though a piece cannot enter a single *eye* (where he cannot immediately take any of his opponent's pieces) without being taken: yet if by voluntarily entering into such *eye* he can surround his enemy, his own piece, instead of being dead, captures all the enemy's pieces which he has thus surrounded. *Black* however would not wait for *White's* attempt to fill in this large *eye*, but would place one piece at 22 and another at 41, and he would thus form five small *eyes* of one point each, 0, 2, 40, 42 and 61. We see then that unless the *eye* is a large one, there must be two small *eyes* to render a camp secure. But these small *eyes* should be in the rear of the camp where the enemy cannot reach them:

for if on the outside, the enemy might plant three men outside *White's eye*, and then boldly putting a man inside the *eye* he would destroy the *eye* by taking off one of the pieces, and at the same time would gain an *eye* for himself: and this would lead to a see-saw.[1]

From this it will appear that—

A piece is lost which enters an enemy's single *eye*, if he cannot by so doing take any of his opponent's pieces; but if by so doing he takes any of his opponent's pieces, his own is not lost;

Any number of pieces when surrounded and entirely shut in by the enemy, as *Black's* 94, 193 and 283, and *White's* 2, 22, 40, 41, 42 and 61; and 336, 337, and 357 are taken off immediately they are closed in;

Pieces enclosed, but not entirely shut in, and which have no *eyes*, as *Black's* 113, 132 and 133, and *White's* 251 and 274 are taken off immediately before counting;

Pieces enclosed, but having two small *eyes*, or one large one, are perfectly safe.

It must be remembered that 94, 193 and 283 were originally covered with *Black's* men, and that 94 and 283 were afterwards covered with *White's* men.

When each player has completed his operations, and the further playing in of more pieces will not affect the game, it is said—*Huan leao*, It is finished.

[1] Mr. Giles's Essay on *Wei-Ch'i* gives an exhaustive account of these *eyes*, their modes of a ack, and their defence.

THE GAME.

Black.	White.	Black.	White.
{ 63	{ 75	73	93
{ 315	{ 303	94	92
53	45	52	71
49	85	70	51
122	136	31	74
176	162	50	114 (94)
262	326	229	308
328	276	309	289
275	255	310	290
296	277	311	307
254	274	231	103
295	235	102	123
253	297	83	143
317	336	24	282
316	234	281	301
233	213	283	302
212	192	202	25
193	214	44	61
191	172	81	48
211	171	28	27
116	115	68	47
96	95	33	242
137	135	241	263
97	251	261	243
273	189	222	181
170	190	204	201
150	175	221	228
156	131	164	145
151	152	245	284 (263)
132	112	165	146
133	173	187	249
113	155	250	209
130	111	230	207
110	72	188	208

Black.	*White.*	*Black.*	*White.*
147	127	3	41
148	337	216	236
335	318	358	84
356	357	43	266
355	197	246	267
196	217	169	167
56	76	168	107
77	55	86	106
36	205	89	64
224	225	23	182
163	142	183	223
244	166	203	5
185	186	62	66
226	206	178	67
280	42	88	298
21	22	338 (336, 337, 357)	129
1	121		
60	177	265	285
157	291	264	283
292	348	268	247
349	327	195	194 (193)
329	35	198	238
300	341	144	124
377	128	100	140
15	14	200	210
16	34	158	180
10	8	220	120
29	347	20 (2, 22, 40, 41,42,61)	109
269	248		
271	288	90	94
270	369	32	7
370	368	9	215
350	13	108	218
12	320	149	227
87	40	91	54
80	101	4	
82	2		

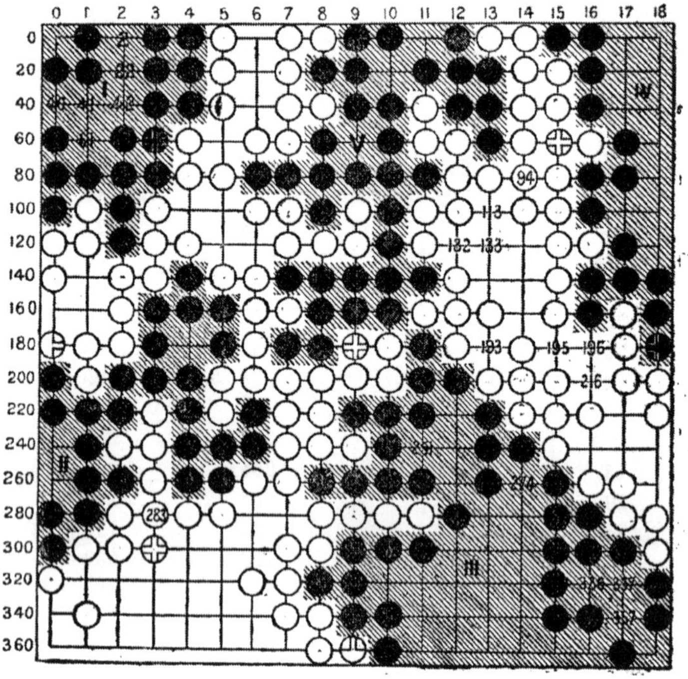

STATE OF THE GAME WHEN FINISHED.

Each player now declares how many camps he has made. *Black* claims five, and *White* two: so *White* takes off three of *Black's* men, say 195, 196 and 216. They then take off the pieces enclosed by the opposite side, as *Black's* 113, 132 and 133, and *White's* 251 and 274.

The game is now ready for counting.

The vacant points of each camp of one of the players, say *Black's*, are now filled in with spare pips of the same colour, and the following is the result.

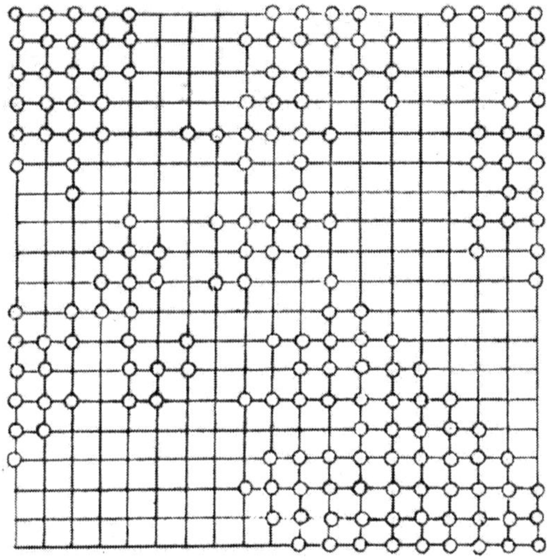

As it is not necessary to count both sides, the *Whites* are now pushed aside where in the way, so as to arrange the *Blacks* in a solid mass in each camp, which is done, where possible, in rows of five, to facilitate counting; and we then have this form.

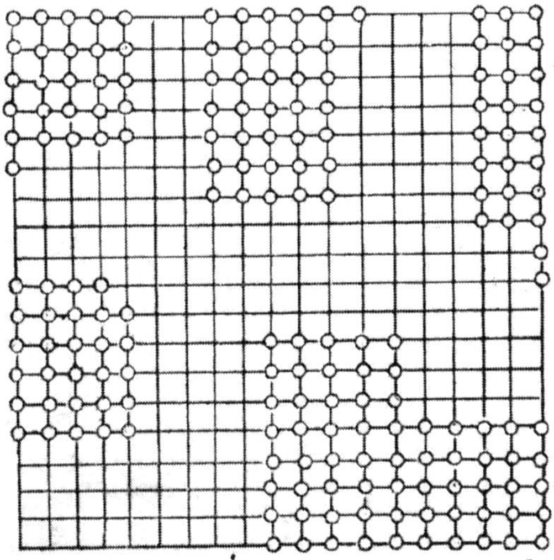

By this we see that

Black's camp I has	$5 \times 5 + 1 = 26$			
" " II "	$5 \times 5 + 4 = 29$			
" " III "	$\left.\begin{matrix} 8 \times 5 \\ 5 \times 5 \end{matrix}\right\} = 65$			
" " IV "	$8 \times 3 + 2 = 26$			
" " V "	$7 \times 5 + 1 = 36$		Total number	361
				182
Therefore *White* has				179

The difference between the two being 5, the *Whites* are said to lose $2\frac{1}{2}$, and the *Blacks* to win $2\frac{1}{2}$.

We have thus given a game by the study of which anyone may be able to play Wei-Ki. But "the very look of the game will be enough to frighten" some: for who would not suppose that if the game consists in surrounding the enemy, the *Whites* have the best of it, and indeed that they have surrounded, and therefore taken every one of the *Blacks*. But the *Blacks* equally surround the *Whites*. This however is not the game: but, as we have seen, each camp or group of pieces may be considered as a fortress, which must have court-yards, however small, called *eyes*, for the forces to move about in. Then it is impregnable, and hostile forces around it are powerless to take it; but if it has no court-yards, then the garrison is considered to be so crowded together with men, women and children, that they cannot move, and the enemy takes the fortress and all within it.

In the game we have given as an example the *Whites* have two camps or fortresses, the left one of which has five *eyes*, 6, 26, 46; 65; 104, 105, 125, 126; 141, 160, 161; and a larger one at the bottom; and the right one three *eyes*,[1] 75; 134, 153, 154, 174; and 237, 256, 257, 258, 278; and, as we have seen, the *Whites* are only five fewer than the *Blacks*. It is therefore a very even game and well fought.

The game however is so intricate that it requires great practice to play it well, and accordingly it is not a game for idle play; it must be made a study; and thus Mr. Giles, who as Consul has long dwelt in China, and is a practised player, assures us—"None but the educated play at Wei-ch'i. A knowledge of this difficult game stamps a man in China as somewhat more than an ordinary person. Its subtleties are beyond the reach of the lazy; its triumphs too refined for the man of gross material tastes. Skill in Wei-ch'i implies the astuteness and versatility so prized amongst the Chinese. They could hardly believe a man to play Wei-ch'i well, and yet be possessed of only indifferent abilities as a practical man of the world. It would amount to a contradiction of terms. All the more so, as nearly all those who enter upon a literary career make a point of attempting to learn the game; but many faint by the way. To a beginner a mere knowledge of the rules for a long time seems hopeless: and subsequent application of them more hopeless still. The persevering ones play on day by day, until at last —suddenly as it were—the great scheme of Wei-ch'i dawns upon them in all its fullness and beauty; and from that day they are ardent enthusiasts in support of its unquestionable merits."

The photograph at the beginning of this article represents a diminutive board and men in my posses-

[1] 113, 132 and 133 were occupied, and 193 and 195, 196, 216 are not *eyes*, but were occupied by the enemy.

sion, the board being only $7\frac{3}{4}$ inches square, and the pieces $\frac{3}{8}$ of an inch in diameter. It stands $3\frac{3}{4}$ inches high, and is japanned with the same design as that of the Japanese chess-board. It is however generally played by the natives on large wooden folding boards about 20 inches square, with pieces of about the size of a shilling, which are kept in japanned bowls. Ladies, however, sometimes appear to play on small japanned boards with china cups.

The photograph at the end is from the dossier of a Chinese draught and backgammon table in my possession, representing a Chinese gentleman and lady playing the game, with another lady looking on. The gentleman has evidently got the best of the game, at which his wife sitting behind him is greatly pleased; while the lady consoles herself with her delicate pipe of tobacco.

BACKGAMMON.

XXIV.

BACKGAMMON.

The board is divided into two *Tables* by the *Bar*. On each side of the Bar is a compartment of six points. One of these compartments is called the *Home*, or *Inner Table*; the other the *Outer Table*. The *Entering Division* is opposite the Home, the two Homes are opposite each other, and the two Entering Divisions also. Consequently all the pieces meet each other.

Two men are placed upon the first point of the opponent's Inner Table, five on the sixth of his Outer Table, three on the second point of the player's Outer Table, and five on the sixth point of his Inner Table. The placing of the opponent's pieces will correspond.

The pieces are entered according to the throws of two dice, and the throws generally have French names. In throwing doublets you have twice the number thrown, and the numbers can be played separately. Any throw which you are not able to throw is lost, but you must play when you can.

A piece taken up must be played before any other piece.

When a point is covered with a single piece it is called a *blot*.

In *bearing off*, on throwing a number corresponding with an uncovered point, you must play up a piece behind it, but if none, you then bear off a piece in front of it.

If you have *borne off* all your pieces before your opponent you win a *hit*, or game; if before all his pieces have entered his *home*, a *gammon*, or two hits; if before they left your *table*, a *Backgammon*, or three hits.

XXV.

GERMAN BACKGAMMON.

The Entering division and the *Home* are common to both players. The Entering division must be either the right-hand near division, or the left-hand opposite division.

The pieces enter by throws, and all pieces must be entered before any leave the Entering division.

On throwing doublets the player, after playing those doublets, is entitled to play the doublets underneath, which are always the complement of seven. Should he forget to do so, or should he not be able to do so, his opponent says—"I play your aces," or whatever the number may be.

On throwing 1, 2, the player can call for any doublets he chooses: but should he forget to do so, his opponent may say—"I play your doublets" But this must be done after throwing his dice, but not lifting up the dice-box.

This is an amusing game, not merely from the frequency of taking up, owing to the pieces all travelling in the same direction, but also from a player being permitted to play whatever his opponent cannot play; and also whatever his opponent forgets to play. The game is much longer than the ordinary backgammon, and the fluctuations of the game much greater, thus producing greater excitement.

XXVI.

TURKISH BACKGAMMON.

The Author—as he played it in Asia Minor - 1845

The Entering divisions are the opposite right-hand divisions, and the Homes are the near right-hand divisions: consequently all the pieces move in the same direction, though they do not start from the same point: and such direction is, like their writing, from right to left, instead of from left to right.

Two pieces are entered on opposite right-hand corner before commencing the game, and these pieces cannot be moved till all the other pieces are entered, and have left the opposite division.

New men are entered on points 1 to 6, counting from, but not including, that of the two men in the corner, but the points for pieces taken up include this point: but as there may never be more than two men on this point, a piece taken up cannot enter with a 1 till one of the two pieces has moved.

It is not permitted to double the pieces on any of the points of the opposite division, either in entering or playing, except the left-hand corner, but they may be doubled in the home divisions.

It is optional in beginning the game, either to enter

new pieces, or to play those already entered: but pieces taken up must be re-entered before other pieces are played.

When an adversary's piece is taken up in his entering division a blot or an open point must be left for any man so taken up: but his pieces may be taken up in any other part of the board, though he have no point to enter at.

In throwing for first move, the higher plays the numbers thrown. After winning a game the conqueror enters a 5 and 6 and then throws for first move.

If all the pieces are taken home, and one taken off, while his adversary has all his points 1—6 occupied by his men, and one captive which he cannot enter, it is a *capote*, which is equal to seven games.

XXVII.

PACHISI.

Hyde—De ludis Orientalibus, II, 68 - - - - 1694
Personal play with natives - - - - - 1860
Calcutta Review, Communicated, with remarks, by the late A. F. Bellasis, Civil Service, Bengal - - - - 1867
E. B. Tylor, D.C.L., F.R.S., On the game of Patolli in ancient Mexico, and its probably Asiatic origin. In *Anthropological Institute Journal* - - - - 1878

Futteypore Sikri Palace—Pachisi Court.

Pachisi is the national game of India. It is played in palaces, zenanas, and the public caffés.

M. L. Rousselet, speaking of the Court of the Zenana in the palace at Futteypore, says—"The game of Pachisi was played by Akbar in a truly regal manner.

The Court itself, divided into red and white squares, being the board, and an enormous stone raised

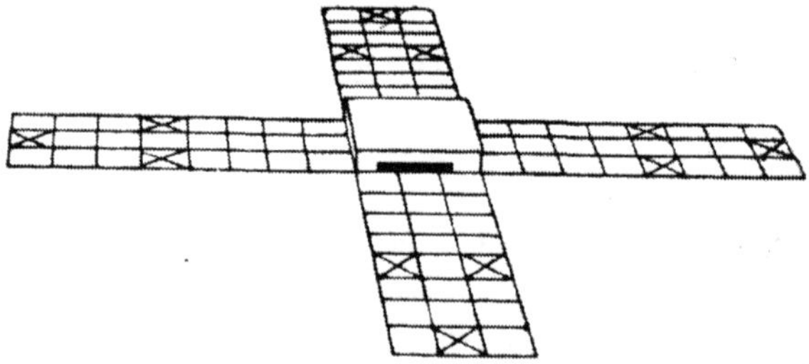

on four feet, representing the central point. It was here that Akbar and his courtiers played this game; sixteen young slaves from the harem wearing the players' colours, represented the pieces, and moved to the squares according to the throw of the dice. It is said that the Emperor took such a fancy to playing the game on this grand scale that he had a court for pachisi constructed in all his palaces, and traces of such are still visible at Agra and Allahabad."[1] Mr. Bellasis says—" There is a gigantic pachishee board at the palace at Agra, where the squares are inlaid with marble on a terrace,[2] and where the Emperors of Delhi used to play the game with live figures,—a similar board existed within one of the courts of the palace at Delhi; but it was destroyed in the alterations after the Mutiny."

In one of the early numbers of the *Calcutta Review* we read—and this boisterous excitement in playing the author has seen in his own experience—" The

[1] India and its Native Princes, 1876.

[2] I applied at the India Office, but could get no information as to whether it still exists ! Ought we not to have an officer charged to keep a record, and where possible, to assist in keeping in repair the magnificent and exquisite monuments of India, as we are endeavouring to get for the stupendous remains in Egypt; and one to whom the public could apply when information is required for any purpose ? The same remark applies to that of Allahabad.

INDIAN PA

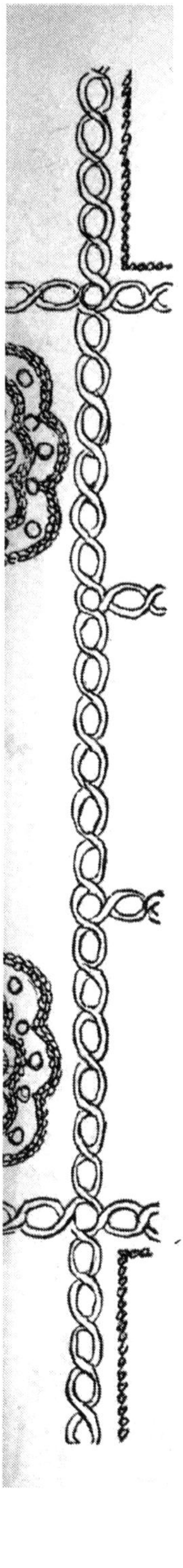
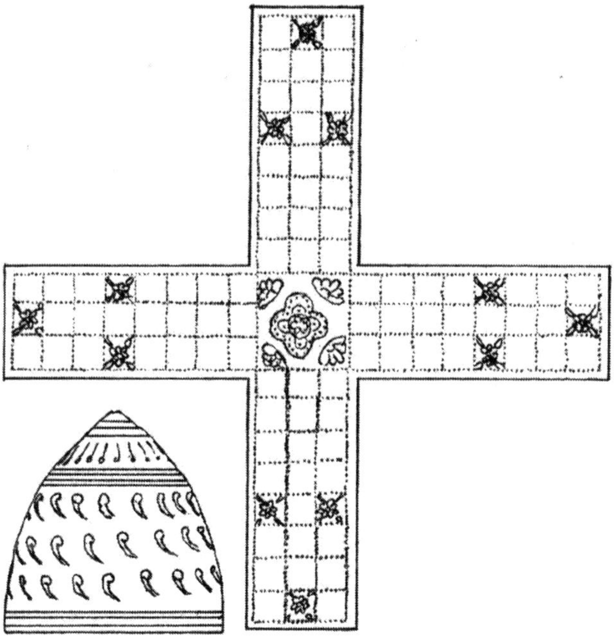

combatants breathe hatred and vengeance against each other: the throws of the dice are accompanied with tremendous noise, and the sounds of "*Kache-Baro*" and and "*Karo-Pauch*" and "*Baro-Pauch*" are heard from a considerable distance. It is altogether a lively scene, in strong contrast with the apathy generally attributed to the Bengalis. . . . In the cool of the evening parties of respectable natives may be not unfrequently seen sitting under the umbrageous *Bakul,* and amusing themselves with chess, pasha, or cards. Laying aside ɔr a season the pride of wealth and even the rigorous istinctions of caste, Brahmins and Sudras may be ɟeen mingling together for recreation. The noisy ɤociferations and the loud laugh betoken a scene of nerriment and joy. The *huhah,* a necessary furniture f a Bengali meeting place, is ever and anon by its ıgant vollies ministering to the refreshment of the sembly: while the plaudits of the successful player se higher than the curling smoke issuing from the ɔcoanut vessel."[1]

The board is generally made of cloth cut into the shape of a cross, and then divided into squares with embroidery; one such in my possession, as seen in accompanying engraving, is of red cloth embroidered with yellow silk: another, as seen in photograph at beginning of this article, is from Delhi, and is made of glass beads beautifully worked, and having both sides alike, and even the men and dice are worked with beads in like manner. Each limb has three rows of eight squares. The outer rows have roses or ornaments at certain distances, which serve as castles, in which pieces are free from capture. The extreme square of

[1] *Calcutta Review*, vol. xv, 1851.

central row is also a castle. The castles are open to both partners. Pieces may double on other squares, but it is at their own peril. These castles are placed on the board so that from the centre or home, where all the pieces start from, going down the middle row, returning on the outside, and then on to end of next limb, will be exactly 25, hence the name of the game; and from the castle in middle of nearer side of one limb to middle of further side of next limb will be 25; from middle of further side of one limb to middle of nearer side of opposite limb will be 25 + 1 (grace) which grace may be played separately; and from extreme end of fourth limb to the home of first limb will also be 25, and out. From ignorance or forgetfulness of this arrangement, the castles, in modern modifications of this game are not put in the right places. Any number of pieces of a player or of his partner are safe in these castles, and an enemy cannot enter: but, if pieces double in any other squares, they can be taken off by a single piece at one stroke on throwing that number.

The game is played by four players each having four pieces. The two opposite sides are partners, and they win or lose together. In order to distinguish them better, the *yellow* and *green* should play against the *red* and *black*. Each enters from the centre, and goes down the middle of his own limb, and then round the board, returning up the centre of his own limb from whence he started. On going up the central line of one's own home, the pieces are turned over on their side, to show that they have made the circuit. They can only get out by throwing the exact number. The pieces move by throw of six cowries; these throws count as follows:—

6 with mouths down	- -	= 25	and grace, and play again.
5 ,, ,,	and 1 up	= 10	,, ,, ,,
4 ,, ,,	,, 2 ,,	= 2	
3 ,, ,,	,, 3 ,,	= 3	
2 ,, ,,	,, 4 ,,	= 4	
1 ,, ,,	,, 5 ,,	= 5	
	6 ,,	= 6	and play again.

Here again there is a diversity in different parts of India. In some parts seven cowries are used instead of six, and the throws also are different: sometimes they are 1, 2, 3, 4, 5, 6, 12, and 25; sometimes 2, 3, 4, 6, 10, 12, 25; and sometimes 2, 3, 4, 7, 10, 14, 25 and 30.

The cowries and dice are thrown by the hand, but the latter generally roll down an inclined plane, the natives shouting as they roll for good luck.

When graces are thrown the grace may be played separately. On taking a piece the player may throw again; and, consequently, if a piece is taken by a 25, a 10, or a 6, the player will have two more throws, one for the throw, and one for taking a piece.

In commencing the game the first piece may be entered whatever throw is made, but the other pieces can enter only with a grace. So, likewise, a piece taken up can enter only with a grace. The pieces move against the sun. A player may refuse to play when it comes to his turn, or he may throw and then refuse to take it. He may do this either because he is afraid of being taken, or to help his partner. On reaching the extremity of the fourth limb he may wait there till he gets a "twenty-five" and thus gets out at one throw. Should his partner be behind in the game, he must keep his own pieces back in order to assist him, and so by blocking up the way, prevent the adversaries from following close behind him, and thus hinder their moving, or taking them if they do move. Tyros in the game, forgetting this principle that both parties must win or lose together, or intent solely upon their own desire of being first, make haste to get their own pieces out, thus leaving their partners in the lurch ; who, if much in the rear are sure to lose the game, as their opponents have two throws to their one, and are enabled to keep close behind them, and thus trip them up. Sometimes the forward player, on arriving at his own limb instead of turning his piece over and going up the centre, may, if permittad, run all round the board a second time, in order to assist his partner. Sometimes the player who is out first is permitted to give his throws to his partner, but this is not the game.

The ladies of the harem who play this game are said to call it *Das-Pauchish*, taking this name from the two principal throws, *ten* and *twenty-five*.[1]

Two games, being modifications of the Pachisi, are so distinct as to acquire specific names, Chausar and Chauput, which will be described immediately. Hyde calls the game Tchupur, but he gives no rules for playing it ; while Mr. Tylor[2] describes a game which was played by the ancient Mexicans, called Patolli, the account of which is most interesting, showing a very early migration, accidental or otherwise, from Asia to South America. He supposes that this game originated from the primitive game of *Tab*, which is still played in Egypt and the Holy Land, and described by Hyde, ii, 217 : and this primitive game is supposed to be an imitation of war.

[1] *Calcutta Review*.

[2] On the game of Patolli, in ancient Mexico, and its probably Asiatic origin, by E. B. Tylor, Esq., D.C.L., F.R.S. From the *Journal of the Anthropological Institute*, Nov., 1878.

XXVIII.

CHAUSAR AND CHAUPUT.

Slight varieties of Pachisi in move and play, in different parts of India

---

The varieties in these games may be thus described in general; some adopting one alteration, some another.

Green.

Black. 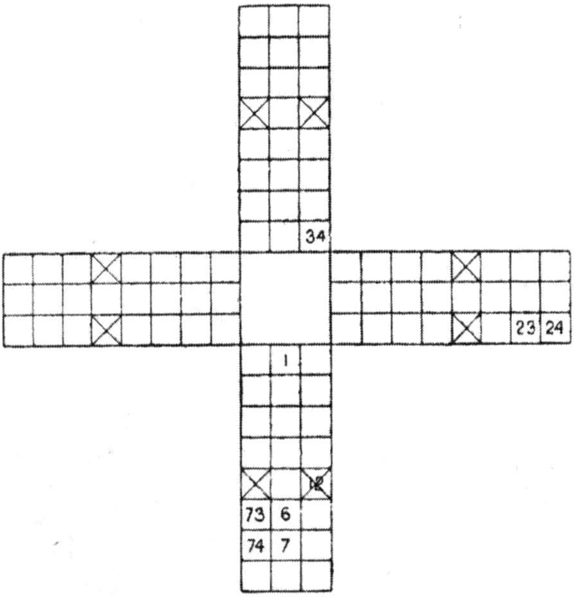 *Red.*

Yellow.

Chauput is played with cowries as in Pachisi, but there is no "25," and no "10," and no "grace" in these games; and there is no option in playing: whatever the throw, the pieces must move if they can. Two pieces enter by coming down the centre and then round the board. Two pieces start from squares 6 and 7, one from 12, while the other enters from the centre at first throw, whatever that may be. Sometimes the two latter pieces are placed at 22 and 24, in order to catch *Red's* pieces, while those at 6 and 7 are in wait to catch *Black's* pieces. And so the same with the other colours. Sometimes the pieces are entered by placing two pieces on 6, and two on 7: or else the pieces stand on 6, 7, 73 and 74.

Chausar is played with three oblong dice having

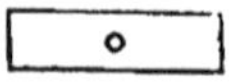 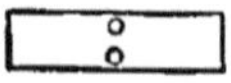 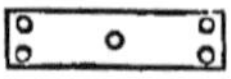 and 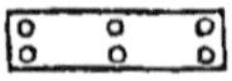

on their four faces. If two of these are thrown with the same number, they are doublets, and if given to a single piece it moves only twice the throw, but if given to two pieces standing on the same square, each of such pieces moves twice the throw. There are no castles in this game, though the ordinary Pachisi board is used, but the castles are useful for counting. On arriving at 34 the pieces may double, and then they cannot be taken except by doubles. The game is played by two or four persons, at pleasure. If with two players, the *black* and *yellow* against the *red* and *green*. All the *black* pieces must get out before the *yellow*, and the *red* before the *green*. If four are playing, when one player has got out all his pieces, his partner has his throws.

These games, however, have variations in different parts of India: so that one native gives one description of the game, and another another.

XXIX.

ASHTA-KASHTE.

ONE-EIGHT.

A modification of Pachisi.

16	15	14	13	12	11	10
17	29	30	31	32	33	9
18	28	43	44	45	34	8
19	27	42	49	46	35	7
20	26	41	48	47	36	6
21	25	40	39	38	37	5
22	23	24	1	2	3	4

The game can be played by two, three, or four players. Each player has four men which he enters in castle in front of him. The men move according to the numbers shown on diagram. When the outer circuit is completed against the sun, to square 24, the course is reversed till they arrive at the centre 49, when they are taken off.

Pieces occupying a castle cannot be taken.

Pieces may enter on their entering castle, even though occupied by an opponent.

If doubles are made on any other square, they can be taken only by doubles.

The moves are regulated by four cowries: all mouths down reckon as 8 and a grace, and throw again; all mouths up reckon as a grace, and throw again; all other numbers reckon by the number of mouths up. On throwing 8 and a grace, they may be played separately. A player is not obliged to play his throws. On taking an opponent, you throw again.

It will thus be seen that though the form of the board is different, the moves and rules are very nearly the same as those of Pachisi.

MAGIC SQUARES.

XXX.

MAGIC SQUARES.

Agrippa—De Occulta Philosophia (II, 42) -	1510
Bachet—Problems plaisans et delectables - - -	1624
Prestet—Nouveaux Elemens des Mathématiques - -	1689
De la Loubere—Relation du Royaume de Siam - -	1693
Frenicle—Des Quarrez Magiques. Acad. R. des Sciences -	1693
Ozonam—Récréations Mathématiques - - -	1697
Violle—Traité complet des Carrés Magiques - -	1837-8

A magic square is a square the cells of which add up to the same amount, whichever way they are taken. They were called magic, because they were said to be used by the Egyptians and Pythagoreans[1] for the purpose of imposing on the credulous. The squares of two, or four cells, being incapable of forming a magic square, were said to represent chaos. Squares of three, four, five or more cells to be dedicated to the sun, the moon and the different planets. These squares were then supposed to be placed in a polygon, having the same number of sides as the root of the square, and this polygon in a circle; while in the space between the polygon and the circle were inscribed the signs of the zodiac, and the good or evil name of the planet, according as the talisman was required for the purpose

[1] M. De la Loubere gives them an Indian descent.

of good or evil: and, according as this was the case the talisman was projected and engraved in different materials selected from their supposed or pretended efficacy.

The principle upon which Pythagoras is said to have founded his philosophy was that all things are regulated by numbers. In some things the unit is discernible; in others, the triangle, the square, the hexagon or some other figure. In some instances they are odd, in others even; in some straight, in others curved: and that from meditating on this, he believed that numbers were the animate principle of all things. We will not, however, pretend to explain that which the philosopher did not understand himself, but will turn to the subject immediately before us.

Magic squares are divisible into two classes, odd and even, according as the sides consist of an equal or an unequal number of cells. Again, the even squares are further divisible into two classes, according as the sides, when divided by two, are even or uneven: these are called evenly even, and unevenly even. As the methods of executing these are all different, we must treat each separately. The numbers may be in any kind of progression, natural or arithmetical, geometrical, harmonic, or serial.

XXXI.

ODD SQUARES.

The odd squares are not only the most easy to fill up, but the same principle may be applied to all odd squares, whatever may be the number of their sides. The most simple and easiest method is that by Agrippa. Place the first number immediately below the centre; then place the others, one by one, in a diagonal line inclining downwards to the right. When beyond a line, whether vertical or horizontal, carry it to the commencement of that line. When the diagonal march leads to a cell already occupied, take a diagonal direction from the cell so occupied towards the left, and then proceed as before to the right. The same rule applies when the number falls outside both of the vertical and horizontal lines. The mean number will always occupy the centre, and the highest number the cell immediately above the centre.

4	9	2
3	5	7
8	1	6

11	24	7	20	3
4	12	25	8	16
17	5	13	21	9
10	18	1	14	22
23	6	19	2	15

In these squares it is observable that the diagonals from left to right are in natural progression, 11, 12, 13, &c.; while those from right to left, 3, 8, 13, &c., are in a progression equal to the root of the square, or the number of cells in each side; while in every case the mean number occupies the centre; the first number the cell below the centre, and the highest the cell above the centre; while the numbers equally distant from the centre, added together, are exactly the double of the centre.

From this it follows that we can construct the square without any additional aid. First, on the central number, 13, we fill in the two diagonals, 11, 12, 13, 14, 15; and 3, 8, 13, 18, 23; then the shorter diagonals, 7, 8, 9; 17, 18, 19; and 7, 12, 17; 9, 14, 19. Then on 25, the highest number, the diagonals 20, 25, 5, 10; 24, 25; and 24, 4; and then on 1, the lowest number, the diagonals 16, 21, 1, 6; 1, 2; and 22, 2; and thus complete the square.

On examining these squares, Bachet perceived that the numbers are inverted, and that by transposing them he could get the numbers in their natural sequence.

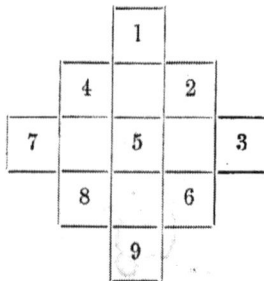

		1		
	4		2	
7		5		3
	8		6	
		9		

				1				
			6		2			
		11		7		3		
	16		12		8		4	
21		17		13		9		5
	22		18		14		10	
		23		19		15		
			24		20			
				25				

In the first example, that of a square of three, each number beyond the square is removed three cells; the 1 three cells below; the 9 three cells above; the 3 three cells to the left; and the 7 three cells to the right. In the other example, that of a square of five, each number beyond the square is removed five cells: the 1, 2 and 6 downwards; the 20, 24 and 25 upwards; the 4, 5 and 10 to the left; and the 16, 21 and 22 to the right; while the numbers in the diagonals remain the same.

M. de la Loubere's method, taken from the Indians, is slightly different. The first number is placed in the middle of the top band. The march is upward instead of downward; and when arriving at a cell already occupied, the next number is placed immediately below the last one played. Other things remain the same.

8	1	6
3	5	7
4	9	2

17	24	1	8	15
23	5	7	14	16
4	6	13	20	22
10	12	19	21	3
11	18	25	2	9

It will be observed that the central column of this last method is exactly the same as that of Bachet's; and that the vertical columns consist of the same numbers, but differently placed: and with this guide we have no difficulty in offering a similar key to his method.

Arrange the numbers, 1 to 25, in arithmetical progression in horizontal rows in the following manner:—

	viii			
	iii	1	2	3
	4	5	6	
7	8	9	vii	
			ii	

		xvii						
		xxiii	xxiv					
		iv	v	1	2	3	4	5
		x	6	7	8	9	10	
		11	12	13	14	15		
	16	17	18	19	20	xvi		
21	22	23	24	25	xxi	xxii		
					ii	iii		
						ix		

Transpose the numbers outside the square to their corresponding positions inside of the square: the 3 to iii, and 7 to vii, in the square of three; and the 4, 5, 10; 16, 21, 22 to the iv, v, x; xvi, xxi, xxii, in the square of five. Then, taking the middle column as correct, transpose the upper number of the first column on the right of centre 2, to the bottom of that column, ii; the two upper numbers of the second column of the square of five, 3 and 5, to bottom of that column, iii and ix; the lowest number of first column on the left of centre, 24 to the top of that column, xxiv; and the two lowest numbers of second column, 17 and 23, to top of that column, xvii and xxiii. Then, in like manner transpose 4, 5 and 10 on right side to iv, v and x on left; and 16, 21 and 22 on left side to xvi, xxi and xxii on right; and the square is complete when the perpendicular columns of each square are pushed into position.

A still easier way, because involving only one change is obtained by placing the numbers seriatim in a

		2
viii	1	6
3	5	7
4	9	ii
8		

				3
			2	9
xvii	xxiv	1	8	15
xxiii	5	7	14	16
4	6	13	20	22
10	12	19	21	iii
11	18	25	ii	ix
17	24			
23				

diagonal direction, beginning from top of central column, and completing each diagonal row before commencing another. When such row is completed, the next row must commence under the last number of the row above it; and, so on, till the five rows are completed. The numbers outside of the square are then put in their proper places and the square is complete.

Another method was invented by Poignard, and improved by M. de la Hire, which, however, it is not necessary to give, as the following method, based upon it, will, I think, be found more simple.

Form two squares, one of numbers in an arithmetical progression; the other, of multiples of those numbers, but substituting a cipher for the highest number, and disposing them in a different order to the first square.

In the first square make the first vertical column correspond with the top horizontal row, and then complete each row in the same order as the top one.

1	2	3	4	5
2	3	4	5	1
3	4	5	1	2
4	5	1	2	3
5	1	2	3	4

20	15	10	5	0
0	20	15	10	5
5	0	20	15	10
10	5	0	20	15
15	10	5	0	20

In the second square reverse the order of the top row for the first column, and then complete each row in the same order as the top one.

Now add these two squares together, and the result will be a magic square.

21	17	13	9	5
2	23	19	15	6
8	4	25	16	12
14	10	1	22	18
20	11	7	3	24

By changing the order of the numbers in the second square, an endless variety of magic squares might be found. It was, probably, in this way that Caetano Gilardono framed the following magic square which is on an incised tablet let into a wall at the Villa Albani, at Rome.

15	58	29	34	63	49	74	41	6
7	27	31	81	23	76	80	18	26
38	8	30	71	47	20	21	78	56
73	19	25	42	10	33	50	65	52
22	55	72	1	45	60	28	16	70
79	35	39	66	2	48	17	24	59
14	64	69	12	77	3	51	68	11
46	36	61	53	40	43	4	54	32
75	67	13	9	62	37	44	5	57

Lector si doctus admirator si ignarus scito, Quadratus hic mathematico constructus ab uno usque ad octoginta unum 3321 unitates includit qualibet ipsius columnæ tam in linea plana quam in recta et transversali unitates 369 quæ ductæ per novem easdem 3321 unitates restituunt et appellatur maximus quia maximam possidet extensionem. Vale.

Caietanus Gilardonus Romanus philotechnos inventor. A.D. MDCCLXVI.

XXXII.

EVEN SQUARES.

WHOSE HALVES ARE EVEN.

The most simple example is that invented by Agrippa. It is a square of four, containing sixteen cells. This square has afforded an amusing puzzle in almost every household. Place the numbers in their natural order.

1	2	3	4
5	6	7	8
9	10	11	12
13	14	15	16

1	15	14	4
12	6	7	9
8	10	11	5
13	3	2	16

Then change the top and bottom central numbers alternately, the 2 and 15; and the 3 and 14; then the left and right central numbers, the 5 and 12; and the 8 and 9; and we get a magic square.

It will be observed that the numbers on the two diagonals, 1, 6, 11, 16, and 4, 7, 10 and 13 remain unchanged. Consequently, we form the magic square, beginning at 1, passing over all cells not on a diagonal; so we get 1, 4, 6, 7, 10, 11, and 13, 16. We then begin at the bottom and work backwards towards the top, 2, 3, 5, 8, 9, 12, 14 and 15; which is, of course, the easiest and most simple way, and which will apply to all even squares whose halves are even.

The combinations of this square are wonderful, all of which amount to 34. We begin with the four horizontal and four perpendicular rows; we then take the two diagonals; then the two diamonds, 1, 7, 16, 10; and 4, 6, 13, 11; then the squares, 1, 4, 16, 13; 6, 7, 11, 10; 1, 15, 6, 12; 14, 4, 9, 7; 8, 10, 3, 13; 11, 5, 16, 2; 15, 9, 2, 8; 14, 5, 3, 12; 1, 14, 11, 8; 15, 4, 5, 10; 12, 7, 2, 13; 6, 9, 16, 3: then the oblongs, 15, 14, 2, 3; 9, 5, 8, 12; 1, 15, 10, 8; 14, 4, 5, 11; 12, 6, 3, 13; 7, 9, 16, 2; 1, 14, 7, 12; 8, 11, 2, 13; 15, 4, 9, 6; 5, 16, 3, 10; 14, 9, 3, 8; 5, 2, 12, 15: and then the rhomboids, 1, 15, 2, 16; 14, 4, 13, 3; 4, 9, 8, 13; 5, 16, 1, 12; 1, 14. 3, 16; 15, 4, 13, 2; 4, 5, 12, 13; 9, 16, 1, 8; 12, 6, 11, 5; 7, 9, 8, 10; 14, 7, 10, 3; 11, 2, 15, 6; 12, 7, 10, 5; 6, 9, 8, 11; 14, 11, 6, 3; 7, 2, 15, 10; 15, 7, 10, 2; 14, 6, 11, 3; 9, 11, 6, 8; 5, 7, 10, 12: in all 56 combinations of 34 each.

So with any larger squares whose halves are equal, we first fill up the diagonals, passing over the other cells, and then beginning at the bottom, and working backwards and above, we fill in the other numbers.

1			4	5			8
	10	11			14	15	
	18	19			22	23	
25			28	29			32
33			36	37			40
	42	43			46	47	
	50	51			54	55	
57			60	61			64

1	63	62	4	5	59	58	8
56	10	11	53	52	14	15	49
48	18	19	45	44	22	23	41
25	39	38	28	29	35	34	32
33	31	30	36	37	27	26	40
24	42	43	21	20	46	47	17
16	50	51	13	12	54	55	9
57	7	6	60	61	3	2	64

Ozanam gives us another method, but far less simple: he places the higher and lower numbers in corresponding

	1	2	3	4	4	3	2	1	
ROWS	1	2	3	4	5	6	7	8	ROWS
I.	64	63	62	61	60	59	58	57	VIII.
	4	1	2	3	3	2	1	4	
II.	9	10	11	12	13	14	15	16	VII.
	56	55	54	53	52	51	50	49	
	3	4	1	2	2	1	4	3	
III.	17	18	19	20	21	22	23	24	VI.
	48	47	46	45	44	43	42	41	
	2	3	4	1	1	4	3	2	
IV.	25	26	27	28	29	30	31	32	V.
	40	39	38	37	36	35	34	33	

groups or couplets, over each of which he places the guide numbers, 1, 2, 3, &c., up to half the root of the square, and then the same numbers in a reversed order, and changing the order of the guide numbers for every row.

To fill up the first four rows, take the bottom number when the guide number is odd, and the upper number when the guide number is even. For the four lower rows, reverse the process, beginning at the bottom, taking the bottom number when even, and the top number when odd. We thus get the following; the result of which is very similar to Agrippa's, many of the numbers being the same, but reversing the diagonals, and changing over the remaining corresponding numbers—

64	2	62	4	5	59	7	57
9	55	11	53	52	14	50	16
48	18	46	20	21	43	23	41
25	39	27	37	36	30	34	32
33	31	35	29	28	38	26	40
24	42	22	44	45	19	47	17
49	15	51	13	12	54	10	56
8	58	6	60	61	3	63	1

On investigating this it will be found that the square is divided into four quarters; and the numbers are filled in in their natural positions in alternate cells only; each quarter beginning at an alternate cell to that of the adjacent quarter.

	2		4	5		7	
9		11			14		16
	18		20	21		23	
25		27			30		32
33		35			38		40
	42		44	45		47	
49		51			54		56
	58		60	61		63	

The remaining numbers are then filled in precisely in the same way, beginning at the bottom. This now is as easy a method as that invented by Agrippa, and a much more simple one than Ozanam's.

Another way of executing the square is by the method discovered by Poignard and De la Hire. First form an arithmetical square, placing the numbers in any order in the first row, reversing them in the next, and so on alternately for half the square; then fill in the lower half, but making the first row coincide with the last of the upper half. Then form a geometrical square with 0 and the multiples of the root, in vertical columns, reversing the numbers in each row, except that the fifth row is to be the same as the fourth.

1	6	5	2	7	4	3	8
8	3	4	7	2	5	6	1
1	6	5	2	7	4	3	8
8	3	4	7	2	5	6	1
8	3	4	7	2	5	6	1
1	6	5	2	7	4	3	8
8	3	4	7	2	5	6	1
1	6	5	2	7	4	3	8

48	8	48	8	8	48	8	48
16	40	16	40	40	16	40	16
32	24	32	24	24	32	24	32
0	56	0	56	56	0	56	0
56	0	56	0	0	56	0	56
24	32	24	32	32	24	32	24
40	16	40	16	16	40	16	40
8	48	8	48	48	8	48	8

Adding these together forms a magic square:—

49	14	53	10	15	52	11	56
24	43	20	47	42	21	46	17
33	30	37	26	31	36	27	40
8	59	4	63	58	5	62	1
64	3	60	7	2	61	6	57
25	38	29	34	39	28	35	32
48	19	44	23	18	45	22	41
9	54	13	50	55	12	51	16

On examining this we find that the square is divided into two horizontal halves, and the horizontal rows are grouped together according to their distance from the centre; the first and eighth together, the second and seventh, and the fourth and fifth. To begin with the middle. First place two opposites of one division, then two means of the second, then two means of the first, and then two opposites of the second; the order of filling up each being reversed.

8		4			5		1
	3		7	2		6	

Now fill in the first numbers of the other rows: the two extreme ones together, the second and seventh, and the third and sixth. Then reverse the order, completing the third and sixth, then the second and seventh, then the two extremes, and then the central rows.

But we gain nothing by this process: for it is as cumbrous and complicated as that of Poignard and De la Hire. But the fault lies in the confused order adopted by them, which simply shows that a magic square can be formed by any arrangement of the numbers. Let us, therefore, take the natural arrangement of the numbers, in both squares :—

1	2	3	4	5	6	7	8
8	7	6	5	4	3	2	1
1	2	3	4	5	6	7	8
8	7	6	5	4	3	2	1
8	7	6	5	4	3	2	1
1	2	3	4	5	6	7	8
8	7	6	5	4	3	2	1
1	2	3	4	5	6	7	8

0	56	0	56	56	0	56	0
8	48	8	48	48	8	48	8
16	40	16	40	40	16	40	16
24	32	24	32	32	24	32	24
32	24	32	24	24	32	24	32
40	16	40	16	16	40	16	40
48	8	48	8	8	48	8	48
56	0	56	0	0	56	0	56

Then the magic square becomes :—

1	58	3	60	61	6	63	8
16	55	14	53	52	11	50	9
17	42	19	44	45	22	47	24
32	39	30	37	36	27	34	25
40	31	38	29	28	35	26	33
41	18	43	20	21	46	23	48
56	15	54	13	12	51	10	49
57	2	59	4	5	62	7	64

And the result is a most unexpected one, exhibiting a perfectly new arrangement of the numbers, and a more simple method than that of Agrippa. The

1		3			6		8
16		14			11		9
17		19			22		24
32		30			27		25
40		38			35		33
41		43			46		48
56		54			51		49
57		59			62		64

figures are arranged in the first, third, sixth and eighth columns only, but counting in all the vacant squares; and reversing the order in each alternate row: but beginning the fifth row at the further end and reversing the order to complete the square.

It will be seen that in each of these methods the secret consists in balancing the numbers. Any method may be used which has the result of placing the corresponding numbers in opposite cells, taking care at the same time that the order of the march be in just progression. When this is carried out, not only are the opposite numbers complementary to each other, but if we divide the square in two halves perpendicularly, we shall in each horizontal line perceive that there is a constant difference of one between the two inside numbers; a difference of three between the second numbers right and left of the centre; of five between the third numbers right and left; and of seven between the outside numbers: and if we divide the square in two horizontal halves, and examine the vertical columns, we shall find in each case a difference of eight times the former numbers: viz., a difference of 8 between the two central numbers, of 24 in the next; then of 40; and, lastly, of 56, between the outside numbers. But in Poignard and De la Hire's magic square, p. 285, though there is the same correspondence of numbers, they are differently placed in the horizontal rows. This square therefore is not so perfect as the others.

XXXIII.

EVEN SQUARES

WHOSE HALVES ARE UNEVEN.

These squares have hitherto been found much more difficult to execute than the preceding.

One way of accomplishing the task was to reduce the square, whose half is uneven, to one whose half is even, by taking off a border all round. Thus the square of six was reduced to a square of four, with a border round it; and the square of ten to one of eight, and so on. Let us take a square of six: for all such squares, of whatever size, can be done by the same method.

After filling in all the squares seriatim with the natural numbers, make the inner square of four cells magic by leaving the diagonals, and removing and replacing in proper order the other numbers, according to previous rule. We thus get No. 1—

1

1	2	3	4	5	6
7	8	28	27	11	12
13	23	15	16	20	18
19	17	21	22	14	24
25	26	10	9	29	30
31	32	33	34	35	36

2

1	35	34	3	32	6
30	8	28	27	11	7
19	23	15	16	14	24
18	17	21	22	20	13
12	26	9	10	29	25
31	2	4	33	5	36

We now proceed with the borders. Letting the angle cells remain the same, of the four remaining numbers of the top row the first and fourth go to the bottom; and the fourth and first bottom numbers taken away are then made to pair with them, so as to make the same vertical total, 37. The second number of the top, not including the angle, is then changed with the second number of the bottom; the third of top with the second of bottom, and the second of top with the third of bottom. Then with the sides, the first and fourth of left go to the right, and the fourth and first of right pair with them; the third of left side is exchanged with the third of right; the second of left with the third of right; and the third of left with the second of right. Finally, reverse the mean numbers of bottom row of inner square; and the mean numbers of right side: and we then get No. 2.

Poignard and De la Hire devised the following method. They formed an arithmetical and a geometrical square, as before, and added them together:—

5	6	3	4	1	2
2	1	4	3	6	5
5	6	3	4	1	2
5	6	3	4	1	2
2	1	4	3	6	5
5	6	3	4	1	2

24	6	24	24	6	24
0	30	0	0	30	0
12	18	12	12	18	12
18	12	18	18	12	18
30	0	30	30	0	30
6	24	6	6	24	6

29	12	27	28	7	26
2	31	4	3	36	5
17	24	15	16	19	14
23	18	21	22	13	20
32	1	34	33	6	35
11	30	9	10	25	8

In a square of six, or 36 cells, the following modifications were made. The third figure of top line was transferred with the third of bottom line; and the third of left column with the third of right: the four middle numbers of the top row were then reversed; and the four middle numbers of left column; the two middle figures of right column; and the two middle figures of bottom row. Lastly, the two middle figures of top row of inner square were reversed, and the two middle figures of left column.

29	7	28	9	12	26
32	31	3	4	36	5
23	18	15	16	19	20
14	24	21	22	13	17
2	1	34	33	6	35
11	30	10	27	25	8

Both these methods are ingenious, but very complicated; and as so many alterations were made before the result could be obtained, it is impossible to deduce any simpler process from them. We will attempt, therefore, to solve the difficulty by other methods.

A more easy way is to balance the numbers of the four outside rows, and to change the order in the two central rows, as shown :—

1	34	2	35	3	36
28	7	29	8	30	9
24	14	22	16	20	18
13	23	15	21	17	19
12	27	11	26	10	25
33	6	32	5	31	4

17
20

1	32	3	34	5	36
26	7	28	9	30	11
18	20	16	22	14	24
19	17	21	15	23	13
12	29	10	27	8	25
35	6	33	4	31	2

1	96	2	97	3	98	4	99	5	100
86	11	87	12	88	13	89	14	90	15
21	76	22	77	23	78	24	79	25	80
66	31	67	32	68	33	69	34	70	35
41	59	43	57	45	55	47	53	49	51
60	42	58	44	56	46	54	48	52	50
40	65	39	64	38	63	37	62	36	61
75	30	74	29	73	28	72	27	71	26
20	85	19	84	18	83	17	82	16	81
95	10	94	9	93	8	92	7	91	6

54	48	52
47	53	49

On examining the two middle rows it is evident that as in the series 13—18, and 19—24 in the square of six; and of 41—50, and 51—60 in the square of ten, the lowest number of each series begins in the same row, the other row in each square must have a greater number by the number of cells in each row. In the square of six there must be a difference of six between the two middle rows; and in the square of ten a difference of ten: consequently, in the square of six we reverse the numbers 17 and 20, making a difference of 3; and in the square of ten the numbers 54, 48, 52 and 47, 53, 49, making a difference of 5, thus making both rows equal. So in a square of 14, there will be a difference of 14 between the two middle rows: so the numbers 103, 95, 101 and 94, 102, 106 making a difference of 7, have to be reversed to make such a square magic.

Another easy way is to divide the square into as many small squares as the square of half the root of the given square. Thus a square of six cells on every side will be divided into nine small squares, each containing four cells; and a square of ten cells into twenty-five small squares: and these now being squares of an odd number will be filled in according to the rule for odd squares.

But in these small squares of four cells each it is evident that if all these cells are filled in in the order of

1	2
4	3

all the vertical columns will be alike, but the horizontal rows will be alternately too little, and too much. What we have to do, therefore, is to change the vertical numbers of some of the cells, so as to make them equal. Thus, in a square of six cells, on each side, which now is reduced to a square of three, we fill in the three columns in the following order:—

4	2	1	2	4	2	15
1	3	4	3	1	3	15

16	14	33	34	8	6
13	15	36	35	5	7
12	10	17	18	28	26
9	11	20	19	25	27
32	30	1	2	24	22
29	31	4	3	21	23

In a square of ten cells on each side the five columns will be:—

1	3	4	3	1	2	4	3	1	3	25
4	2	1	2	4	3	1	2	4	2	25

In a square of fourteen :—

4	2	4	3	1	2	1	2	1	2	4	3	4	2	35
1	3	1	2	4	3	4	3	4	3	1	2	1	3	35

and so on for squares of any number of cells.

41	43	96	95	25	26	80	79	9	11
44	42	93	94	28	27	77	78	12	10
13	15	48	47	97	98	32	31	61	63
16	14	45	46	100	99	29	30	64	62
65	67	20	19	49	50	84	83	33	35
68	66	17	18	52	51	81	82	36	34
37	39	72	71	1	2	56	55	85	87
40	38	69	70	4	3	53	54	88	86
89	91	24	23	73	74	8	7	57	59
92	90	21	22	76	75	5	6	60	58

XXXIV.

MAGIC SQUARES BEGINNING AT ANY CELL.

We have stated that the ways of forming a magic square are endless: and so there is no difficulty in making such magic square begin at any cell desired. Let us take the magic square of 4 cells on each side, already given. If we transpose one of the rows of such square, or one of the columns, with any other of such rows or columns, the square will still remain magic. The law of combinations shows us the immense number of alterations which may be made, still preserving the property of the magic square. But any equal number of combinations might be made by beginning with any other square of 4 cells, of which many might be formed. By changing the rows and columns of the given square, we obtain:—

1

1	15	14	4
12	6	7	9
8	10	11	5
13	3	2	16

2

13	3	2	16
1	15	14	4
8	10	11	5
12	6	7	9

3

4	9	5	16
14	7	11	2
1	12	8	13
15	6	10	3

4

12	6	7	9
13	3	2	16
8	10	11	5
1	15	14	4

5

15	1	4	14
6	12	9	7
3	13	16	2
10	8	5	11

6

16	4	5	9
13	1	8	12
3	15	10	6
2	14	11	7

7

16	4	9	5
2	14	7	11
13	1	12	8
3	15	6	10

8

2	14	7	11
3	15	6	10
16	4	9	5
13	1	12	8

9

14	15	1	4
2	3	13	16
11	10	8	5
7	6	12	9

10

11	7	14	2
8	12	1	13
5	9	4	16
10	6	15	3

11

5	9	4	16
10	6	15	3
8	12	1	13
11	7	14	2

12

3	6	15	10
16	9	4	5
2	7	14	11
13	12	1	8

13

12	13	8	1
7	2	11	14
9	16	5	4
6	3	10	15

14

5	11	10	8
4	14	15	1
16	2	3	13
9	7	6	12

15

9	6	7	12
16	3	2	13
4	15	12	1
5	10	11	8

16

6	10	3	15
9	5	16	4
7	11	2	14
12	8	13	1

Of these squares only six are magic in their diagonals, 6, 8, 9, 12, 13 and 14.

Although these squares are changed about so as to get the number 1 in every one of the cells, they still obtain a harmonious relation in their movements, as will be exhibited in the following diagrams:—

1 . 14

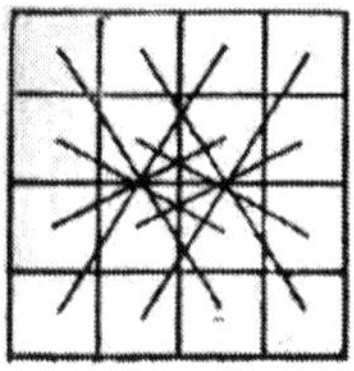

2 6 9 12 13

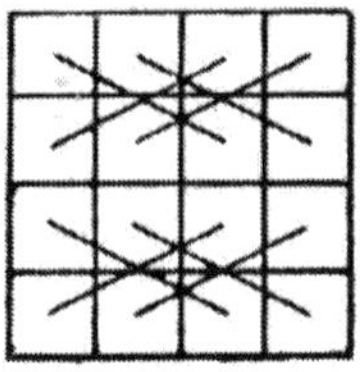

3

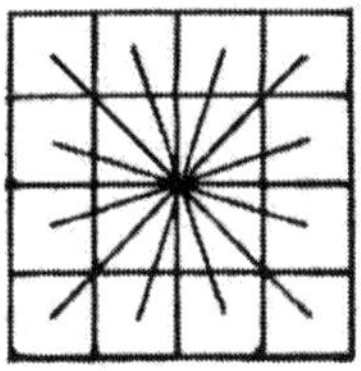

7 8 15

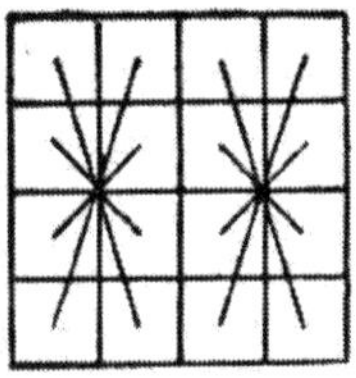

4 5

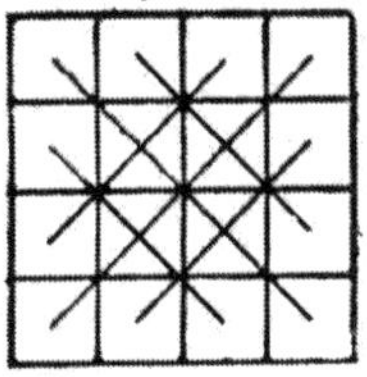

10 11 16

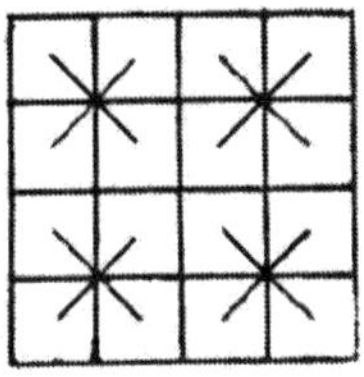

The following is an example of the variety which may be made in these squares. Arrange the numbers in squares of five, overlapping each other, as in the following diagram. We have entered only half the numbers so as more easily to distinguish the squares.

1			14	2			15
	24	27			21	28	
32			19	31			18
	9	6			12	5	
3			16	4			13
	22	25			23	26	
30			17	29			20
	11	8			10	7	

On filling in the other numbers we get this result :—

1	59	56	14	2	60	53	15
46	24	27	33	47	21	28	34
32	38	41	19	31	37	44	18
51	9	6	64	50	12	5	63
3	57	54	16	4	58	55	13
48	22	25	35	45	23	26	36
30	40	43	17	29	39	42	20
49	11	8	62	52	10	7	61

Here it will be found that not only are all the horizontal rows, and the vertical columns, and the two diagonals alike, amounting to 260 : but the half row, and the half columns, and the half diagonals, are also alike, amounting to 130 ; and each of the sixteen small squares, into which the square is divided, also amounts to 130. It is, therefore, the most perfect magic square which can be constructed. One nearly as perfect will

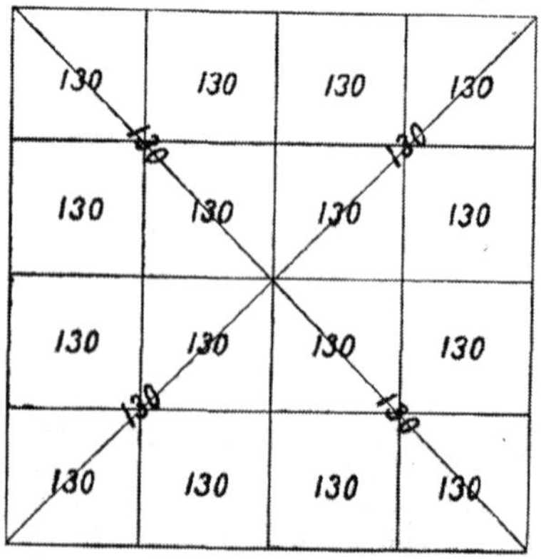

be found further on, invented by Mr. Beverley, the numbers of which are regulated by the knight's move. But in that the diagonals are unequal.

XXXV.

MAGIC SQUARES IN COMPARTMENTS.

Any square which is capable of being subdivided into a number of compartments, the cells of which can form a magic square, may, by the arrangement of such compartments or smaller squares, be made magic also. Thus, a square of nine, or of 81 cells, may not only be

49	63	62	52	129	143	142	132	17	31	30	20
60	54	55	57	140	134	135	137	28	22	23	25
56	58	59	53	136	138	139	133	24	26	27	21
61	51	50	64	141	131	130	144	29	19	18	32
33	47	46	36	65	79	78	68	97	111	110	100
44	38	39	41	76	70	71	73	108	102	103	105
40	42	43	37	72	74	75	69	104	106	107	101
45	35	34	48	77	67	66	80	109	99	98	112
113	127	126	116	1	15	14	4	81	95	94	84
124	118	119	121	12	6	7	9	92	86	87	89
120	122	123	117	8	10	11	5	88	90	91	85
125	115	114	128	13	3	2	16	93	83	82	96

made a magic square, but it may be divided into nine compartments of 9 cells each, each of which compartments or smaller squares can be made magic: and the compartments themselves can be so arranged as to make the square itself magic; a square of twelve, or 144 cells, is divisible into nine magic compartments of 16 cells; or of sixteen magic compartments of 9 cells

4	9	2	130	135	128	121	126	119	31	36	29
3	5	7	129	131	133	120	122	124	30	32	34
8	1	6	134	127	132	125	118	123	35	28	33
103	108	101	49	54	47	58	63	56	76	81	74
102	104	106	48	50	52	57	59	61	75	77	79
107	100	105	53	46	51	62	55	60	80	73	78
67	72	65	85	90	83	94	99	92	40	45	38
66	68	70	84	86	88	93	95	97	39	41	43
71	64	69	89	82	87	98	91	96	44	37	42
112	117	110	22	27	20	13	18	11	139	144	137
111	113	115	21	23	25	12	14	16	138	140	142
116	109	114	26	19	24	17	10	15	143	136	141

each; a square of fifteen, or 225 cells, into nine magic compartments of 25 cells each; or of twenty-five compartments of 9 cells, and be itself magic; and a square of sixteen, or 256 cells, into sixteen compartments of 16 cells, and be itself magic.

XXXVI.

MAGIC SQUARES IN BORDERS.

To form these commence with the outer border, half of the numbers of which are to be taken from the lowest series, and the other half from the highest. The border of the next square will be filled up in like manner; one half of the numbers being composed of the next lowest numbers in succession, and the other half of the next highest; and so on to the centre square, the numbers of which, will, of course, be the mean numbers of the whole, and which numbers will be arranged according to the preceding rules for magic squares. To arrange the numbers in the borders place the lowest number in one corner, and the highest in the opposite angle. In the even squares the other two angles are to be filled in with their natural numbers, or those which would fall into them were all the numbers placed seriatim. This will be found a great advantage in the even squares, as it gives four numbers to start with instead of two, as in the odd squares. For other cells the sum of any opposite numbers, whether vertical or horizontal, is to be equal to the sum of these two numbers. The numbers must then be so balanced that the sum of each side makes up the number of the square, which in a square of ten is 505, and in a square of nine is 369. For the rest it is perfectly indifferent in what order the numbers are placed, when once the series is discovered, as each of these numbers with its complement makes up the same sum.

1	3	6	71	70	72	68	73	5
2	17	21	60	55	58	57	19	80
4	18	29	47	50	48	31	64	78
8	20	30	40	45	38	52	62	74
66	59	49	39	41	43	33	23	16
67	54	46	44	37	42	36	28	15
69	56	51	35	32	34	53	26	13
75	63	61	22	27	24	25	65	7
77	79	76	11	12	10	14	9	81

ODD SQUARES.

1	95	99	89	5	9	88	98	11	10
17	19	76	80	70	28	24	81	26	84
87	79	33	67	66	37	62	38	22	14
18	74	42	43	57	56	46	59	27	83
15	72	40	54	48	49	51	61	29	86
4	30	65	50	52	53	47	36	71	97
85	23	60	55	45	44	58	41	78	16
93	32	63	34	35	64	39	68	69	8
94	75	25	21	31	73	77	20	82	7
91	6	2	12	96	92	13	3	90	100

EVEN SQUARES.

XXXVII.

HOLLOW AND FANCY SQUARES, AND MAGIC CIRCLES.

Many ingenious combinations of Magic Squares have been invented from time to time. Indeed, it would be curious to see a collection of fancy squares. The Chev. Violle, is pre-eminent for such discoveries. It would take too much space, and be trespassing too much on his labours were we to give all the varieties of these squares which he has discovered. It will suffice to give the following as examples. We give below the full title of his work to show its comprehensiveness.[1]

56	2	113	4	115	121	117	8	119	10	6
12										110
33		58	92	27	97	29	96	28		89
34		42						80		88
55		47		60	73	50		75		67
11		31		51	61	71		91		111
77		69		72	49	62		53		45
78		86						36		44
99		94	30	95	25	93	26	64		23
100										22
116	120	9	118	7	1	5	114	3	112	66

[1] Chevalier B. Violle, Traité complet des Carrés Magiques, pairs et impairs simples et composés, à bordures, campartimens, croix, chassis, équerrés, bandes détachées; &c., ainsi d'un Traité des Cuhes Magiques, et d'un Essai sur les Cercles Magiques. 2 tomes 8vo., et 1 tome fol. Paris 1837-8.

82	35	87	81	42	33	36	80	86	41	68
57					62					64
65					60					58
38					79					66
88					51					44
47	72	50	53	74	61	70	48	52	69	75
34					71					78
84					43					56
37					63					83
85					59					39
54	76	46	49	67	89	77	55	45	73	40

	12					53	
61	62	60	6	9	51	10	1
	11					54	
	8					57	
	58					7	
	2					63	
4	55	5	59	56	14	3	64
	52					13	

	24		29	36		41	
20	9	46	55	54	37	12	27
	25		35	30		40	
21	52	48	14	15	43	49	18
44	16	17	50	51	22	13	47
	42		32	33		23	
45	53	19	11	10	28	56	38
	39		34	31		26	

1	10	48	39	47	26	4
12	37	14	9	36	29	38
45	16	6	32	7	27	42
28	17	30	25	20	33	22
8	40	43	11	44	24	5
35	21	31	41	19	13	15
46	34	3	18	2	23	49

In the last example it will be noticed that the cells in shade form the magic square of four similar to the first of the Even Squares whose halves are even.

The following example of a *Magic Circle* was invented by Dr. Franklin. In it the numbers in each of the intersecting circles, having 12, A, B, C, or D, as centres, added to 12, make 360. The half of any of these, as divided by either the perpendicular or horizontal line, added to the half of 12, makes 180. The numbers of any *cuneus* added to 12, make 360; and the half of any *cuneus* added to the half of 12, makes 180. Any four adjacent numbers, forming a square, as 73, 15, 72, 14, with half of 12, make 180; as also any four opposite numbers forming a square, as 73, 14, 41, 46, added to the half of 12.

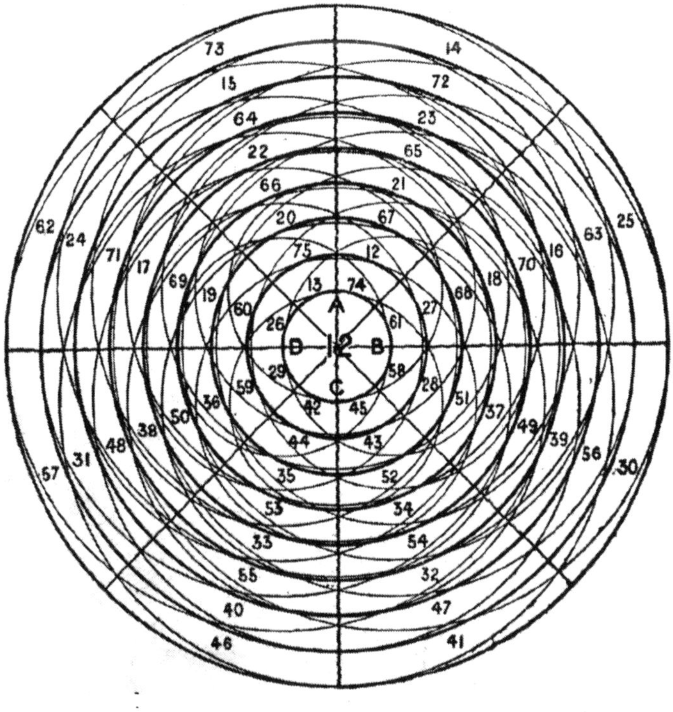

The following Magic Pentagon has been invented by M. Frolow,[1] exhibiting a spider's web.

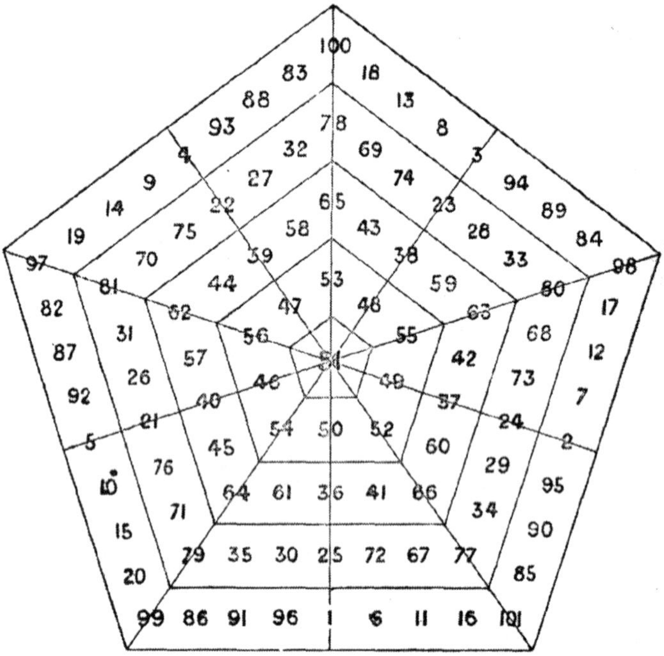

It will be observed that the five sides of each pentagon are all equal, and that the five diameters, from one angle to the centre of the opposite side, are each 459, which is nine times the central number 51, which is also the mean number, the series being 1—101. And, further, that the inner pentagon is 510, or 10 times the mean number; the next pentagon 1020, or 20 times the mean; the next 1530, or 30 times the mean; and the outside pentagon 2040, or 40 times the mean.

[1] *Les Carrés Magiques*, 8vo., Paris, 1886.

XXXVIII.

THE KNIGHT'S TOUR.

Ozanam—Récréations Mathématiques et Physiques -	1750
Euler—Histoire de l'Academie Royale des Sciences et Belles Lettres - - - - - -	1766
Ozanam—Physical Recreations, translated by Hutton with additions - - - - - -	1803
La Corso del cavallo per tutti gli Scacchi della Scacchiera—Bologna - - - - - -	1766
Lettre addressée aux auteurs du Journal Encyclopédique sur un problème de l'Echiquier. Prague - -	1773
Collini—Solution du problème du Cavalier - -	1775
Essai sur les problèmes de Situation. Rouen - -	1783
Dollinger—24 Verschiedene arten den Springer - -	1806
Chess, an attempt to annalyze the Knight's move - -	1821
Von Warnsdorf—Des Sprunge's einfachste und allgemeinste Losung - - - - - -	1823
Billig, E. Der Rossensprung - - - - -	1831
Ciccolini—Del Cavallo degli Scacchi . - -	1836
Dr. Roget—Philosophical Magazine - - -	1840
Le Palamède—Seconde Series, vols. ii, iv, and vi - -	1842-6
Tomlinson—Amusements in Chess - - -	1845
Schachzeitung—Vols. i, ii, iv, v, vii, and ix - -	1846-54
Brede—Almanach for Freunde von Schachspiel - -	n.d.

The attempt to cover all the squares of the chess-board with a knight's move, without going over the same square a second time, is, perhaps, as old as the invention of the game itself. The anonymous author of the Persian MS. in the Library of the Royal Asiatic Society, No. 260, written subsequently to 899, writes:—"Finally, I will show you how to move a knight from any individual square on the board, so that it may cover each of the remaining squares in as many moves;

and, finally rest on that square whence it started. I will also show you how the same thing may be done by limiting yourself only to one half, or even to one quarter of the board." Unfortunately, the MS. breaks off there. Another MS. in the British Museum, No. 16,856, written about 1550, but copied and abridged from an older work, also contains a description of this move.

At first the difficulty was how to perform the task in any manner, then to find out the principle of doing so; then to make the course re-entering; then to begin and end at any given square; and, finally, to make the course a magic square.

The mathematician Euler was the first, in modern times, to improve on the random efforts of his predecessors, by preparing an ingenious though sometimes complicated and laborious process of effecting his purpose. He first filled up as many cells of the square as he could,[1] as in the following figure, in which two cells are vacant, which we will call *a* and *b*.

34	21	54	9	32	19	48	7
55	10	33	20	53	8	31	18
22	35	62	*a*	40	49	6	47
11	56	41	50	59	52	17	30
36	23	58	61	42	39	46	5
57	12	25	38	51	60	29	16
24	37	2	43	14	27	4	45
1	*b*	13	26	3	44	15	28

[1] This forms a very good game for anyone who has not tried it.

On examining these numbers he perceived that 62, the last number, governs the cell 9; and that 10 governs *a*. He, therefore, took the series 1—9; then crossed into 62, from which he traversed backwards all the numbers successively till he came to 10, from which he was enabled to pass into the upper blank cell *a*. This course is represented by 1—9; 62—10: *a*. He perceived also that some of the other numbers would have given him the same result, as 1—53: 62—54: *a*. And 1—53: 62—56; *a*.

Another cell governed by *a* is 58, and 57 governs *b*. He therefore got 1—9: 62—58: *a*: 10—57: *b*; thus producing the square.

40	27	60	9	38	25	54	7
61	16	39	26	59	8	37	24
28	41	10	15	46	55	6	53
17	62	47	56	13	58	23	36
42	29	14	11	48	45	52	5
63	18	31	44	57	12	35	22
30	43	2	49	20	33	4	51
1	64	19	32	3	50	21	34

His next desire was to make it re-entering. After several other transmutations he at length obtained from the last square 1—9: 46—64: 31—45: 22—19: 30—23: 12—17: 10, 11, 18, thus forming a re-entering square which would enable him to cover the board when beginning at any square he chose.

38	51	24	9	36	53	18	7
25	60	37	52	23	8	35	54
50	39	62	59	10	19	6	17
61	26	11	20	57	22	55	34
40	49	58	63	12	43	16	5
27	64	29	42	21	56	33	44
48	41	2	13	46	31	4	15
1	28	47	30	3	14	45	32

This method, however, was too elaborate for general use. At length it was perceived that the board of 64 cells resolved itself into four quarters of 16 cells each; and that these 16 cells arranged themselves into two squares and two diamonds, forming a knight's move between each point. Dr. Roget communicated this

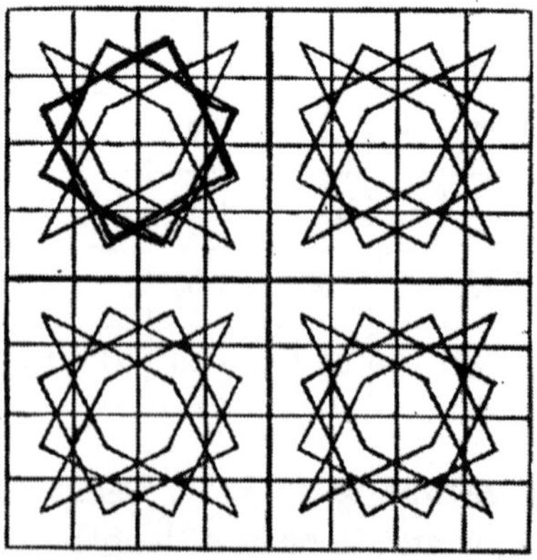

discovery to the *Philosophical Magazine and Journal*, vol. xvi, in a letter dated 1840; and he thought so much of it that he had a card printed for circulation among his friends with this diagram, having the squares in black and the diamonds in red, and with the figures in black and red on the diagram, and not as shown here separately; and underneath this "Key to the Knight's Move as a Magic Square" was printed —"With best compliments of the author."

22	11	36	53	20	13	38	51
35	54	21	12	37	52	17	14
10	23	56	33	16	19	50	39
55	34	9	24	49	40	15	18
26	7	48	57	32	1	42	63
47	58	25	8	41	62	31	2
6	27	60	45	4	29	64	43
59	46	5	28	61	44	3	30
260	260	260	260	260	260	260	260

Naturally such a star can also be formed in the centre, and we shall presently see such a central star made use of in one of the following problems.

The reader must make himself fully conversant with this process before he attempts any further analysis. He will note how in forming each diamond care is taken to fill up the outer cells before the more central ones, and that in forming either squares or diamonds care is taken to end the figure where it is most easy to pass on to the next quarter.

Reasoning upon this principle, and perceiving, as we have shown, that the last-filled cell is exactly a Knight's move from the first cell, or starting point,

Dr. Roget conceived that it is immaterial in what cell the march is commenced; and that by skipping some cells connected with the terminal one, but still preserving the same order of squares and diamonds, he would be able, after completing the other figures, to fill up the cells so omitted, and thus end in any desired cell, provided that that cell is of a different colour to the starting cell.

As this exercise forms a very good game or puzzle to show a friend, we will take a few instances; and in order to explain the method more easily, we will divide the board into four quarters.

iii	iv
ii	i

To begin and end in the same series of diamonds, but in the first and third quarters, say 1 and 64.

It is evident that it is more difficult to end at the last quarter than at the second or fourth, because the order of forming these diamonds i, ii, iii, iv, will be interrupted in the middle. There are two ways of proceeding, one by forming diamonds in i, ii, and iv, leaving out iii; the other by leaving out the diamonds iii and iv to the last.

In the first method we complete diamonds i and ii, form a square in iii, and a diamond in iv, then squares in iv, i and ii. We now form diamonds in ii, i, iv, iii; and squares in iv, i, ii, iii; leaving out cells of 59 and 60 (which would have been filled up with 52 and 55), because they lead to the last diamond in iii: then fill up these numbers 59 and 60, and thus enter upon the last diamond.

63	56	11	44	13	46	17	38
10	43	64	57	18	39	14	47
55	62	41	12	45	16	37	20
42	9	58	61	40	19	48	15
7	54	25	32	3	60	21	36
28	31	8	59	24	33	2	49
53	6	29	26	51	4	35	22
30	27	52	5	34	23	50	1

In the second method we complete diamonds in i and ii; form squares in iii, iv, i and ii; diamonds in ii, i, iv, iii; squares in iv, i, ii, iii; leaving out, while doing so, the places of 55 and 56—which would have been filled up with 48 and 49—for the same reason as before, and then fill up 55 and 56, so as to lead to diamonds in iv and iii.

63	52	11	40	59	42	15	34
10	39	64	53	14	35	58	43
51	62	37	12	41	60	33	16
38	9	54	61	36	13	44	57
7	50	21	28	3	56	17	32
24	27	8	55	20	29	2	45
49	6	25	22	47	4	31	18
26	23	48	5	30	19	46	1

To begin and end in adjoining cells and adjoining quarters, both diamonds, say 1 and 64.

Complete diamonds ii, i, iv, 3; and squares ii, i, iv, 3; then diamonds iv and i, leaving out cell 56 which ought to have been filled in with 40, because this cell commands cell 57 which leads up to the last diamond, then squares i, iv, iii, 2; then by means of 56 proceed to fill up the remaining diamonds ii, iii.

62	31	48	13	34	27	46	11
49	14	63	32	47	12	35	26
30	61	16	51	28	33	10	45
15	50	29	64	9	44	25	36
60	17	52	1	56	21	40	7
53	2	57	20	43	8	37	24
18	59	4	55	22	39	6	41
3	54	19	58	5	42	23	38

Another way, making a star in the centre.

Form diamond in centre, and run round the board with half squares, then form square in middle, which will complete these half squares. Then run round the board with half diamonds, and then with half squares. Form square in middle completing the half squares; then half diamonds in ii and iii, and whole diamonds in iv and i: thus making a half central diamond. Then complete the half diamonds in ii and iii, and centre.

52	43	10	29	54	33	12	31
9	28	53	44	11	30	55	34
42	51	2	19	46	57	32	13
27	8	45	64	3	20	35	56
50	41	18	1	58	47	14	21
7	26	63	48	17	4	59	36
40	49	24	5	38	61	22	15
25	6	39	62	23	16	37	60

To begin and end in adjoining quarters, and adjoining cells, both in squares, say 1 and 64.

Complete squares ii, i, iv, iii; diamonds iv, i, ii, iii; squares iv, i, ii, iii; leaving out 64 which ought to have been filled in with 48, place 48 in iv, so as to begin the last course of diamonds in iii, and then finish in 64.

51	46	13	32	53	34	11	18
14	31	52	47	12	17	54	35
45	50	29	16	33	48	19	10
30	15	64	49	20	9	36	55
63	44	1	28	59	40	7	22
2	27	60	41	8	21	56	37
43	62	25	4	39	58	23	6
26	3	42	61	24	5	38	57

To begin and end in the same quarter, and in adjoining cells, both squares. say 1 and 64.

Form squares i. ii. iii. iv: diamonds iv. iii. ii. i:

squares ii, iii, iv. Then cover 45, leaving the rest of the square, and proceed with diamonds i, ii, iii, iv, from the last point of which complete square in i.

22	11	40	57	20	13	42	59
39	56	21	12	41	58	17	14
10	23	54	37	16	19	60	43
55	38	9	24	61	44	15	18
26	7	36	53	32	3	62	47
35	52	25	8	45	48	31	2
6	27	50	33	4	29	46	63
51	34	5	28	49	64	1	30

To begin and end in opposite corners, say 1 and 64.

Form diamonds i, ii, iii, iv; and squares i, ii, iii, iv. Then, as 64 is at the point of the diamond, close up one of the approaches 33, and form the squares iv, iii, ii, i; and diamonds i, ii, iii, iv, previously filling up 50.

11	40	27	60	13	36	31	64
26	59	12	39	30	33	14	35
41	10	61	28	37	16	63	32
58	25	38	9	62	29	34	15
7	42	21	50	3	46	17	52
24	57	8	45	20	51	2	47
43	6	55	22	49	4	53	18
56	23	44	5	54	19	48	1

XXXIX.

THE KNIGHT'S MAGIC SQUARE.

The first approach to a Knight's magic square was to place the numbers in such a manner that there should be a constant difference of the same amount between any two corresponding numbers. By the system adopted by Euler, that mathematician perceived that if he could go on to 32 without entering any of the corresponding cells, he could then fill up these corresponding cells seriatim, beginning at that corresponding to 1, and thus have a constant difference of 32 between any corresponding numbers. To accomplish this he endeavoured, at random, to fill in as many consecutive cells as he could, filling in the corresponding numbers at the same time. He thus obtained the numbers 1—19 and 33—51. Then beginning again at 1 and 33, he filled in, in a retrograde manner, the numbers 64—58 and 32—26.

10	29	48	35	8	31	46	33
49	36	9	30	47	34	7	58
28	11				45	32	19
37	50				6	59	44
12	27	38				18	5
51	64	13				43	60
26	39	2	15	62	41	4	17
1	14	63	40	3	16	61	42

The twelve vacant cells he gradually filled in by transposition, in the manner already indicated, and as we shall see exhibited again presently. He thus obtained the following:—

A Knight's magic square, the difference between any opposite numbers of which is equal to 32.

14	59	42	35	16	31	54	33
41	36	15	58	55	34	17	30
60	13	56	43	18	53	32	7
37	40	19	12	57	6	29	52
20	61	38	25	44	51	8	5
39	64	21	50	11	24	45	28
62	49	2	23	26	47	4	9
1	22	63	48	3	10	27	46

Having obtained one, his system easily enabled him to obtain others, of which he gives us several examples, of which the following is a specimen. Instead of 1—32, take the numbers 3—34. Now as 34 governs 7, we obtain 3—7, and 34—8, which reversed is 8—34 and 7—3. But 3 governs 24, therefore we get 8—24, 3—7 34—25; and their opposites 40—56, 35—39; 2, 1 64—57.

Employing the same process, he then attempted

To fill in a square with a Knight's move, so that the difference between any opposite numbers shall be 32; and the first 32 numbers shall be on the same half of the board.

To accomplish this he filled up as many numbers as

he could in one half of the board, getting as far as 28: to the remaining four cells he attached the letters, *a*, *b*, *c*, *d*.

							33
1	*a*	*b*	28	7	14	19	16
24	27	8	*c*	20	17	6	13
9	2	25	22	11	4	15	18
26	23	10	3	*d*	21	12	5

He began by observing that as 28 governs 27, 25, 11 and 17: he was able to take choice of any one of the following orders of progression:—1—25, 28—26; or 1—11, 28—12; or 1—17, 28—18. Selecting one of them, and then making many more transpositions, he obtained—1—8; 23—21; 18—20; *b*, 24—28; 17—19; *a*, *c*, and *d*. But as this did not connect itself with 33, he made other transpositions, till he got—1—8; 23—21; 18—20; *b*, 24—28; 17—15; *d*, *c*, *a*; 9—14; giving this result:—

37	62	43	56	35	60	41	50
44	55	36	61	42	49	34	59
63	38	53	46	57	40	51	48
54	45	64	39	52	47	58	33
1	26	15	20	7	32	13	22
16	19	8	25	14	21	6	31
27	2	17	10	29	4	23	12
18	9	28	3	24	11	30	5

He then, by the manner shown in the last example, obtained several varieties of this, which the reader will understand.

To fill up a square with a Knight's move, so that the difference between any opposite numbers shall be 16.

In Tomlinson's "Amusements in Chess," p. 127, is an example of such a square, but of which the author says—"This route is not a re-entering one; and we do not think it could be made so, with a constant difference of 16."

17	8	43	38	15	10	45	36
42	39	16	9	44	37	14	11
7	18	41	48	5	12	35	46
40	49	6	19	34	47	4	13
29	20	63	50	3	22	33	56
62	51	28	21	64	57	2	23
27	30	53	60	25	32	55	58
52	61	26	31	54	59	24	1

The difficulty is solved easily by Euler's process, 64 governs 31, and 31 of course governs 32, the position of the last desired cell,

17	8	52	58	15	10	51	60
54	57	16	9	52	59	14	11
7	18	55	48	5	12	61	50
56	47	6	19	62	49	4	13
29	20	33	46	3	22	63	40
34	45	28	21	32	39	2	23
27	30	43	36	25	64	41	38
44	35	26	31	42	37	24	1

Which being re-entering, can be varied now in 63 different ways.

To fill up a square with a Knight's move, so that the difference between any opposite numbers shall be 8.

To do this we have to take care that 9 shall be in the opposite cell to 1; 25 to 17; 41 to 33; and 57 to 49.

18	11	34	59	32	13	46	63
35	58	17	12	47	62	31	14
10	19	60	33	16	29	64	45
57	36	9	20	61	48	15	30
22	7	40	53	28	1	44	49
37	56	21	8	41	52	27	2
6	23	54	39	4	25	50	43
55	38	5	24	51	42	3	26

The next approach to a magic square was effected by arranging the numbers in such a manner that all the vertical columns shall be equal.

To fill up a square with a Knight's move, so that the difference between any opposite numbers shall be 32; the first 32 numbers being in the same half of the board; and all the vertical columns of each half shall be equal; the whole column being 260.

1	30	3	20	5	24	11	26
16	19	14	29	12	27	8	23
31	2	17	4	21	6	25	10
18	15	32	13	28	9	22	7
33	62	35	52	37	56	43	58
48	51	46	61	44	59	40	55
63	34	49	36	53	38	57	42
50	47	64	45	60	41	54	39
260	260	260	260	260	260	260	260

XL.

We now come to the last and most difficult operation of the Knight's tour.

To form a Magic square with a Knight's move, so that all the perpendicular columns and horizontal rows shall be equal, beginning at any square of the chessboard.

This was first accomplished by Mr. Beverley, and was published by him in the *Philosophical Magazine*, in 1848. It is not only the first discovered, but is at the same time the most perfect. For not only is the entire square magic, but it divides into four magic quarter squares, and each of these with four minor quarter magic squares. It divides also into eight perpendicular, and eight horizontal magic parallelograms; and the two halves of any line, whether perpendicular or horizontal, are equal.

1

1	30	47	52	5	28	43	54
48	51	2	29	44	53	6	27
31	46	49	4	25	8	55	42
50	3	32	45	56	41	26	7
33	62	15	20	9	24	39	58
16	19	34	61	40	57	10	23
63	14	17	36	21	12	59	38
18	35	64	13	60	37	22	11

In the following year Herr Carl W . . . s, of P. published another, the discovery of which was celebrated by several poetic effusions in the Schach zeitung.

2

2	11	58	51	30	39	54	15
59	50	3	12	53	14	31	38
10	1	52	57	40	29	16	55
49	60	9	4	13	56	37	32
64	5	24	45	36	41	28	17
23	48	61	8	25	20	33	42
6	63	46	21	44	35	18	27
47	22	7	62	19	26	43	34

In 1862 M. de Jaenisch's elaborate treatise appeared, in which we find the four following solutions :—

3

3	6	59	48	61	10	23	50
58	47	4	7	22	49	62	11
5	2	45	60	9	64	51	24
46	57	8	1	52	21	12	63
31	44	53	20	33	40	25	14
56	19	32	41	28	13	34	37
43	30	17	54	39	36	15	26
18	55	42	29	16	27	38	35

4

18	43	58	3	46	39	22	31
59	2	19	44	21	30	47	38
42	17	4	57	40	45	32	23
1	60	41	20	29	24	37	48
16	5	56	61	52	9	28	33
55	64	13	8	25	36	49	10
6	15	62	53	12	51	34	27
63	54	7	14	35	26	11	50

5

15	2	31	52	17	54	43	46
30	51	16	3	42	45	18	55
1	14	49	32	53	20	47	44
50	29	4	13	48	41	56	19
27	64	33	40	5	12	21	58
36	39	28	61	24	57	6	9
63	26	37	34	11	8	59	22
38	35	62	25	60	23	10	7

6

27	30	3	40	5	42	55	58
2	39	28	31	54	57	6	43
29	26	37	4	41	8	59	56
38	1	32	25	60	53	44	7
15	36	61	52	17	24	9	46
64	51	16	33	12	45	18	21
35	14	49	62	23	20	47	10
50	63	34	13	48	11	22	19

Lastly, the author discovered the three following some thirty years ago when he was studying these squares :—

7

15	42	55	4	17	6	59	62
54	3	16	43	58	61	18	7
41	14	1	56	5	20	63	60
2	53	44	13	64	57	8	19
51	40	25	32	45	12	21	34
28	31	52	37	24	33	46	9
39	50	29	26	11	48	35	22
30	27	38	49	36	23	10	47

8

42	3	16	55	6	61	18	59
15	54	43	4	17	58	7	62
2	41	56	13	64	5	60	19
53	14	1	44	57	20	63	8
40	31	52	25	12	33	46	21
51	28	37	32	45	24	9	34
30	39	26	49	36	11	22	47
27	50	29	38	23	48	35	10

8*a*

6	47	4	59	10	49	62	23
3	58	7	48	61	22	11	50
46	5	60	1	52	9	24	63
57	2	45	8	21	64	51	12
44	19	32	53	40	13	34	25
31	56	41	20	33	28	37	14
18	43	54	29	16	39	26	35
55	30	17	42	27	36	15	38

In 1884 a French gentleman, of Orleans, published the following in a brochure, under the pseudonym of Palamède :—

9

43	30	53	4	45	28	51	6
54	1	44	29	52	5	48	27
31	42	3	56	25	46	7	50
2	55	32	41	8	49	26	47
63	34	9	24	57	40	15	18
10	23	62	33	16	19	58	39
35	64	21	12	37	60	17	14
22	11	36	61	20	13	38	59

And he formed duplicate arrangements of 2, 3, 4, 5, 6 and 7; and a second one of 4, of beautiful design.

2

2	27	50	43	6	23	62	47
51	42	1	26	63	48	7	22
28	3	44	49	24	5	46	61
41	52	25	4	45	64	21	8
14	29	40	53	20	9	60	35
39	54	13	32	57	36	19	10
30	15	56	37	12	17	34	59
55	38	31	16	33	58	11	18

3

3	58	5	30	55	40	27	42
6	31	2	57	28	43	54	39
59	4	29	8	37	56	41	26
32	7	60	1	44	25	38	53
61	46	17	36	9	52	15	24
18	33	64	45	16	21	12	51
47	62	35	20	49	10	23	14
34	19	48	63	22	13	50	11

4

18	43	54	3	46	39	30	27
55	2	19	44	29	26	47	38
42	17	4	53	40	45	28	31
1	56	41	20	25	32	37	48
16	5	64	57	52	9	24	33
63	60	13	8	21	36	49	10
6	15	58	61	12	51	34	23
59	62	7	14	35	22	11	50

4

46	55	26	3	58	43	6	23
27	2	45	56	5	24	59	42
54	47	4	25	44	57	22	7
1	28	53	48	21	8	41	60
52	33	16	29	40	61	20	9
15	30	49	36	17	12	39	62
34	51	32	13	64	37	10	19
31	14	35	50	11	18	63	38

5

43	2	45	28	39	30	55	18
26	47	42	3	54	19	38	31
1	44	27	46	29	40	17	56
48	25	4	41	20	53	32	37
5	64	21	52	9	36	57	16
24	49	8	61	14	59	12	33
63	6	51	22	35	10	15	58
50	23	62	7	60	13	34	11

6

43	46	3	22	5	60	19	62
2	23	42	45	20	63	6	59
47	44	21	4	57	8	61	18
24	1	48	41	64	17	58	7
49	40	25	32	9	56	15	34
26	29	52	37	16	33	12	55
39	50	31	28	53	10	35	14
30	27	38	51	36	13	54	11

7

43	26	51	2	15	30	39	54
50	3	42	27	40	53	14	31
25	44	1	52	29	16	55	38
4	49	28	41	56	37	32	13
45	24	61	8	17	12	57	36
64	5	48	21	60	33	18	11
23	46	7	62	9	20	35	58
6	63	22	47	34	59	10	19

6[1]

59	38	3	32	5	62	27	34
2	31	60	37	28	33	6	63
39	58	29	4	61	8	35	26
30	1	40	57	36	25	64	7
41	56	13	20	45	52	9	24
16	19	44	53	12	21	46	49
55	42	17	14	51	48	23	10
18	15	54	43	22	11	50	47

On examining these it will be found that the squares are re-entering, with the exception of Mr. Beverley's, Palamèdes' 2, 4, 6, 7 and 9; and Mr. Caldwell's.

As these squares all commence in the same quarter of the board, what we find in this quarter will apply to all the other quarters: and what we find in any quarter will apply to the corresponding cells of that

1				
x	9			
5	2	7		
4	6	8	3	

[1] Was published by Mr. E. C. Caldwell in the "English Mechanic," in 1879.

quarter. Consequently there remains only the cell marked x, the solution from which has not been discovered, and which remains, therefore, for the study and amusement of lovers of chess, and for the exercise of the scientific research of mathematicians.

The following are approximate efforts for the cell x. In each case the changing of two cells would make the square right.

64	33	2	31	60	37	18	15
1	30	61	36	19	16	59	38
34	63	32	3	40	57	14	17
29	4	35	62	13	20	39	58
50	47	28	5	56	41	22	11
27	6	49	46	21	12	55	42
48	51	8	25	44	53	10	23
7	26	45	52	9	24	43	54

50	47	2	31	54	43	18	15
1	30	49	46	19	16	55	42
48	51	32	3	44	53	14	17
29	4	45	52	13	20	41	56
64	33	28	5	40	57	12	21
27	6	61	36	9	24	39	58
34	63	8	25	60	37	22	11
7	26	35	62	23	10	59	38

58	39	2	31	42	55	18	15
1	30	57	40	19	16	43	54
38	59	32	3	56	41	14	17
29	4	37	60	13	20	53	44
64	33	28	5	52	45	12	21
27	6	61	36	9	24	51	48
34	63	8	25	46	49	22	11
7	26	35	62	23	10	47	50

6	59	2	29	38	27	36	63
1	30	5	60	33	64	39	26
58	7	32	3	28	37	62	35
31	4	57	8	61	34	25	40
56	9	52	45	24	41	18	15
51	48	55	12	17	14	21	42
10	53	46	49	44	23	16	19
47	50	11	54	13	20	43	22

XLI.

INDIAN MAGIC SQUARES.

Rev. A. H. Frost, M.A.—Invention of Magic Cubes and Construction of Magic Squares. In "Quarterly Journal of pure and applied Mathmatics," No. 25 - - 1865
—Supplementary Note on Nasik Cubes, ditto, No. 29 1866
—On the construction and properties of Nasik Squares and Cubes - - - - Cambridge, 1877
—Magic Squares - - - - "Enc. Brit." 1882
H. J. Kesson—On Magic Squares, and Caïssan Magic Squares - - (Ursus) In the "Queen," 1879-1881

Since writing, some thirty years ago, what we have described relative to Magic Squares, a great development of the subject has been made by the discovery of other properties of Magic Squares as practised in India. The Rev. A. H. Frost, while a Missionary for many years in India, of the Church Missionary Society, interested himself in his leisure hours in the study of these squares and cubes; and in the articles which he published on the subject gave them the name of *Nasik*, from the town in which he resided. He has also deposited "Nasik Cubes" in the South Kensington Museum; and he has a vast mass of unpublished materials of an exhaustive nature, most carefully worked out, which we should be glad to see published. Mr. Kesson has treated the same subject in a different way, and in a more popular form, in the *Queen*, and we hope he will collect these scattered papers, and publish them in a concrete form, so as to render them more easy of reference. He gives his, very appropriately, the name of *Caissan* Squares, a name given to these squares, he says, by Sir Wm. Jones.

The proper name, however, for such squares should rather be *Indian*. For not only have the Brahmins been known to be great adepts in the formation of such squares, from time immemorial; not only does Mr. Frost give his an Indian name, and Mr. Kesson give his Caissa a location in Eastern Europe; not only is one of these squares represented over the Gate of Gwalior, while the natives of India wear them as amulets; but La Loubère, who wrote in 1693, expressly calls them *Indian* squares.

Though the study of these squares would not be in keeping with the object of this book, which is to enable anyone to take up the pursuit of the games and problems we have given, as a half hour's amusement and recreation, and not as a mathematical study requiring long and continued work; we think it desirable to give an example of such a square, in order to show how these squares differ from the ordinary magic square.

In these Indian squares it is necessary not merely that the summation of the rows, columns and diagonals should be alike, but that the numbers of such squares should be so harmoniously balanced, and that the summation of any eight parts in one direction, as in those of a bishop or knight, should also be alike.

We will take as an example a square of 8, as being that of the chess-board; though this square is not so perfect in all its paths as a square of 10; but it is quite sufficiently so to answer our purpose. The square is supposed to be surrounded in all directions by other squares filled in with the same figures or numbers. The following diagram shows the square, and a portion of eight surrounding squares, by which it will be seen that the numbers on these portions are identical with those of the corresponding cells of the central square: consequently it is obvious that it is not necessary to go into these surrounding squares, but to continue working from the corresponding cells of the central square.

28	40	31	38	29	33	26	35	28	40
61	1	58	3	60	8	63	6	61	1
52	16	55	14	53	9	50	11	52	16
45	17	42	19	44	24	47	22	45	17
36	32	39	30	37	25	34	27	36	32
5	57	2	59	4	64	7	62	5	57
12	56	15	54	13	49	10	51	12	56
21	41	18	43	20	48	23	46	21	41
28	40	31	38	29	33	26	35	28	40
61	1	58	3	60	8	63	6	61	1

Let us suppose that we require eight moves equal to the distance from 40 to 7. This would require six adjoining squares:—

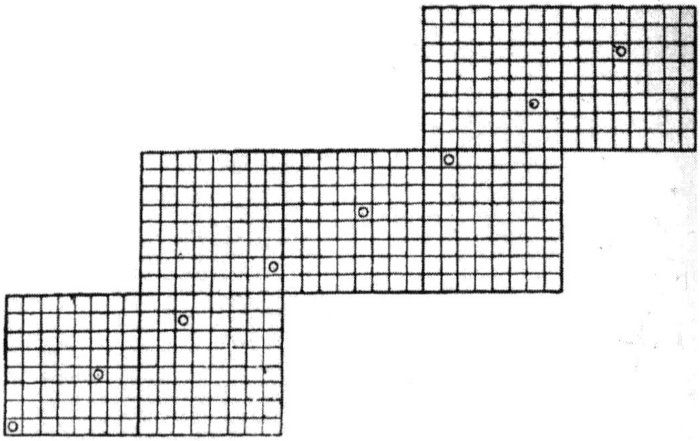

The move 40—7 is three diagonal cells to the NE, and then two to the E, or right; and that cell in the second square will correspond with 14 in the first square. The next three diagonal and two to the right will lead us into cell corresponding with 21 in the first square; and the cells in the remaining squares will correspond with numbers 25, 58, 51 and 44 in the first square. And thus, instead of having these additional squares, we proceed from 40 to 7 in the previous diagram: then three diagonals will bring us to cell outside corresponding with 16, and then taking two to the right will give us 14: from which two diagonals will bring us to cell corresponding with 33, and one more will be 23 from which two to the right will give us 21: from which three diagonals and two to the right will give us 25, and so on. These, when put in their proper places, will produce this pattern, being the Bishop's move from 21 consecutively to 58, and its complement, on the other side of the diagonal, 40; thus making a summation of 260.

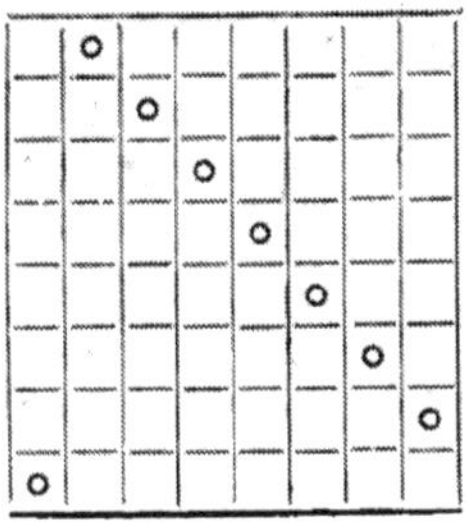

As each *path* consists of eight cells, it is immaterial whether a piece moves any number of cells forwards, or the complement of eight backwards.

Thus, in the Bishop's move 40 to 47, the *path* will be :—

		40
5 forwards	...	47
3 backwards	...	54
5 forwards	...	61
3 backwards	...	25
3 ———	...	18
5 forwards	...	11
3 backwards	...	4
		260

And in the Knight's extended move, 40 to 46, the *path* will be :—

		40
6 forwards	...	46
2 backwards	...	49
2 ———	...	59
2 ———	...	32
6 forwards	...	22
2 backwards	...	9
2 ———	...	3
		260

The following are the properties of this square:—

1. All the rows and columns, and the two diagonals have an equal summation.

2. Any square of four cells = 130.

3. The four corner cells of any square of 16, 36 or 64 cells = 130.

4. The two cells on each side of any such square, or of a double square = 130.

As	16	53	or	16	50	or	16	50	=	130.
	17	44		17	47		57	7		

5. Every alternate group of two figures is equal, as will be seen in following diagram.

6. The *path* of each Bishop's shortest move = 260.
As 16 . 58 . 38 . 20 . 49 . 7 . 27 . 45 = 260.

7. The *path* of each Bishop's extended move = 260
As 56 . 44 . 35 2 . 9 . 21 . 30 . 63 = 260.

8. The *path* of each Knight's move = 260
As 40 . 43 . 49 . 62 . 32 . 19 . 9 . 6 = 260.

9. The *path* of each Knight's extended move (with some exceptions) = 260
As 40 . 46 . 49 . 59 . 32 . 22 . 9 . 3 = 260.

10. Many endless imaginary *paths* will also make 260.
As 40 . 7 . 14 . 21 . 25 . 58 . 51 . 44 = 260 (as in p. 340).
40 . 45 . 51 . 63 . 25 . 20 . 14 . 2 = 260.
40 . 53 27 . 15 . 33 . 52 . 30 . 10 = 260.

11. When any such *path* repeats itself half-way it is 130.

12. As the square is of regular formation, it will have all the same properties if one or more columns are taken from one side and put on the other; or if the same be done with the top and bottom rows.

An easy way of forming this particular square is exhibited in the following diagram, in which it will be seen that four figures in one quarter are balanced by four figures in another quarter, each of which is exactly opposite to the corresponding one. Then two groups of four others are placed in the same manner, till half the board is covered.

1		3		8		6	
16		14		9		11	
17		19		24		22	
32		30		25		27	
	2		4		7		5
	15		13		10		12
	18		20		23		21
	31		29		26		28

The other cells are filled in in the reverse way, and the square is complete.

We will now show how the square can be transposed without destroying its magical character.

We will first take its diagonal, 1—28 for its first vertical column, and we get:—

1	58	3	60	8	63	6	61
55	14	53	9	50	11	52	16
19	44	24	47	22	45	17	42
37	25	34	27	36	32	39	30
64	7	62	5	57	2	59	4
10	51	12	56	15	54	13	49
46	21	41	18	43	20	48	23
28	40	31	38	29	33	26	35

We will now turn the square sideways, making the top row 61—35, and will then work it downwards with a Knight's move, 61, 17, 2, 43, which will make the first column, and we then get—

61	16	42	30	4	49	23	35
17	39	59	13	48	26	6	52
2	54	20	33	63	11	45	32
43	29	8	50	22	36	57	15
60	9	47	27	5	56	18	38
24	34	62	12	41	31	3	53
7	51	21	40	58	14	44	25
46	28	1	55	19	37	64	10

The left diagonal of the original, counting from the top, is now horizontal; the right diagonal is two diagonal squares and one straight; the horizontal rows are now a Knight's move, and the columns are a diagonal to the left; while the present diagonal to the right is two diagonals and one downwards: and the original square is not recognised.

Thus we see that in the original square, p. 339, we can begin the second row with the diagonal 55, the Knight's move 14, or with any extended Knight's move, as 53, 9, 50, 11, or 52, and then fill up the numbers in each row: and this in either of these operations, thus producing great variety. And we can do the same if we select any other number of the square, as 1—7, four diagonal and one horizontal.

XLII.

FIGURES OF THE KNIGHT'S TOUR.

A further exercise of ingenuity afforded by the Knight's tour is exhibited by tracing the figure of its march. In this exercise not only must every square of the board be filled up with a Knight's move, but the track, when figured out, must exhibit some regular or striking form. The following illustrations will serve as examples of the great variety of figures which may be produced. Those on the double chess-board are still more regular. These figures show, at the same time, the great variety of ways in which the Knight's tour may be accomplished, and the harmonious order of its march.

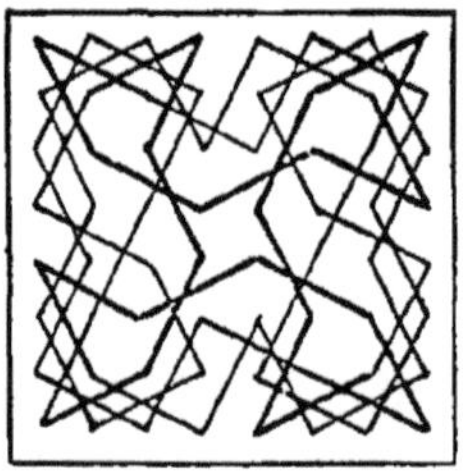

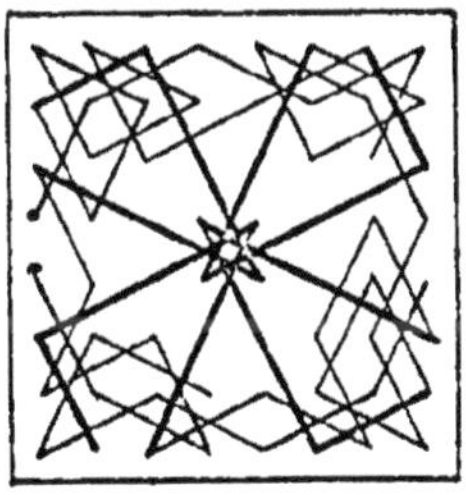

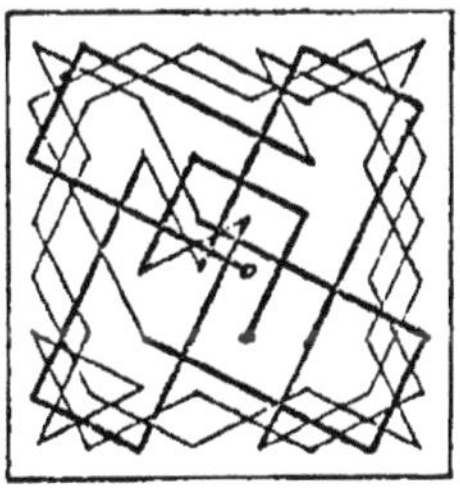

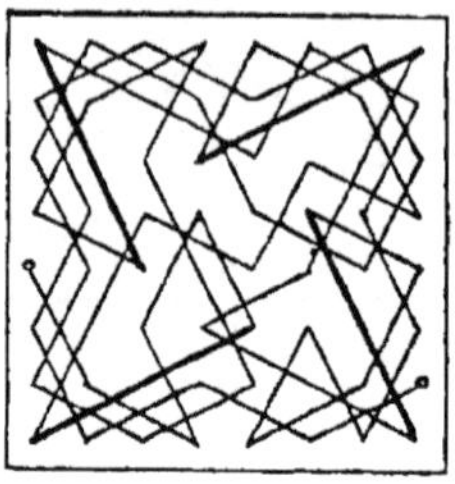

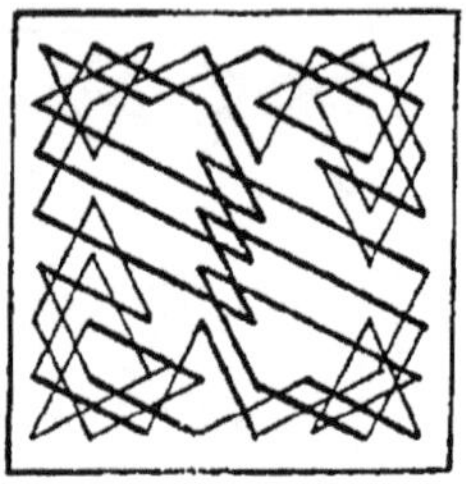

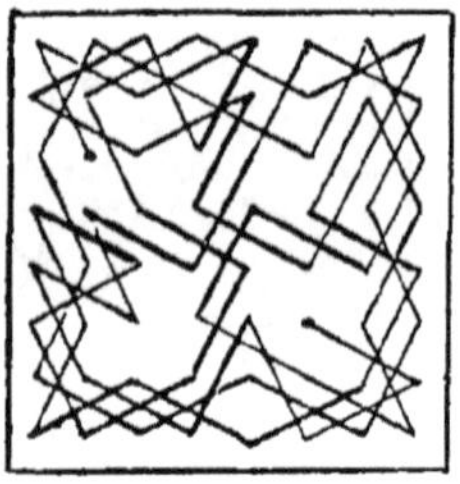

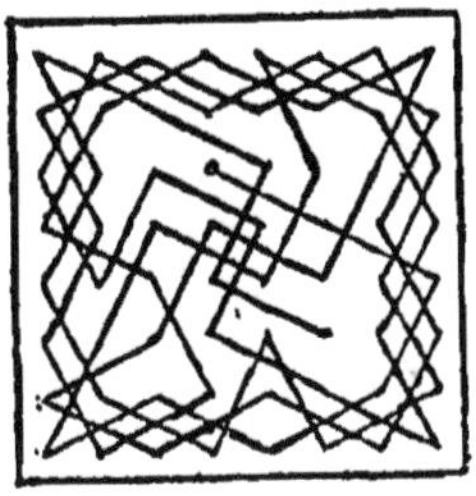

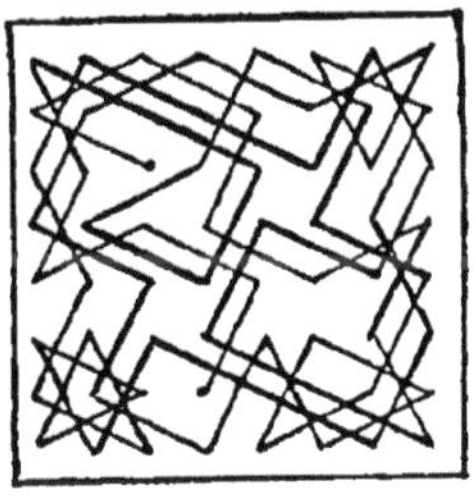

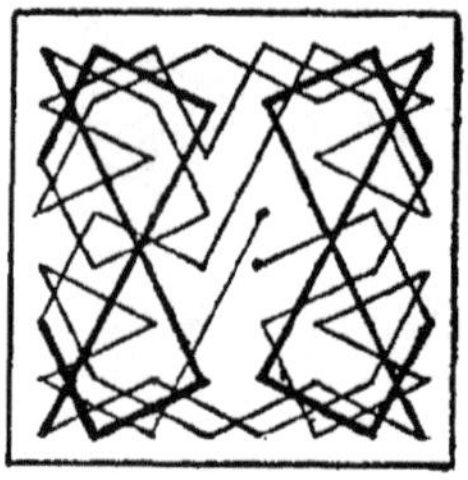

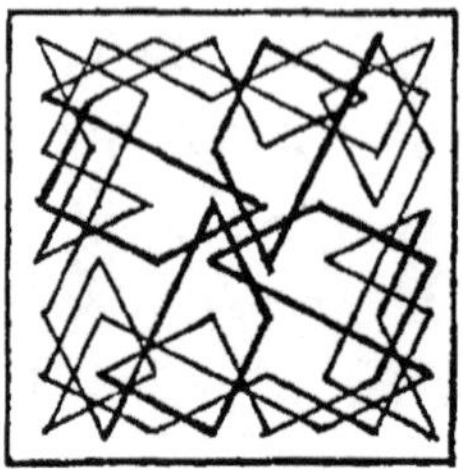

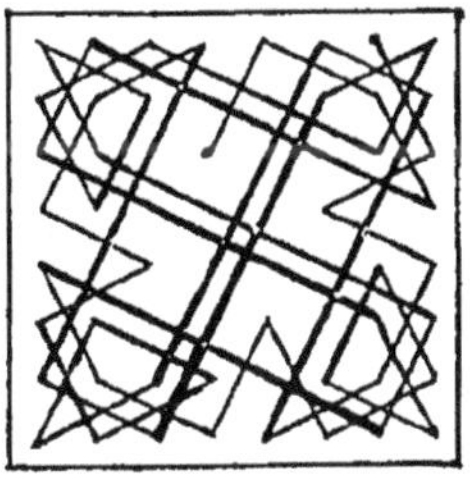

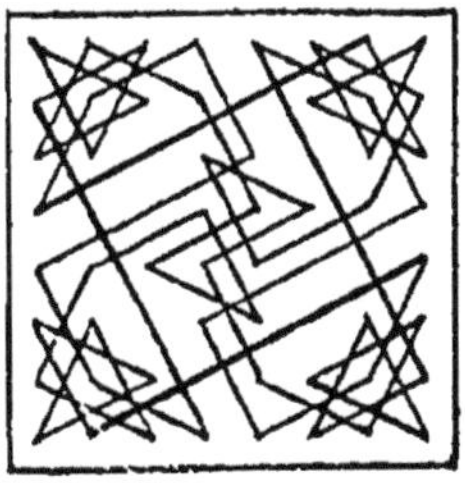

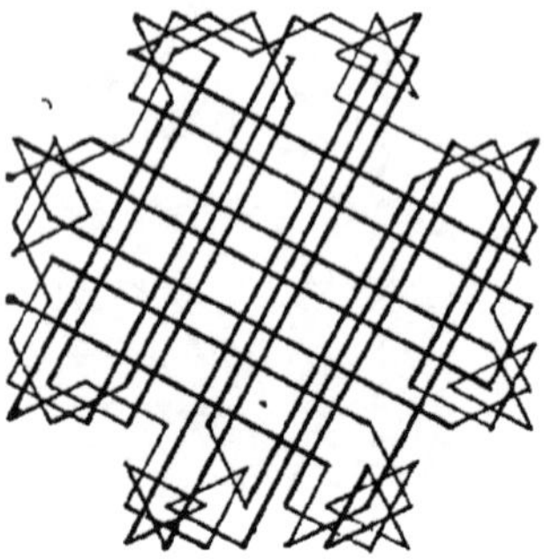

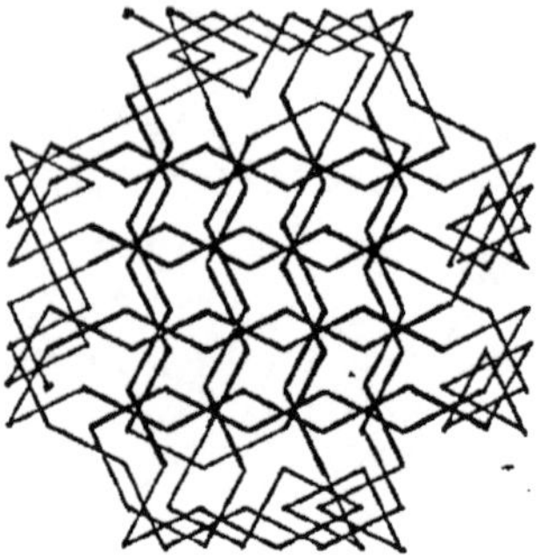

APPENDIX

No. I.

RULES OF THE EGYPTIAN GAMES.

I.

LUDUS LATRUNCULORUM.

The game is played on a twelve-square board, having 144 cells or squares.

Each player has five rows of six pieces, beginning at the left hand corner, and placed alternately.

The pieces move and take in all directions, perpendicularly, horizontally, diagonally, forwards and backwards.

The pieces can leap over an adversary if the opposite cell is vacant; but not over one of their own colour.

Pieces attack each other when in contiguous cells; and when another piece comes up on the opposite side the intermediate piece is taken off.

But a piece can go between two adverse pieces without being taken.

When one side is hopelessly beaten, or locks himself in, the game is lost.

II.

THE GAME OF SENAT.

The game was played on a thirteen-square, eleven-square, nine-square, seven-square, or five-square board, according as there was more or less time to play.

But the board must have an odd number of squares, so as to have a central square, which square is to remain vacant till all the other squares are filled in.

The players, by turn, begin by placing two pieces wherever they please, till all the squares are filled in except the central one.

In placing the pieces there is no taking up. When all the pieces are placed the game begins.

The pieces move forwards, backwards and sideways, but not diagonally.

A piece is taken by putting one on each side of it, in a straight line, vertical or horizontal.

But a piece can go between two hostile pieces without being taken.

When a player locks himself in, refusing to come out, he loses the game.

III.

THE GAME OF THE BOWL.

This is a game of stakes, which are placed in the bowl. They may be either counters or small money.

The board consists of twelve concentric rings, having the Bowl in the middle, to hold the stakes, and the pieces which get home.

Each player has twelve pieces, and two counters or cowries.

The counters are coloured on one side, and are white on the other: the coloured side counting as two, the white as one. The cowries if down count as two, if up as one.

A player can either enter his throws, or play pieces already entered.

The principle of the game is the same as that of the other Egyptian games, the Tau or Latrunculi, and Senat, that a piece is taken when attacked on each side.

As the board consists of rings, the pieces on the board are supposed to operate right and left round the ring: and thus, if two pieces are on one side, and only one on the other side of a ring; one of these pieces will operate on the right, and the other on the left, and thus attack the opposite piece on both sides and take it.

But a piece can enter or move into a ring when two or more pieces are on the other side; and cannot be taken till the opponent enters a fresh piece into that ring.

The pieces enter on the outside, and gradually move up to the centre, and then out as they get in the bowl, according to the throw.

When one of the players has no more pieces on the board, the game is ended.

Each player then counts the number of pieces which have got home, and the number of prisoners he has taken; and the victor adds thereto the number of pieces he has remaining on the board.

IV.

THE GAME OF THE SACRED WAY.

The board consists of three lines of squares, the side ones of only four squares, while the middle line has twelve squares

Each player has four pieces, which are entered in the four side squares; which are supposed to be marked 1, 2, 3, and 4, beginning from below.

One dice only is used on either side. This dice is of oblong form, and marked 1, 2, 3, 4.

The pieces move down the sides, and up the centre, and out, according to the throw.

It is optional to move or not, as the player thinks fit.

Prisoners taken by either side are entered on that side, when the player chooses, in 1, 2, 3 or 4, according as 1, 2, 3 or 4 is thrown.

When one player has lost or played out all his pieces, the game is ended: and each player reckons up his pieces out, and the victor adds thereto his pieces on the board, and his prisoners.

APPENDIX

No. II

ADDENDA ET CORRIGENDA.

Page 53, line 13. After the word "result" add—For rules of the game see Appendix I.

,, 75, line 2. Add—For rules of the game see Appendix I.

,, ,, line 7. Add—In page 11 the inscription should read "Lifts three pieces and two," not "three pieces *or* two." So many pieces *and* so many, is just what we find in this game, though in the game we played we did not succeed in taking three pieces in one move. No doubt with good players such a take would occur, and the painting or inscription represents two skilful players, each of whom has captured three pieces at one stroke. But two pieces are frequently taken at one stroke, as in the example we have given; and this stroke is followed up by subsequent moves, taking up other pieces, and thus the inscription "Three pieces and two," wonderfully confirms our interpretation of the game.

,, 87, line 8 from bottom. For "marked" read *masked.*

,, ,, At end. Add—For rules of the game see Appendix I.

,, 99, At end of third paragraph, Add—For rules of the game see Appendix I.

,, 109, Insert 2 before bottom note.

,, 121, line 5 from bottom. For "did" read *mid.*

,, 125, line 3 from bottom. For "Universal" read *University.*

,, 142, line 12. For "Rukh" read *Rook.*

,, 243, Note. For "a ack" read *attack.*

Unlike the Chinese who use paper chess-boards, the Turks who carry their chess-men and chess-cloth in a bag, so as to be always ready, and Europeans who deposit them in closets till wanted; the Japanese pile their games one upon another as ornaments in their rooms. I have two piles of these games the ornamentation of which is very similar. The lower board is that of *Go*, the game of Enclosing; the next is the Chess-board; the next is a game which I have not been able to ascertain, but I believe it is played with a dozen men on each side, black and white, and with diminutive dice only $\frac{3}{16}$ of an inch square, the fritillus, or dice box for which is japanned to correspond with the board, and is $1\frac{1}{2}$ inches high, with an internal diameter of only $\frac{9}{16}$ of an inch. The board itself has twelve oblong divisions on each side, with a space between the two sides. Above this game is a box to hold the pieces.

APPENDIX

No. III.

LOWER EMPIRE GAMES.

In a letter received from my friend Mr. George Dennis, dated January 2nd, 1892, he says:—

Immediately I received your letter I started for the Forum. The excavations at Rome of late years have disclosed the original pavements of many buildings in the Forum, which show circles scratched of old on the slabs, evidently for some game or other. The diagrams I give are all scratched in the pavement of the Basilica Julia, or of other buildings which have been brought to light of late years; and I take it that they must have been made in the Lower Empire, when the temples and basilicas were deserted, and before the capture of Rome by the Goths: because the destruction of the principal buildings at that period would have covered the pavements with debris. I went carefully over all the ruins in the Forum, and could find no other varieties than I here give you. Many of the circles are rudely scratched in the pavement, but a few are geometrically correct: the former are very numerous. There are but few of the squares. I could find no instances of numerous concentric circles. (I had asked him about these.) I remember similar diagrams at Pompeii or elsewhere, but I never paid them much attention. I will not fail to report to you any other instances I may note in my wanderings.

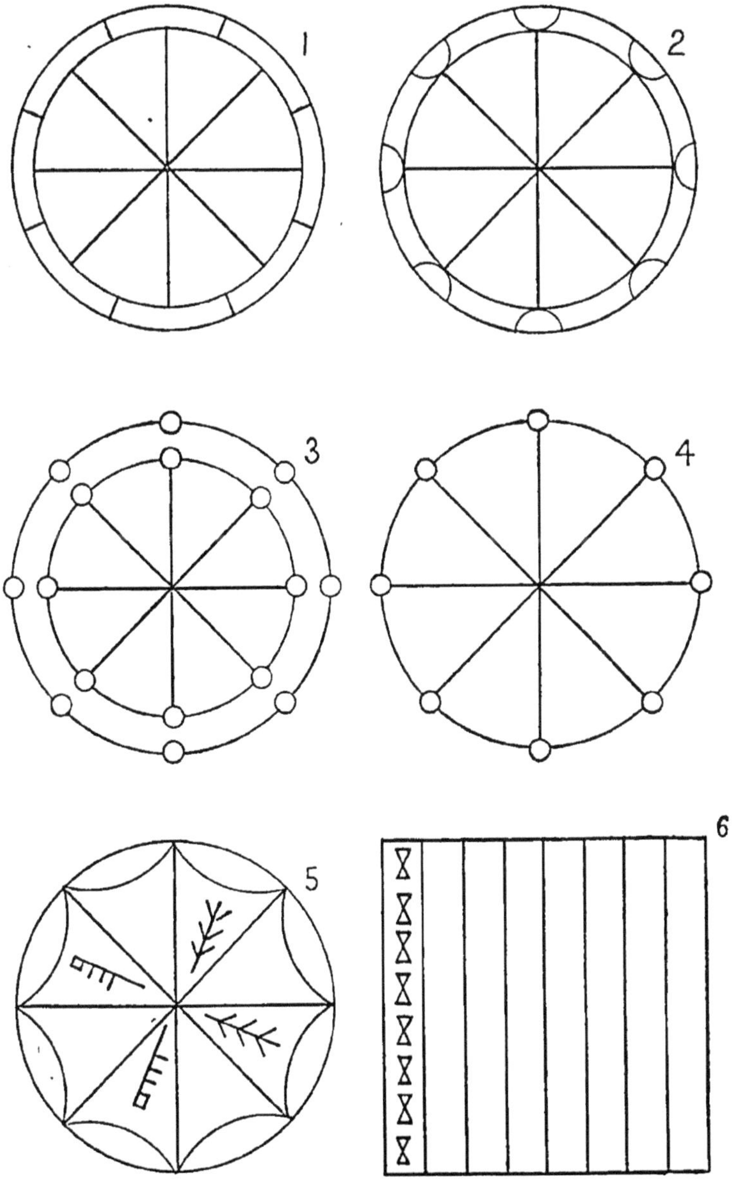

LOWER EMPIRE GAMES.

1. About 3 ft 3 ins in diameter
2. About 2 ft. 8 ins. in diameter, others similar, but without inner circles.
3. About 5ft. in diameter others without the radii, but with holes in outer circle.
4. Others without the holes.
5. About 20 ins in diameter.
6. About 2 ft. square. A similar one about 15 ins. square.

All the circular diagrams appear to represent the same game. During my twelve months' residence in Pompeii in 1847, while excavating the house of Marcus Aurelius, I do not recollect seeing any such diagrams; for, as Mr. Dennis says, I was not then interested in them: and I do not consider it likely that the Ædile of such a modern watering-place as Pompeii then was, would have allowed the pavement of public buildings to be so disfigured, or idle people to be squatting about and playing at such games, to the great discomfort and annoyance of other people, engaged either in public business or at their devotions.

BY THE SAME AUTHOR.

Museum of Classical Antiquities	- -	1851-2.
Theatres in Crete	- - - -	1854.
Dædalus	- - - - -	1860.
Ephesus and the Temple of Diana	-	1862.

William Pollard & Co., Printers, Exeter.
Owen Williams, Photographer, Laugharne.
Waterlow & Sons Ltd., Photo-Engravers, London.

43.

Lightning Source UK Ltd.
Milton Keynes UK
UKHW020501050620
364398UK00005B/57